# Scott Foresman - Addison Wesley
# MIDDLE SCHOOL MATH

## Course 1

# Indiana Math Connections

## A Review and Practice Workbook

We wish to thank the following Indiana teachers:

**Lead Writers**

David Caulfield

Richard Caulfield

Barbara Hawkins

Sharon Horner

**Contributing Writers**

Gloria Baker

Cindy Bilinski

Mike Flattery

Laura Gojderowicz

Marguerite Hart

Shawnita Longstreet

Dorothy May

Julie McNabb

Joyce Miller

Meg Price

Kathy Rieke

Linda Rudlaff

Paul Smith

Deborah Vannater

# Scott Foresman - Addison Wesley

Editorial Offices: Menlo Park, California • Glenview, Illinois
Sales Offices: Reading, Massachusetts • Atlanta, Georgia • Glenview, Illinois
Carrollton, Texas • Menlo Park, California

http://www.sf.aw.com

## Overview

*Indiana Math Connections: A Review and Practice Workbook* consists of these three sections of material.

**Review** worksheets provide practice of key skills and concepts that were covered last year in math class.

**Indiana Connections** worksheets provide interesting applications, problem sets, and puzzles dealing with themes and historical events related to the state of Indiana. There is one worksheet for each section of the Student Edition. Each worksheet applies and reinforces mathematical content from that section.

**Practice** worksheets provide additional exercises for students who have not mastered key skills and concepts covered in the student text. A Practice worksheet is provided for each regular lesson in the student text. In addition, a Practice worksheet is also provided for each Section Review and Cumulative Review lesson. Lesson worksheets provide exercises similar to those in the Practice and Apply section of the student text. Section Review worksheets review the student text section and include application problems that review previous material. Cumulative Review worksheets cover important skills from the chapter at hand and from previous chapters. References to the applicable student text lessons are provided.

## Photo Credits

Photos courtesy of Indiana Department of Commerce, Tourism Division; Visuals Unlimited, Inc.; The Upland Courier; The Free Library of Philadelphia; Indiana State Archives; Jan Kanter; Everett Collection of film stills; The Studebaker National Museum.

ISBN 0–201–34866–7

# Contents

**Review**         1–4

**Indiana Connections**

| | | |
|---|---|---|
| Indiana Connections | 1A | 1 |
| Indiana Connections | 1B | 2 |
| Indiana Connections | 1C | 3 |
| Indiana Connections | 2A | 4 |
| Indiana Connections | 2B | 5 |
| Indiana Connections | 2C | 6 |
| Indiana Connections | 3A | 7 |
| Indiana Connections | 3B | 8 |
| Indiana Connections | 3C | 9 |
| Indiana Connections | 4A | 10 |
| Indiana Connections | 4B | 11 |
| Indiana Connections | 4C | 12 |
| Indiana Connections | 5A | 13 |
| Indiana Connections | 5B | 14 |
| Indiana Connections | 6A | 15 |
| Indiana Connections | 6B | 16 |
| Indiana Connections | 7A | 17 |
| Indiana Connections | 7B | 18 |
| Indiana Connections | 8A | 19 |
| Indiana Connections | 8B | 20 |
| Indiana Connections | 8C | 21 |
| Indiana Connections | 9A | 22 |
| Indiana Connections | 9B | 23 |
| Indiana Connections | 10A | 24 |
| Indiana Connections | 10B | 25 |
| Indiana Connections | 10C | 26 |
| Indiana Connections | 11A | 27 |
| Indiana Connections | 11B | 28 |
| Indiana Connections | 12A | 29 |
| Indiana Connections | 12B | 30 |

**Practice**

**Chapter 1: Statistics—Real-World Use of Whole Numbers**

| | | |
|---|---|---|
| Practice | 1-1 | 1 |
| Practice | 1-2 | 2 |
| Practice | 1-3 | 3 |
| Section 1A Review | | 4 |
| Practice | 1-4 | 5 |
| Practice | 1-5 | 6 |
| Practice | 1-6 | 7 |
| Section 1B Review | | 8 |
| Practice | 1-7 | 9 |
| Practice | 1-8 | 10 |
| Practice | 1-9 | 11 |
| Section 1C Review | | 12 |
| Cumulative Review Chapter 1 | | 13 |

**Chapter 2: Connecting Arithmetic to Algebra**

| | | |
|---|---|---|
| Practice | 2-1 | 14 |
| Practice | 2-2 | 15 |
| Practice | 2-3 | 16 |
| Practice | 2-4 | 17 |
| Section 2A Review | | 18 |
| Practice | 2-5 | 19 |
| Practice | 2-6 | 20 |
| Practice | 2-7 | 21 |
| Practice | 2-8 | 22 |
| Practice | 2-9 | 23 |
| Section 2B Review | | 24 |
| Practice | 2-10 | 25 |
| Practice | 2-11 | 26 |
| Practice | 2-12 | 27 |
| Practice | 2-13 | 28 |
| Section 2C Review | | 29 |
| Cumulative Review Chapters 1–2 | | 30 |

**Chapter 3: Decimals**

| | | |
|---|---|---|
| Practice | 3-1 | 31 |
| Practice | 3-2 | 32 |
| Practice | 3-3 | 33 |
| Practice | 3-4 | 34 |
| Section 3A Review | | 35 |
| Practice | 3-5 | 36 |
| Practice | 3-6 | 37 |
| Practice | 3-7 | 38 |
| Section 3B Review | | 39 |
| Practice | 3-8 | 40 |
| Practice | 3-9 | 41 |
| Practice | 3-10 | 42 |
| Practice | 3-11 | 43 |
| Practice | 3-12 | 44 |
| Section 3C Review | | 45 |
| Cumulative Review Chapters 1–3 | | 46 |

**Chapter 4: Measurement**

| | | |
|---|---|---|
| Practice | 4-1 | 47 |
| Practice | 4-2 | 48 |
| Practice | 4-3 | 49 |
| Section 4A Review | | 50 |
| Practice | 4-4 | 51 |
| Practice | 4-5 | 52 |
| Practice | 4-6 | 53 |
| Section 4B Review | | 54 |
| Practice | 4-7 | 55 |
| Practice | 4-8 | 56 |
| Practice | 4-9 | 57 |
| Section 4C Review | | 58 |
| Cumulative Review Chapters 1–4 | | 59 |

## Chapter 5: Patterns and Number Theory

| | | |
|---|---|---|
| Practice | 5-1 | 60 |
| Practice | 5-2 | 61 |
| Practice | 5-3 | 62 |
| Section 5A Review | | 63 |
| Practice | 5-4 | 64 |
| Practice | 5-5 | 65 |
| Practice | 5-6 | 66 |
| Practice | 5-7 | 67 |
| Practice | 5-8 | 68 |
| Section 5B Review | | 69 |
| Cumulative Review Chapters 1–5 | | 70 |

## Chapter 6: Adding and Subtracting Fractions

| | | |
|---|---|---|
| Practice | 6-1 | 71 |
| Practice | 6-2 | 72 |
| Practice | 6-3 | 73 |
| Section 6A Review | | 74 |
| Practice | 6-4 | 75 |
| Practice | 6-5 | 76 |
| Practice | 6-6 | 77 |
| Section 6B Review | | 78 |
| Cumulative Review Chapters 1–6 | | 79 |

## Chapter 7: Multiplying and Dividing Fractions

| | | |
|---|---|---|
| Practice | 7-1 | 80 |
| Practice | 7-2 | 81 |
| Practice | 7-3 | 82 |
| Section 7A Review | | 83 |
| Practice | 7-4 | 84 |
| Practice | 7-5 | 85 |
| Practice | 7-6 | 86 |
| Section 7B Review | | 87 |
| Cumulative Review Chapters 1–7 | | 88 |

## Chapter 8: The Geometry of Polygons

| | | |
|---|---|---|
| Practice | 8-1 | 89 |
| Practice | 8-2 | 90 |
| Practice | 8-3 | 91 |
| Section 8A Review | | 92 |
| Practice | 8-4 | 93 |
| Practice | 8-5 | 94 |
| Practice | 8-6 | 95 |
| Practice | 8-7 | 96 |
| Section 8B Review | | 97 |
| Practice | 8-8 | 98 |
| Practice | 8-9 | 99 |
| Practice | 8-10 | 100 |
| Section 8C Review | | 101 |
| Cumulative Review Chapters 1–8 | | 102 |

## Chapter 9: Integers and the Coordinate Plane

| | | |
|---|---|---|
| Practice | 9-1 | 103 |
| Practice | 9-2 | 104 |
| Practice | 9-3 | 105 |
| Practice | 9-4 | 106 |
| Section 9A Review | | 107 |
| Practice | 9-5 | 108 |
| Practice | 9-6 | 109 |
| Practice | 9-7 | 110 |
| Section 9B Review | | 111 |
| Cumulative Review Chapters 1–9 | | 112 |

## Chapter 10: Ratio, Proportion, and Percent

| | | |
|---|---|---|
| Practice | 10-1 | 113 |
| Practice | 10-2 | 114 |
| Practice | 10-3 | 115 |
| Section 10A Review | | 116 |
| Practice | 10-4 | 117 |
| Practice | 10-5 | 118 |
| Practice | 10-6 | 119 |
| Practice | 10-7 | 120 |
| Section 10B Review | | 121 |
| Practice | 10-8 | 122 |
| Practice | 10-9 | 123 |
| Practice | 10-10 | 124 |
| Practice | 10-11 | 125 |
| Section 10C Review | | 126 |
| Cumulative Review Chapters 1–10 | | 127 |

## Chapter 11: Solids and Measurement

| | | |
|---|---|---|
| Practice | 11-1 | 128 |
| Practice | 11-2 | 129 |
| Practice | 11-3 | 130 |
| Practice | 11-4 | 131 |
| Section 11A Review | | 132 |
| Practice | 11-5 | 133 |
| Practice | 11-6 | 134 |
| Practice | 11-7 | 135 |
| Section 11B Review | | 136 |
| Cumulative Review Chapters 1–11 | | 137 |

## Chapter 12: Probability

| | | |
|---|---|---|
| Practice | 12-1 | 138 |
| Practice | 12-2 | 139 |
| Practice | 12-3 | 140 |
| Section 12A Review | | 141 |
| Practice | 12-4 | 142 |
| Practice | 12-5 | 143 |
| Practice | 12-6 | 144 |
| Section 12B Review | | 145 |
| Cumulative Review Chapters 1–12 | | 146 |

Name _____

# Review From Last Year

**In 1–3, use the line graph.**

1. What was the temperature on December 4?

_____

2. How much higher was the temperature on December 7 than December 8?

_____

3. **a.** Between which two consecutive days was the change in temperature the greatest?

_____

   **b.** What was the change in temperature?

_____

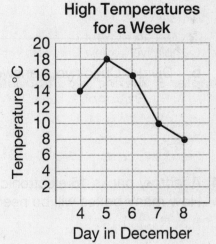

**High Temperatures for a Week**

4. Write 41,206,031 in word form.

_____

5. Write five and seven hundredths in decimal form. _____

6. Find the difference between 12.3 and 4.16. _____

Find each product.

7. $\begin{array}{r} 230 \\ \times\ 50 \\ \hline \end{array}$

8. $\begin{array}{r} \$2.75 \\ \times\ 12 \\ \hline \end{array}$

9. At the Ortiz garage sale, paperback books cost $0.75 and hardback books cost $1.50. How much would you spend if you bought 3 paperback books and one hardback book? _____

Divide.

10. $6\overline{)455}$

11. $4\overline{)23.548}$

Name _____

**12.** The 3 Ortiz children earned $49.50 selling their old books at their garage sale. If they want to split the money equally, how much should each child receive? _____

**13. a.** Estimate the quotient using compatible numbers. $42\overline{)35{,}268}$

_____

**b.** Divide. Check your answer. Show your check. $42\overline{)3\,5,\,2\,6\,8}$

**14.** A factory packs 15 electronic games in a box. How many boxes will be needed for 5445 games? _____

**In 15-17, use the figure at the right.**

**15.** Name a set of perpendicular lines. _____

**16.** Name a right angle. _____

**17.** Name an obtuse angle. _____

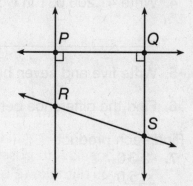

**18.** Circle the figures that are congruent.

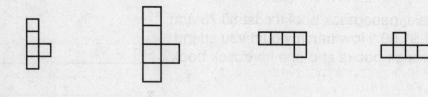

**19.** Write the fractions in order from least to greatest. $\frac{5}{6}, \frac{5}{9}, \frac{5}{8}$

_____

Name _____

**20.** Write $\frac{36}{8}$ as a mixed number in simplest form.

_____

**21.** Write $\frac{7}{10}$ as a percent. _____

Find each sum or difference. Simplify, if possible.

**22.** $2\frac{2}{5}$
$+ 1\frac{3}{10}$
_____

**23.** $2\frac{5}{7}$
$- 2\frac{1}{7}$
_____

**24.** $4\frac{3}{4}$
$- 3\frac{1}{6}$
_____

**25.** At a fabric store, one package of material is marked 3 yards 6 inches for $3 and another package is marked 10 feet for $3. Which package has more material?

_____

**26.** Shequille and Maria hiked $3\frac{1}{4}$ miles before lunch and $2\frac{3}{8}$ miles between lunch and their afternoon rest stop. If their trail is 8 miles long, how much farther do they have to go?

_____

**27.** The bronze Statue of Freedom on top of the United States Capitol building is $19\frac{1}{2}$ feet high. If it is possible to polish 3 feet an hour, how long would it take to polish the statue?

_____

**28.** The Library of Congress contains more than 80 million items in 470 languages. If $\frac{4}{5}$ of the items are in English, how many are in other languages?

_____

**29.** The base of the Washington monument is a square 55.125 feet on a side. What is its perimeter?

_____

base

**30.** The shape of Lake Superior approximates that of a right triangle. Its legs are 350 miles and 160 miles.

   **a.** Use the formula for the area of a triangle, $A = \frac{1}{2} \times (b \times h)$, to approximate the surface area of Lake Superior.

   _____

   **b.** The actual surface area is 31,700 square miles. Was your approximation relatively close?

   _____

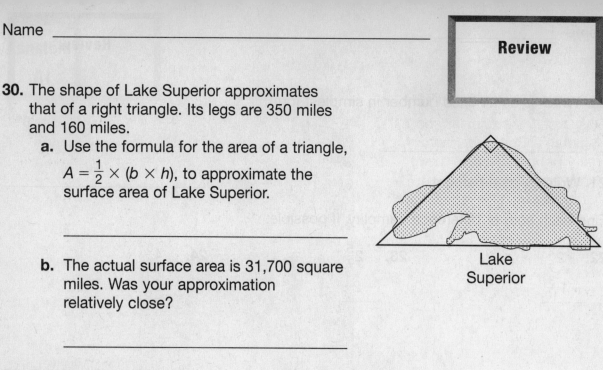

Lake Superior

**31.** Find the circumference. Use 3.14 for π.

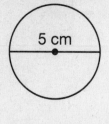

5 cm

$C =$ _____

**32.** Find the surface area of the box.

Corn Flakes

33 cm

20 cm    8 cm

_____

**33.** Find the change in temperature from −5°C to 18°C. _____

**34.** A chef combines 250 mL of melted butter, 187 mL of melted brown sugar, 50 mL of cream, and 563 mL of water. How many liters are there all together? _____

On a field trip to Washington D.C., a group of sixth graders visited 8 different sites of interest. They visited 5 memorials and 3 government institutions.

**35.** Of the sites visited, what is the ratio of memorials to government institutions?

_____

**36.** What percent of the sites of interest listed are memorials?

_____

**37.** If you wrote each of the names of the 8 sites on different slips of paper, put them in a bag, and selected one without looking, what is the probability of selecting a government institution?

_____

Name _____

# Hoosier Hysteria

Basketball is a popular sport in Indiana. One team that many people follow is the men's basketball team from Indiana University.

**Indiana's Brian Evans blocks a drive attempt by Purdue's Justin Jennings.**

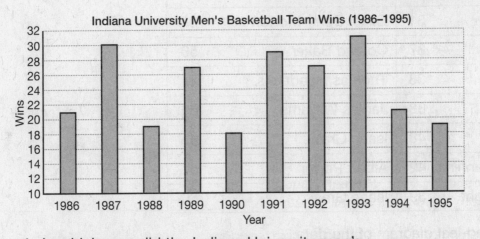

Indiana University Men's Basketball Team Wins (1986–1995)

1. In which year did the Indiana University men's basketball team win the greatest number of games? _____

2. When did the Indiana University men's basketball team win the fourth greatest number of games? _____

3. In which years did the Indiana University men's basketball team win fewer than 20 games? _____

4. How many more games did the team win in 1987 compared to 1995? _____

5. What is the total number of games won shown in the graph? _____

**Extension:** Using the same data, make a bar graph so that it looks like there is a great difference in the number of wins from year to year.

**Indiana Mathematics Proficiency:** (10b) Data Analysis

Indiana
1B

# Governing Indiana

Indiana's first Governor was Jonathan Jennings. He served from 1816 to 1822. The data below show the age each of the first 20 governors of Indiana turned during the year they took office.

| Governor | Age | Governor | Age |
|---|---|---|---|
| Jonathan Jennings | 32 | Ashbel Willard | 37 |
| Ratliff Boom | 41 | Abram Adams Hammond | 46 |
| William Hendricks | 40 | Henry Smith Lane | 50 |
| James Brown Ray | 31 | Oliver Perry Morton | 38 |
| Noah Noble | 37 | Conrad Baker | 50 |
| David Wallace | 38 | Thomas Hendricks | 54 |
| Samuel Bigger | 38 | James Williams | 69 |
| James Whitcomb | 48 | Isaac Gray | 55 |
| Paris Chip-man Dunning | 42 | Albert Porter | 57 |
| Joseph Albert Wright | 39 | Isaac Gray | 60 |

**1.** Make a stem-and-leaf diagram of the data.

| Stem | Leaf |
|---|---|
|  |  |

**2.** What is the range of the ages? _____

**3.** What age did the greatest number of governors turn during the year they took office? _____

*Extension:* Make a line plot or a bar graph using either the 1st or 2nd column of data from the table above.
*Indiana Mathematics Proficiency:* (10b and d) Data Analysis

# Brickyard Data

In 1994, the first annual Brickyard 400 NASCAR stock car race was held at the Indianapolis Speedway. In 1995, Dale Earnhardt won the race with an average speed of 155.218 mph.

**Dale Jarrett leads the pack through the first turn during the running of the third Brickyard 400 in 1996. He went on to win the race.**

### Lap Reports from the 1995 Brickyard

| Lap | Average Speed (in mph) |
| --- | --- |
| 1 | 161 |
| 2 | 165 |
| 4 | 167 |
| 10 | 166 |
| 20 | 165 |
| 30 | 165 |
| 40 | 161 |
| 50 | 162 |
| 60 | 162 |

The data above shows the average speed for selected laps. Use this data to answer the following questions.

**1.** Find the median of the speeds. _____

**2.** Find the mode of the speeds. _____

**3.** Find the mean of the speeds to the nearest whole number. _____

**4.** Does there appear to be an outlier? If so, what is it? _____

_____

***Extension:*** Explain your answer to Problem 4.
***Indiana Mathematics Proficiency:*** (7d) Computation and Estimation; (10b and f) Data Analysis

Name _____

# How Many People?

Indiana's population was estimated at 5,712,799 in 1993. Indiana is the fourteenth most populous state in the United States. A list of Indiana's major cities and their estimated 1993 populations are listed below.

| City | Population |
| --- | --- |
| Evansville | 130,496 |
| Fort Wayne | 172,349 |
| Gary | 151,953 |
| Hammond | 93,714 |
| Indianapolis | 700,807 |
| South Bend | 109,727 |

**Fort Wayne skyline**

Name the place-value position of the given digit.

**1.** The 9 in Gary's population

_____

**2.** The 3 in Hammond's population

_____

**3.** The 1 in Fort Wayne's population

_____

Round the 1993 population of Indiana to the given place.

**4.** millions

_____

**5.** ten-thousands

_____

**6.** hundreds

_____

Write the 1993 population of each city in words.

**7.** Indianapolis _____

**8.** Hammond _____

Compare the populations, using < or >.

**9.** Evansville ◯ South Bend          **10.** Hammond ◯ Fort Wayne

**11.** Write the 1993 population of Indiana in number-word form.

_____

---

**Extension:** Find the populations of the five largest cities in the United States. Place the cities in order from least to greatest population.

**Indiana Mathematics Proficiency:** (5c and e) Whole Number and Decimal Place Value

Use with Chapter 2, Section A.

Indiana
2B

Name _____

# Flowering Numbers

Indiana's first state flower, the carnation, was adopted in 1913. Since then the state flower has changed several times. The state flower from 1931 to 1957 was the zinnia. In 1957, a different state flower was adopted and is still the state flower today.

**Zinnias, former Indiana state flower**

Estimate or simplify to find each answer. Write the letter on the blank that corresponds to each answer to learn the name of the current state flower. You will not use all of the letters.

**1.** Estimate 3446 + 6873.　　　　　　　　　_____ **Y**

**2.** Simplify 81,000 ÷ 90　　　　　　　　　_____ **M**

**3.** Estimate 23 × 48.　　　　　　　　　　_____ **P**

**4.** Estimate 689 − 118　　　　　　　　　_____ **B**

**5.** Simplify $6^2$ + 8.　　　　　　　　　　_____ **0**

**6.** Estimate 487 ÷ 72　　　　　　　　　　_____ **C**

**7.** Simplify (8 − 4) × 5.　　　　　　　　_____ **N**

**8.** Simplify 50 × 4 × 2.　　　　　　　　_____ **E**

Indiana's state flower is the _____ _____ _____ _____ _____ .
　　　　　　　　　　　　　　　1000　　400　　44　　20　　10,000

---

***Extension:*** Create a puzzle of your own. Have a classmate solve your puzzle.
***Indiana Mathematics Proficiency:*** (7b, d, and j) Computation and Estimation

© Scott Foresman • Addison Wesley 6

Name _____

# The State Bird

In 1933, the Indiana General
Assembly adopted the cardinal
as Indiana's state bird. These
birds stay in Indiana all year
and are well-known for their
distinctive color and their
flute-like songs.

Solve each equation.

**1.** $4 + x = 20$ _____

**2.** $y - 10 = 19$ _____

**3.** $\frac{36}{z} = 12$ _____

**4.** $8x = 48$ _____

**5.** $w + 8 = 18$ _____

**6.** $7p = 35$ _____

**7.** $\frac{24}{k} = 3$ _____

**8.** $n - 2 = 18$ _____

**9.** $\frac{x}{12} = 5$ _____

**10.** $9c = 117$ _____

**Extension:** Create ten different equations that have the same solutions as those above.
**Indiana Mathematics Proficiency:** (12b) Algebra

Use with Chapter 2, Section C.

**Indiana
3A**

# Popping Big Numbers

Indiana is home to the world's largest
popcorn producer, Weaver Popcorn
Company. This company is located
in Van Buren, Indiana and produces
popcorn that is sold throughout
the United States and in 29 foreign
countries. About 100,000,000 pounds
of popcorn are produced each year
on about 36,000 acres of land
on 400 farms.

Write each number in scientific notation.

**1.** 100,000,000                                    _____

**2.** 36,000                                          _____

**3.** 29                                              _____

**4.** 400                                             _____

About 2777.78 pounds of popcorn
are produced per acre.

**5.** Round this decimal to the nearest whole number.   _____

**6.** Round this decimal to the nearest tenth.          _____

An American family of five consumes about ten pounds
of popcorn per year. It takes about $\frac{4}{1000}$ of an acre to
produce ten pounds of popcorn.

**7.** Write this fraction as a decimal.                 _____

**8.** Write the decimal in word form.                   _____

Order these decimals from least to greatest.

**9.** 5.86, 5.63, 6.04                                 _____

**10.** 0.413, 0.409, 0.148                             _____

**11.** 7.055, 7.0555, 7.55                             _____

**12.** 0.13, 0.03, 0.31                                _____

**Extension:** Find another product produced in large amounts in Indiana. Write the numbers in scientific notation.
**Indiana Mathematics Proficiency:** (5b, c, d, and e) Whole Number and Decimal Place Value

Name _____

# The State Tree

In 1931, the Indiana General Assembly adopted a state tree. It produces flowers that are greenish-yellow and grows in all parts of the state. To find out which tree it is, solve each equation. Write the letter on the blank below that corresponds to each solution. You will not use all of the letters.

**State tree of Indiana**

**1.** $x - 4.75 = 2.51$ _____ **E**     **2.** $1.1 + y = 5.9$ _____ **I**

**3.** $z - 55.45 = 5.01$ _____ **T**     **4.** $7.3 - n = 1.2$ _____ **L**

**5.** $0.07 - v = 0.03$ _____ **T**     **6.** $y + 2.44 = 3$ _____ **R**

**7.** $k + 0.066 = 0.088$ _____ **E**     **8.** $1.5 + x = 9.2$ _____ **C**

**9.** $w + 3.002 = 9$ _____ **P**     **10.** $m - 47.5 = 50$ _____ **U**

____  ____  ____  ____  ____    ____  ____  ____  ____
60.46   97.5   6.1   4.8   5.998    0.04   0.56   0.022   7.26

**Extension:** What is your favorite tree that grows in Indiana? Create a puzzle of your own about your favorite tree.
**Indiana Mathematics Proficiency:** (7d) Computation and Estimation; (12) Algebra

Use with Chapter 3, Section B.

Name _____

# Lincoln's Indiana Years

Abraham Lincoln, our nation's sixteenth president, lived in Indiana one-fourth of his life. The Lincolns moved to Indiana in 1816 and stayed until 1830. To find out the county in which the Lincolns lived, solve each equation. Write the letter on the blank below that corresponds to each solution. You will not use all of the letters.

**Painting of young Abe Lincoln**

**1.** $1.3x = 5.2$ _____ **R**     **2.** $0.7m = 4.2$ _____ **N**

**3.** $0.08r = 6.4$ _____ **S**     **4.** $\frac{n}{0.4} = 0.8$ _____ **U**

**5.** $\frac{t}{2.3} = 22.01$ _____ **P**     **6.** $y + 0.091 = 2.5$ _____ **C**

**7.** $0.04z = 2.8$ _____ **E**     **8.** $a - 8.14 = 29.003$ _____ **E**

Abraham Lincoln lived in

_____ _____ _____ _____ _____ _____ _____ County, Indiana.
80   50.623   37.143   6   2.409   70   4

---

**Extension:** Write eight different problems that will have the same solutions as those above.
**Indiana Mathematics Proficiency:** (7d) Computation and Estimation; (12) Algebra

Name _____

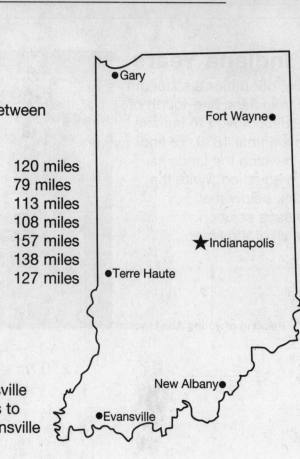

Indiana
4A

# Finding Your Way Around Indiana

Below is a list of distances between selected cities in Indiana.

| | |
|---|---|
| Evansville to Terre Haute | 120 miles |
| Terre Haute to Indianapolis | 79 miles |
| Indianapolis to New Albany | 113 miles |
| New Albany to Evansville | 108 miles |
| Indianapolis to Gary | 157 miles |
| Gary to Fort Wayne | 138 miles |
| Fort Wayne to Indianapolis | 127 miles |

You plan to travel from Evansville to Terre Haute to Indianapolis to New Albany and back to Evansville next week.

1. Use a colored pencil to draw the path of your trip on the map.

2. Find the perimeter of the figure you drew. _____

3. How many miles will you travel on the trip? _____

4. How many feet will you travel on the trip? _____

Your friend plans to travel from Indianapolis to Gary to Fort Wayne and back to Indianapolis.

5. Use a different colored pencil to draw the path of your friend's trip on the map.

6. Find the perimeter of the figure you drew. _____

7. How many miles will your friend travel on the trip? _____

8. How many feet will your friend travel on the trip? _____

**Extension:** Find the distances between cities in kilometers. Then find the length of each trip in kilometers.
**Indiana Mathematics Proficiency:** (7d) Computation and Estimation; (9f and g) Measurement

Use with Chapter 4, Section A.

Name _____

# County Shapes

The area of a region can be approximated by finding the area of a shape that resembles the region. Approximate these areas of the counties in Indiana by finding the area of a shape that resembles it.

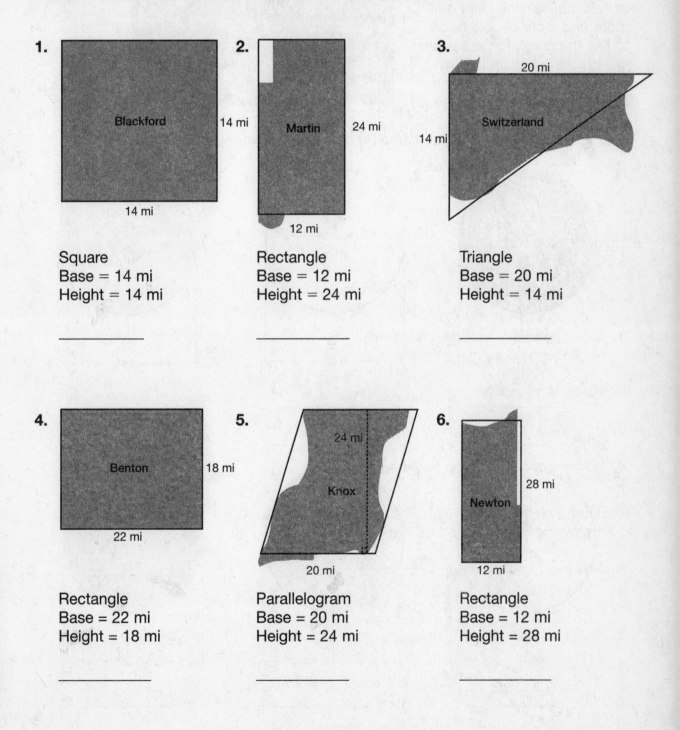

**1.**

Blackford

14 mi

14 mi

Square
Base = 14 mi
Height = 14 mi

_____

**2.**

Martin

24 mi

12 mi

Rectangle
Base = 12 mi
Height = 24 mi

_____

**3.**

20 mi

Switzerland

14 mi

Triangle
Base = 20 mi
Height = 14 mi

_____

**4.**

Benton

18 mi

22 mi

Rectangle
Base = 22 mi
Height = 18 mi

_____

**5.**

24 mi

Knox

20 mi

Parallelogram
Base = 20 mi
Height = 24 mi

_____

**6.**

28 mi

Newton

12 mi

Rectangle
Base = 12 mi
Height = 28 mi

_____

**Extension:** Is there a shape that resembles your county? Approximate the area of your county.
**Indiana Mathematics Proficiency:** (7d) Computation and Estimation; (9g) Measurement

Name _____

# Tomato Tales

Did you know that tomato juice
was invented in Indiana in 1917?
The drink was not very popular
at first, but as time went on,
more and more people began
to like the drink. Tomatoes are
still grown in Indiana today.
Other fruits grown in Indiana
include apples and peaches.

Find the circumference (C) and area (A) of each fruit slice. Use 3.14 for π.

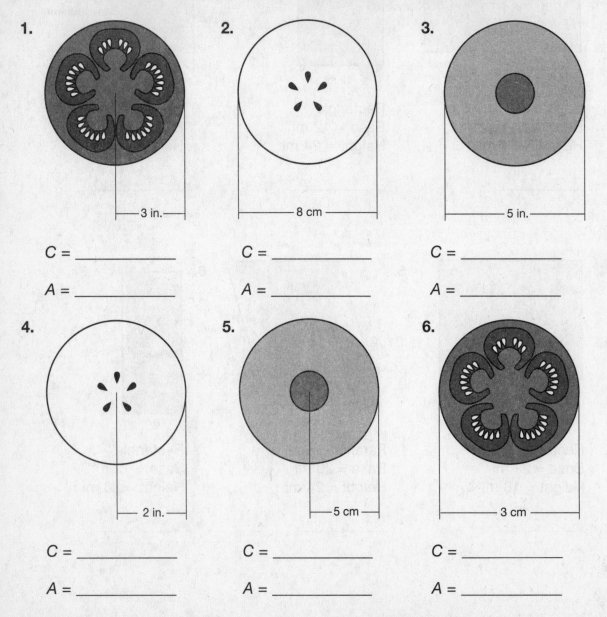

**1.**
├── 3 in. ──┤

C = _____

A = _____

**2.**
├──── 8 cm ────┤

C = _____

A = _____

**3.**
├──── 5 in. ────┤

C = _____

A = _____

**4.**
├── 2 in. ──┤

C = _____

A = _____

**5.**
├──── 5 cm ────┤

C = _____

A = _____

**6.**
├──── 3 cm ────┤

C = _____

A = _____

© Scott Foresman • Addison Wesley 6

***Extension:*** Bring in an apple, peach, or tomato and find the circumference and area of different slices.
***Indiana Mathematics Proficiency:*** (7d) Computation and Estimation; (9g) Measurement

Use with Chapter 4, Section C.

# Indiana's First Teacher

In 1791, Indiana's first teacher was sent to Vincennes by George Washington to teach, for a salary of $200 a year. He became known as the "father of teaching" in the state.

If the first number is divisible by the second number, write its letter on a blank below. The letters should be in the order of the problems. The letters spell the name of Indiana's first teacher.

**Early Indiana classroom**

**1.** 75, 3    **J**        **2.** 72, 9    **O**        **3.** 56, 6    **D**

**4.** 60, 5    **H**        **5.** 64, 10    **I**        **6.** 92, 5    **Q**

**7.** 38, 2    **N**        **8.** 48, 9    **W**        **9.** 63, 9    **R**

**10.** 58, 3    **Z**        **11.** 81, 3    **I**        **12.** 70, 5    **V**

**13.** 26, 3    **W**        **14.** 96, 6    **E**        **15.** 102, 2    **T**

Indiana's first teacher was

___ ___ ___ ___ ___ ___ ___ ___ ___ .

---

***Extension:*** Create three divisibility problems and exchange them with a classmate.
***Indiana Mathematics Proficiency:*** (6b and d) Fractions, Percents, Integers, and Irrationals

Name _____

# Tall Trees

The heights of some of the largest registered trees
in Indiana are listed below.

| | |
|---|---|
| American Chestnut | $\frac{343}{2}$ ft |
| Aspen | $207\frac{1}{4}$ ft |
| Box Elder | $205\frac{4}{8}$ ft |
| Ohio Buckeye | $217\frac{3}{4}$ ft |
| Red Hickory | $205\frac{4}{16}$ ft |
| Shingle Oak | $281\frac{1}{2}$ ft |
| Sugar Maple | $288\frac{9}{12}$ ft |
| Swamp Cottonwood | $\frac{279}{2}$ ft |
| White Pine | $\frac{871}{4}$ ft |

**Ohio buckeye on Indiana University campus
Bloomington, Indiana**

For each fraction, draw a model and name an equivalent fraction.

**1.** $\frac{1}{4}$ _____     **2.** $\frac{3}{4}$ _____     **3.** $\frac{1}{2}$ _____

Write in lowest terms.

**4.** $\frac{4}{8}$ _____     **5.** $\frac{4}{16}$ _____     **6.** $\frac{9}{12}$ _____

Write each improper fraction as a mixed number.

**7.** $\frac{343}{2}$ _____     **8.** $\frac{279}{2}$ _____     **9.** $\frac{871}{4}$ _____

Write each fraction as a decimal.

**10.** $\frac{1}{4}$ _____     **11.** $\frac{3}{4}$ _____     **12.** $\frac{1}{2}$ _____

*Extension:* Find the heights of several other trees in Indiana. Convert the measurements to another form.
*Indiana Mathematics Proficiency:* (6g and h) Fractions, Percents, Integers, and Irrationals

Use with Chapter 5, Section B.

# Just Where Is the Capital?

Did you know that Indianapolis has not always been the state capital. Corydon was the second capital of the Indiana Territory and remained the capital of Indiana through statehood in 1816 until 1824.

**First capitol of the Indiana Territory**

To find out the name of the first capital of the Indiana Territory, solve each equation and write the answer in lowest terms. Write the letter that corresponds to each answer on the appropriate blank below. You will not use all of the letters.

**1.** $x - \dfrac{1}{10} = \dfrac{7}{10}$ _____ **C**   **2.** $a + \dfrac{7}{16} = \dfrac{11}{16}$ _____ **S**

**3.** $\dfrac{1}{8} + k = \dfrac{7}{8}$ _____ **V**   **4.** $m - \dfrac{2}{5} = \dfrac{9}{20}$ _____ **N**

**5.** $n + \dfrac{2}{3} = \dfrac{5}{6}$ _____ **A**   **6.** $\dfrac{7}{10} - w = \dfrac{1}{4}$ _____ **I**

**7.** $\dfrac{5}{16} + t = \dfrac{3}{4}$ _____ **N**   **8.** $g - \dfrac{1}{5} = \dfrac{7}{10}$ _____ **E**

**9.** $\dfrac{2}{3} + y = \dfrac{3}{4}$ _____ **N**   **10.** $z - \dfrac{1}{3} = \dfrac{3}{8}$ _____ **E**

_____  _____  _____  _____  _____  _____  _____  _____  _____
$\dfrac{3}{4}$  $\dfrac{9}{20}$  $\dfrac{7}{16}$  $\dfrac{4}{5}$  $\dfrac{17}{24}$  $\dfrac{17}{20}$  $\dfrac{1}{12}$  $\dfrac{9}{10}$  $\dfrac{1}{4}$

**Extension:** Write your own fraction equations that have the same solutions as the ones on this page.
**Indiana Mathematics Proficiency:** (6d) Fractions, Percents, Integers, and Irrationals; (7d) Computation and Estimation; (12) Algebra

# Let it Rain

Many crops, including corn and soybeans, are grown in Indiana.
Rain and snow provide the moisture needed to grow these crops.
The monthly precipitation recorded at Berne from January
to May in 1996 is given below.

January     $3\frac{9}{10}$ in.

February    $1\frac{1}{2}$ in.

March      $2\frac{2}{5}$ in.

April       $4\frac{2}{5}$ in.

May        $7\frac{1}{2}$ in.

**Indiana cornfield**

Use the information on precipitation to answer the following questions.

1. Estimate the total precipitation for January
   and February. _____

2. Find the exact total precipitation for January
   and February. _____

3. Estimate the total precipitation for April and May. _____

4. Find the exact total precipitation for April and May. _____

5. How much more precipitation fell in May than
   in March? _____

6. How much more precipitation fell in April than
   in February? _____

7. How much more precipitation fell in January than
   in March? _____

8. Use your answer for Problem 2 to find the exact
   total precipitation for January through March. _____

**Extension:** Find the amount of precipitation that fell in your town during each of the last two months.
Find the total precipitation and the difference in the precipitation.
***Indiana Mathematics Proficiency:*** (4a) Problem Solving; (7b and d) Computation and Estimation;
(10b) Data Analysis

Name _____

# Indiana's Grand Old Flag

In 1917, the Indiana General Assembly adopted the current state flag. Two parts of the flag, the torch and the rays, have a special meaning. Liberty and enlightenment are represented by the torch and their influence by the rays.

Indiana State Flag

To find out the name of the designer of the flag, find each product in simplest form. Write the letter that corresponds to each answer on the appropriate blank below.

1. $\frac{3}{8} \times \frac{2}{3}$ _____ **A**

2. $4 \times \frac{5}{8}$ _____ **H**

3. $\frac{1}{9} \times \frac{1}{8}$ _____ **A**

4. $\frac{7}{12} \times \frac{4}{5}$ _____ **P**

5. $\frac{3}{4} \times 10$ _____ **L**

6. $\frac{5}{8} \times 2\frac{1}{5}$ _____ **D**

7. $\frac{1}{6} \times \frac{2}{3}$ _____ **Y**

8. $\frac{5}{9} \times \frac{2}{7}$ _____ **E**

9. $\frac{3}{4} \times 1\frac{1}{2}$ _____ **U**

10. $\frac{3}{7} \times \frac{1}{6}$ _____ **L**

Indiana's flag was designed by

___ ___ ___ ___   ___ ___ ___ ___ ___ ___ .
$\frac{7}{15}$ $\frac{1}{4}$ $1\frac{1}{8}$ $7\frac{1}{2}$   $2\frac{1}{2}$ $\frac{1}{72}$ $1\frac{3}{8}$ $\frac{1}{14}$ $\frac{10}{63}$ $\frac{1}{9}$

**Extension:** Create your own puzzle involving multiplication of fractions.
**Indiana Mathematics Proficiency:** (6c) Fractions, Percents, Integers, and Irrationals; (7d) Computation and Estimation

© Scott Foresman • Addison Wesley 6

Use with Chapter 7, Section A.

Name _____

# The Car Connection

In 1910, the largest car manufacturer in Indiana sold 22,555 cars. The car was named after its manufacturer, and at that time, Indiana was the fifth largest manufacturer of automobiles in the U.S.

**Car that is answer to this puzzle**

Simplify. Write the letter on the blank that corresponds to each answer to learn the name of this famous car manufacturer.

**1.** $\frac{1}{3} \div 6\frac{1}{3}$  _____ **R**

**2.** $10 \div \frac{3}{5}$  _____ **U**

**3.** $\frac{9}{10} \div \frac{1}{5}$  _____ **S**

**4.** $\frac{5}{8} \div \frac{2}{3}$  _____ **E**

**5.** $2\frac{1}{2} \div \frac{1}{8}$  _____ **B**

**6.** $2\frac{1}{10} \div 1\frac{4}{5}$  _____ **K**

**7.** $5\frac{1}{4} \div 1\frac{2}{5}$  _____ **A**

**8.** $4 \div 1\frac{1}{5}$  _____ **D**

**9.** $9 \div \frac{1}{4}$  _____ **T**

**10.** $\frac{4}{5} \div 5$  _____ **E**

___ ___ ___ ___ ___ ___ ___ ___ ___ ___
$4\frac{1}{2}$    36    $16\frac{2}{3}$    $3\frac{1}{3}$    $\frac{15}{16}$    20    $3\frac{3}{4}$    $1\frac{1}{6}$    $\frac{4}{25}$    $\frac{1}{19}$

***Extension:*** Find more information about this famous car manufacturer.
***Indiana Mathematics Proficiency:*** (6d and g) Fractions, Percents, Integers, and Irrationals; (7d) Computation and Estimation

Name _____

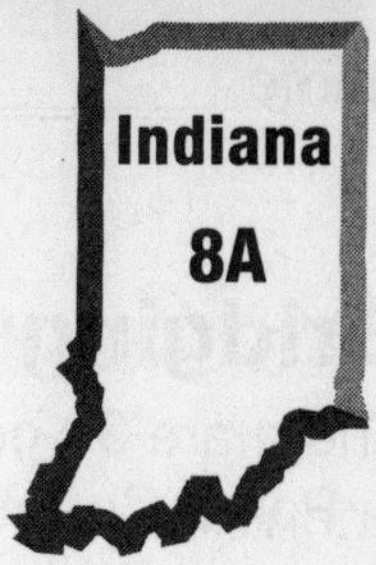

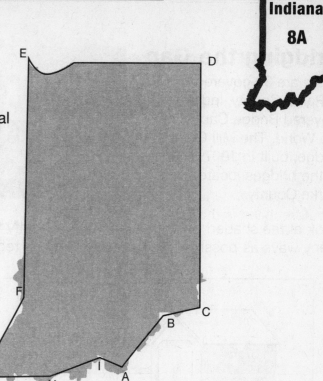

Indiana
8A

# Hoosier Angles

Why is Indiana called the Hoosier state? No one seems to know exactly where the name came from, but several stories are associated with the name. Here is one of them. Many people favor the Samuel Hoosier explanation. Samuel Hoosier was a contractor during the construction of the Ohio Falls Canal in 1826. He liked to hire workers who lived on the Indiana side of the Ohio River. As a result, the name "Hoosier's Men" was given to his crew.

Tell whether each angle in the map above is an acute angle, a right angle, an obtuse angle, or a straight angle.

1. ∠ABC _____

2. ∠FGH _____

3. ∠GHI _____

4. ∠CDE _____

5. ∠IAB _____

6. ∠BCD _____

7. ∠HIA _____

8. ∠GFE _____

Measure each angle with a protractor.

9. ∠ABC _____

10. ∠FGH _____

11. ∠GHI _____

12. ∠CDE _____

13. ∠IAB _____

14. ∠BCD _____

15. ∠HIA _____

16. ∠GFE _____

**Extension:** Look at a map of the United States. Pick four states that appear to have at least 1 right angle in their outlines. Measure all of the angles in these outlines.
**Indiana Mathematics Proficiency:** (9e) Measurement

Name _____

# Bridging the Gap

There are 32 covered bridges in Parke County, Indiana, the Covered Bridge Capital of the World. The Mill Creek bridge, built in 1907, is one of the bridges located in Parke County.

**Parke County covered bridge**

Look at the shaded part of each bridge. Classify the figure in as many ways as possible. Also, tell whether it is regular or irregular.

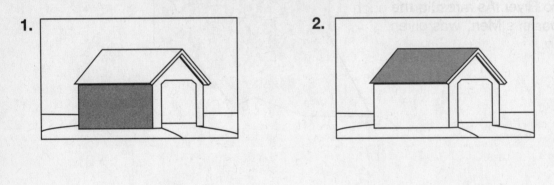

1.

_____

2.

_____

3.

_____

4.

_____

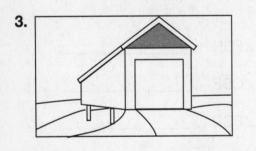

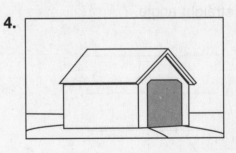

5.

_____

6.

_____

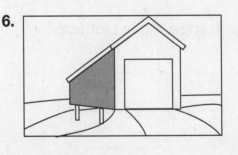

---

***Extension:*** Do you know of any covered bridges in other parts of Indiana? If so, where are they?
***Indiana Mathematics Proficiency:*** (8a) Geometry

Name _____

# Transforming Counties

The outlines of the 92 counties in Indiana show many different shapes, as shown on the state map at the right.

Each figure is the outline of a county in Indiana. Draw the reflection of each outline over the line.

**1.** Clay County

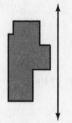

**2.** Fayette County

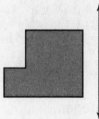

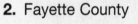

**3.** Orange County

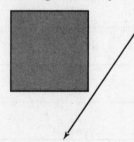

**4.** Adams County

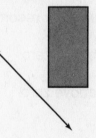

Tell if the outline of each county has lines of symmetry. If it does, tell how many.

**5.** Union County

**6.** Orange County

**7.** Cass County

_____      _____      _____

**Extension:** Draw your own figures and exchange them with a classmate. Tell if the figures have any lines of symmetry, and if they do, how many.
**Indiana Mathematics Proficiency:** (8d and e) Geometry

Name _____

# Highs and Lows

The lowest temperature ever recorded in Indiana was 35°F below zero. The highest temperature ever recorded was 116°F above zero.

**Winter fun in Indiana**

Write each number as an integer.

**1.** The lowest temperature ever recorded in Indiana _____

**2.** The highest temperature ever recorded in Indiana _____

**3.** A temperature of 3°F below zero _____

**4.** A temperature of 8°F above zero _____

**5.** A temperature fall of 6° _____

**6.** A temperature rise of 12° _____

**7.** Find the difference between the highest and the lowest temperatures ever recorded in Indiana. _____

**8.** Which number is farther from zero, the integer for the lowest temperature ever recorded in Indiana or the integer for the highest temperature ever recorded in Indiana? _____

_____

**Extension:** Create three problems of your own about integers and exchange them with a classmate to solve.
**Indiana Mathematics Proficiency:** (6f) Fractions, Percents, Integers, and Irrationals; (7b and e) Computation and Estimation.

Name _____

# Locating Indiana

The northern boundary of Indiana is
Lake Michigan and the state of Michigan.
The southern boundary is the north bank
of the Ohio River. The eastern boundary is
the state of Ohio. The western boundary is
the state of Illinois.

**1.** Plot these points on the coordinate plane below:
   (5, 10), (–5, 10), (–5, –5), (–7, –11), (–3, –10), (5, –5).

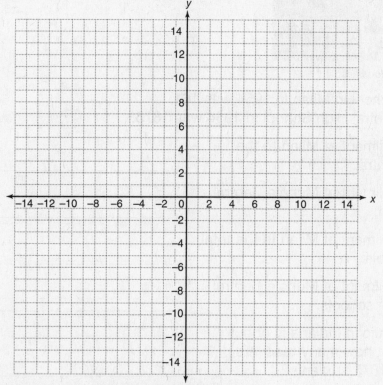

**2.** Connect the points in the order given.
   What does the shape look like?

   _____

   _____

**3.** List all the points in the graph that are located in:

   **a.** Quadrant II        _____

   **b.** Quadrant III       _____

   **c.** Quadrant IV        _____

---

***Extension:*** Add three more points to the graph and give the coordinates of each point.
***Indiana Mathematics Proficiency:*** (6e) Fractions, Percents, Integers, and Irrationals; (12c) Algebra

# Basketball is King

One memorable moment in Indiana basketball occurred in the 1954 Indiana boy's state basketball tournament. In that year, the team from the small town of Milan beat the team from Muncie Central. This fantastic story is told in the movie *Hoosiers*.

**Scene from the movie *Hoosiers***

The enrollment at the high school in Milan in 1954 was 161.
The enrollment at Muncie Central High School in 1954 was 1875.

1. Give the ratio of the enrollment at Milan to the enrollment at Muncie Central. _____

2. Give the ratio of the enrollment at Muncie Central to the enrollment at Milan. _____

3. Give the ratio of the enrollment at Milan to the total enrollment for both schools. _____

4. Give the ratio of the enrollment at Muncie Central to the enrollment for both schools. _____

5. The student to teacher ratio in Indiana is about 18 to 1. At this rate about how many teachers would be in a school of 1875 students? _____

6. Use the information given about the student to teacher ratio in Problem 5. Using this rate, about how many teachers would be in a school of 161 students? _____

7. The ratio of adults to children at a basketball game is expected to be 4 to 1. At this rate how many adults will go to the game if there are 80 children attending? _____

**Extension:** Create two more ratio problems using the enrollment of two high schools in Indiana.
Exchange your problems with a classmate.
***Indiana Mathematics Proficiency:*** (11a) Ratios, Proportions, and Percents

Use with Chapter 10, Section A.

Name _____

# Bringing in the Crops

A large part of the land in Indiana is used for agriculture. Crops and open pasture can be found on about two-thirds of the land.

Some of Indiana's crop production records are given in the table below.

| Crop | Year | Best Yield |
|------|------|------------|
| Corn | 1982 | 129 bushels per acre |
| Soybeans | 1982 | 40 bushels per acre |
| Wheat | 1980 | 49 bushels per acre |
| Oats | 1980 and 1981 | 65 bushels per acre |
| Barley | 1970 | 50 bushels per acre |

Use a proportion to solve each problem.

1. If a farmer can produce 129 bushels of corn on one acre, how many bushels can he produce on 12 acres? _____

2. Given that the ratio of acres to bushels of soybeans is 1 to 40, how many acres would it take to produce 200 bushels of soybeans? _____

3. Given that the ratio of acres to bushels of oats is 1 to 65, how many bushels of oats can be produced on 3 acres? _____

4. Given that the ratio of acres to bushels of barley is 2 to 100, how many bushels of barley will 10 acres produce? _____

**Extension:** Create two problems that can be solved using a proportion. Exchange with a classmate.
**Indiana Mathematics Proficiency:** (7d) Computation and Estimation; (11a, b, and d) Ratios, Proportions, and Percents

Name _____

# Indiana Percents

The total area of Indiana is 36,185 square miles. Water covers
about 1% of the area and land about 99% of the area. Uses
of the land are shown in the table below.

**Land Uses**

| Crops | 60% |
|---------|------|
| Forest | 17% |
| Pasture | 5% |
| Other | 18% |

Convert to a decimal.

**1.** 1% _____     **2.** 99% _____

**3.** 60% _____     **4.** 17% _____

**5.** 5% _____      **6.** 18% _____

Convert to a fraction in lowest terms.

**7.** 1% _____      **8.** 99% _____

**9.** 60% _____     **10.** 17% _____

**11.** 5% _____     **12.** 18% _____

About 36,000 square miles of Indiana is land. Use the table above
to find each of the following.

**13.** The area of land used for crops.      _____

**14.** The area of land used for forest.      _____

**15.** The area of land used for pasture.      _____

**16.** The area of land used for other purposes.      _____

**Extension:** Create two problems of your own from the data. Exchange them with a classmate to solve.
**Indiana Mathematics Proficiency:** (6g and j) Fractions, Percents, Integers, and Irrationals;
(11c and d) Ratios, Proportions, and Percents

Name _____

# A Big Place

Indianapolis is home to the largest covered stadium in Indiana. The stadium, which opened in 1984, can seat 63,000 people. The stadium covers 8 acres and is 193 feet tall at its highest point.

Find the surface area of each solid. Write the letter on the blank that corresponds to each answer to learn the name of the stadium.

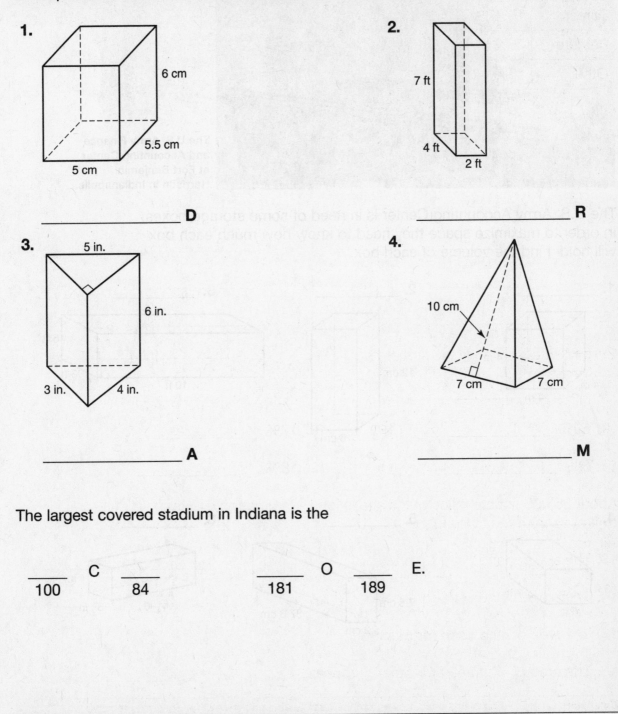

1.

6 cm

5.5 cm

5 cm

_____ D

2.

7 ft

4 ft

2 ft

_____ R

3.

5 in.

6 in.

3 in.    4 in.

_____ A

4.

10 cm

7 cm    7 cm

_____ M

The largest covered stadium in Indiana is the

___ C ___        ___ O ___ E.
100    84          181    189

**Extension:** Have you ever visited this stadium? Describe your experience.
**Indiana Mathematics Proficiency:** (9g) Measurement

Use with Chapter 11, Section A.

Name _____

# Lots of Space

The U.S. Army Finance and Accounting Center at Fort Benjamin Harrison in Indianapolis has the largest floor dimensions of any single structure in Indiana. The building covers 14 acres, is three stories high, and contains 80,000 square feet of windows.

**The U.S. Army Finance and Accounting Center at Fort Benjamin Harrison in Indianapolis.**

The U.S. Army Accounting Center is in need of some storage boxes. In order to maximize space they need to know how much each box will hold. Find the volume of each box.

1. _____

2. _____

3. _____

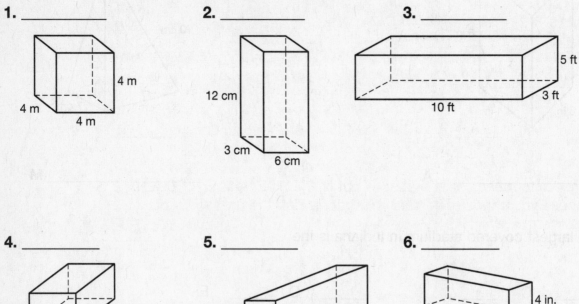

4. _____

5. _____

6. _____

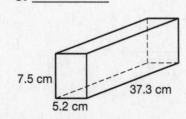

---

**Extension:** Find the volume of your classroom or a room in your house.
**Indiana Mathematics Proficiency:** (9g) Measurement

# What's in a Name?

Native Americans, originally called Indians, first came to what is now known as Indiana over 10,000 years ago to hunt mammoths. Native Americans remained in the area for many years. In fact, most of the area was called Indian territory as late as 1800. The land eventually was called Indiana, which means "land of many Indians."

**Angel Mounds**

There are seven cards that spell out I N D I A N A. Suppose you choose one card at random. Find the probability of each event.

**1.** *P*(N) _____

**2.** *P*(D) _____

**3.** *P*(I) _____

**4.** *P*(A) _____

**5.** *P*(vowel) _____

**6.** *P*(consonant) _____

There are fourteen cards that spell out N A T I V E   A M E R I C A N. Suppose you choose one card at random. Find the probability of each event.

**7.** *P*(N) _____

**8.** *P*(V) _____

**9.** *P*(E) _____

**10.** *P*(A) _____

**11.** *P*(vowel) _____

**12.** *P*(consonant) _____

**Extension:** Create three of your own probability problems using one of the key words in the paragraph at the top of the page.
***Indiana Mathematics Proficiency:*** (10i) Data Analysis

# The Probability of Lincoln

Indiana's connection to Abraham Lincoln, our nation's sixteenth president, is well known. The history of the Lincoln penny may not be so well known. The Lincoln penny was designed by Victor D. Brenner. Pennies before 1959 were called "wheat pennies" because of the wheat designs on the tail side of the coin. In 1959 the tail side was changed to the Lincoln Memorial.

**Wheat penny**

**Penny with Lincoln Memorial**

Two pennies are flipped.

**1.** Draw a tree diagram showing all possible outcomes.

Two pennies are flipped at the same time. Find the probability of each event.

**2.** *P*(H, H)  _____     **3.** *P*(H, T)  _____

**4.** *P*(T, T)  _____     **5.** *P*(T, H)  _____

A penny is flipped and the spinner is spun once. Find the probability of each event.

**6.** *P*(H, 2)  _____     **7.** *P*(T, even number)  _____

**8.** *P*(T, less than 3)  _____     **9.** *P*(H, prime number)  _____

*Extension:* Design a game using two pennies that is not fair.
*Indiana Mathematics Proficiency:* (10 j and l) Data Analysis

# Reading Graphs

Use the Disney Park Attendance pictograph to answer Exercises 1–5.

**1.** Which park had the fewest visitors?

_____

**Disney Park Attendance, 1993**

Disneyland ♥♥♥♥♥♥♥♥♥♥

EPCOT at Disneyworld ♥♥♥♥♥♥♥♥♥

Magic Kingdom at Disneyworld ♥♥♥♥♥♥♥♥♥♥♥

Disney-MGM Studios ♥♥♥♥♥♥♥♥

♥ = 1 million visitors

**2.** Which park had the most visitors?

_____

**3.** How many visitors did EPCOT have? _____

**4.** Which park had more visitors, Disneyland or EPCOT? _____

**5.** What is the total number of visitors to the four parks? _____

Use the Children in U.S. Families graph to answer Exercises 6–7.

**Children in U.S. Families**

**6.** What percent of families include exactly 2 children?

_____

No children, 51%

4 or more children, 3%

1 child, 20%

2 children, 19%

3 children, 7%

**7.** Of the categories shown, which is the largest?

_____

Use the graph of the Five Best-selling Motorcycle Brands to answer Exercises 8–11.

**The Five Best-selling Motorcycle Brands, 1993**

**8.** Which brand sold the most motorcycles?

_____

**9.** Which brand (of the five shown) sold the fewest?

_____

**10.** About how many Honda motorcycles were sold?

_____

Number sold (thousands) — 100, 80, 60, 40, 20, 0

Honda, Suzuki, Yamaha, Harley-Davidson, Kawasaki

Brand

**11.** Which brand sold more motorcycles, Suzuki or Kawasaki? _____

# Misleading Graphs

Use the Number of Jobs in the U.S. graph for Exercises 1–4.

**Number of Jobs in the U.S.,
1990-1992**

1. About how many times taller does the July 1990 bar appear to be than the July 1991 bar?

   _____

2. Read the graph. How many jobs were there

   in July 1990? _____

   in July 1991? _____

3. Compare your answers to Exercises 1 and 2. Could the bar graph be misleading? If so, how would you correct the graph?

   _____

   _____

4. How many more jobs were there in July 1990 than in July 1992?

   _____

Use the Endangered Birds graph for Exercises 5–8.

**Endangered Birds**

5. The number of endangered bird species in Hawaii appears to be how many times greater than the number of endangered bird species in Texas?

   _____

6. Texas has how many endangered bird species?

   _____

7. Hawaii has how many endangered bird species?

   _____

8. Could the bar graph be misleading? If so, how would you correct the graph?

   _____

   _____

Name _____

# Scatterplots and Trends

For each scatterplot, determine if there is a trend. If there is, describe the pattern of the data.

1. _____

_____

2. _____

_____

Use the scatterplot for Exercises 3–8.

3. Is there a trend? If so, describe the pattern of the data.

_____

_____

4. Name two points that represent people who are the

same age. _____ How old are they? _____

5. Which point represents the youngest person? _____ the oldest person? _____

6. Which point represents the shortest person? _____ the tallest person? _____

7. a. Name two points that represent people who are the same height. _____

b. How tall are they? _____

8. Give the approximate age and height represented by each point.

a. A                    b. B                    c. C                    d. D

age _____          age _____          age _____          age _____

height _____        height _____        height _____        height _____

Name _____

# Section 1A Review

Use the bar graph for Exercises 1–3.

**Active-duty Personnel, 1992**

1. Which of the armed services had

   the most active-duty personnel? _____

   the fewest active-duty personnel? _____

2. About how many active-duty personnel were in

   the Navy? _____

3. About how many more active-duty personnel
   were in the Army than in the Air Force?

   _____

Use the line graphs for Exercises 4–6.

**NASA Spending, 1970-1990**

4. How much did NASA spend

   in 1975? _____

   in 1985? _____

5. Describe the change in the data over time.

   _____

   _____

6. How are the two graphs alike? How are they different?

   _____

   _____

7. **Consumer** A clock radio sells for $26.00. If a customer
   pays $30.00 for the radio, how much change should be
   given? Assume there is no tax. *[Previous Course]*       _____

8. Last summer Rolando read 17 books. If each book had
   236 pages, how many pages did Rolando read all together?   _____

© Scott Foresman • Addison Wesley 6

# Tallies, Frequency Charts, and Line Plots

Make a frequency chart for each set of tally marks in Exercises 1–2.

**1.** Number of hours of television watched yesterday

| Hours | Tally |
|-------|-------|
| 0 | III |
| 1 | HHT II |
| 2 | HHT |
| 3 | HHT III |
| 4 | III |
| 5 | II |

**Frequency Chart**

**2.** Number of pets at home

| Pets | Tally |
|------|-------|
| 0 | HHT HHT HHT II |
| 1 | HHT HHT II |
| 2 | HHT III |
| 3 | HHT I |
| 4 | III |
| 5 | I |

**Frequency Chart**

**3.** Make a line plot of the number of books read last month.

| Books | Frequency |
|-------|-----------|
| 0 | 4 |
| 1 | 6 |
| 2 | 3 |
| 3 | 2 |
| 4 | 1 |

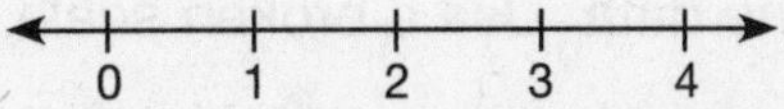

0   1   2   3   4

**4.** The following data set shows the answers people gave when asked how many hours they slept last night: 8, 7, 8, 6, 8, 7, 5, 6, 9, 7, 6, 8, 7, 9, 7

**a.** Make a frequency chart for the data.    **b.** Make a line plot for the data.

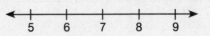

5   6   7   8   9

# Scales and Bar Graphs

**1.** Make a bar graph from the data showing the number of answering machines sold from 1989 to 1993.

| Year | Millions of machines |
|------|---------------------|
| 1989 | 3.7 |
| 1990 | 5.6 |
| 1991 | 8.0 |
| 1992 | 11.1 |
| 1993 | 13.6 |

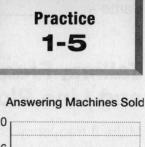
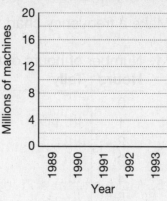

Answering Machines Sold

**2. Social Science** The data shows the average size of U.S. households from 1960 to 1990. Make a bar graph of the data.

| Year | Average household size |
|------|-----------------------|
| 1960 | 3.33 |
| 1970 | 3.14 |
| 1980 | 2.76 |
| 1990 | 2.63 |

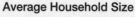
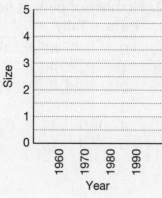

Average Household Size

**3.** What is the range of the data for the average household size in Exercise 2?

_____

**4. Career** The data shows the 1990 average weekly earnings of workers in several industries. Make a bar graph of the data. Use a broken scale, if appropriate.

| Industry | Earnings |
|----------|----------|
| Iron and steel foundries | 484.99 |
| Electric and electric equipment | 420.65 |
| Machinery, non-electrical | 494.34 |
| Hardware, cutlery, hand tools | 440.08 |
| Fabricated metal products | 447.28 |

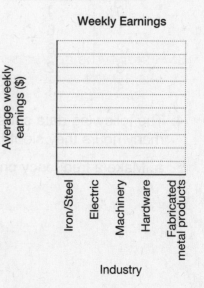

Weekly Earnings

Name _____

# Stem-and-Leaf Diagrams

Use the stem-and-leaf diagram for Exercises 1–4.

| stem | leaf |
|------|------|
| 6 | 7 8 8 |
| 7 | 0 1 2 3 4 9 9 |
| 8 | 1 3 3 3 4 7 |
| 9 | 0 2 5 |

1. What is the range of the values? _____

2. What value appears most often? _____

3. How many times does the value 79 appear? _____

4. What is the largest number in the data that is less than 90? _____

5. Make a stem-and-leaf diagram of the data showing scores on a history test.

| stem | leaf |
|------|------|
| | |

84, 93, 72, 87, 75, 86, 97, 68, 74, 86, 91, 64, 83, 79, 80, 72, 83, 76, 90, 77

6. Make a stem-and-leaf diagram of the data showing the number of badges earned by local scouts.

| stem | leaf |
|------|------|
| | |

7, 12, 9, 2, 17, 24, 0, 3, 10, 20, 12, 3, 6, 4, 9, 15

7. Make a stem-and-leaf diagram of the data showing the number of compact discs owned by some students.

| stem | leaf |
|------|------|
| | |

17, 36, 0, 64, 5, 0, 39, 12, 7, 19, 67, 42, 0, 3, 12, 4, 9, 13, 17, 31, 0

8. **History** The data shows the number of individuals who served as cabinet members for each of the first 21 Presidents. Make a stem-and-leaf diagram of the data.

| stem | leaf |
|------|------|
| | |

Washington: 11   J. Adams: 8   Jefferson: 10
Madison: 16   Monroe: 8   J.Q. Adams: 6
Jackson: 19   Van Buren: 10   W. Harrison: 6
Tyler: 21   Polk: 9   Taylor: 7
Fillmore: 11   Pierce: 7   Buchanan: 14
Lincoln: 13   A. Johnson: 13   Grant: 23
Hayes: 10   Garfield: 7   Arthur: 17

Name _____

# Section 1B Review

**1.** Make a frequency chart and a line plot of the data showing the number of teachers that a set of students have at Monroe Middle School.

3, 7, 4, 7, 3, 5, 6, 4, 6, 4, 5, 6, 4, 7, 5, 6

**Frequency Chart**                                          **Line Plot**

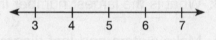

**2. Geography** Make a bar graph of the data showing the five longest rivers in America. Use a broken scale, if appropriate.

| River | Length (mi) |
|-------|-------------|
| Missouri | 2540 |
| Mississippi | 2340 |
| Yukon | 1980 |
| St. Lawrence | 1900 |
| Arkansas | 1460 |

Longest U.S. Rivers

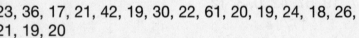

**3.** Make a stem-and-leaf diagram of the data showing the scores that some students received in a spelling bee.

23, 36, 17, 21, 42, 19, 30, 22, 61, 20, 19, 24, 18, 26, 21, 19, 20

stem | leaf

**4.** Give the approximate weight and price for the package of cereal represented by each point in the scatterplot.
*[Lesson 1-3]*

A: weight _____ price _____

B: weight _____ price _____

C: weight _____ price _____

D: weight _____ price _____

E: weight _____ price _____

F: weight _____ price _____

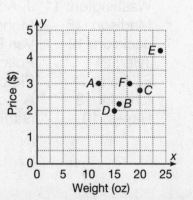

# Median and Mode

Find the median and mode(s).

**1.** median _____

    mode(s) _____

```
        X
        X   X
    X   X   X       X
    X   X   X   X   X
    X   X   X   X   X
 <--+---+---+---+---+-->
   23  24  25  26  27
```

**2.** median _____

    mode(s) _____

```
     X
 X   X
 X   X   X
 X   X   X   X       X
 X   X   X   X   X   X   X
 <--+---+---+---+---+---+---+-->
    6   7   8   9  10  11  12
```

**3.** median _____

    mode(s) _____

| stem | leaf |
|------|------|
| 1 | 8 8 9 |
| 2 | 0 3 5 5 7 9 |
| 3 | 1 3 8 |
| 4 | 2 3 5 |

**4.** median _____

    mode(s) _____

| stem | leaf |
|------|------|
| 3 | 4 6 9 |
| 5 | 0 2 3 7 8 |
| 6 | 1 4 6 7 |
| 7 | 2 3 |

**5.** 13, 19, 20, 22, 24, 19, 14, 18, 20, 19, 32, 17, 40, 27, 25, 35, 28.

    median _____      mode(s) _____

In Exercises 6–7, make a line plot for each data set, and then find the median and mode(s).

**6.** 12, 21, 17, 13, 19, 12, 17, 15, 21, 17, 14, 13

    median _____      mode(s) _____

```
 <--+--+--+--+--+--+--+--+--+--+-->
   12 13 14 15 16 17 18 19 20 21
```

**7.** 6, 12, 8, 7, 10, 12, 8, 9, 11, 8, 7, 10, 11

    median _____      mode(s) _____

```
 <--+---+---+---+---+---+---+-->
    6   7   8   9  10  11  12
```

**8.** Find the median and mode(s) for the number of congressional representatives for the southern states:

Alabama: 7      Georgia: 11      Mississippi: 5      Tennessee: 9
Arkansas: 4      Kentucky: 6      North Carolina: 12      Texas: 30
Delaware: 1      Louisiana: 7      Oklahoma: 6      Virginia: 11
Florida: 23      Maryland: 8      South Carolina: 6      West Virginia: 3

    median _____      mode(s) _____

# The Meaning of Mean

Find the mean of each set of data.

**1.** mean _____

```
          X
      X   X
  X   X   X
X X   X   X   X
7   8   9  10  11
```

**2.** mean _____

```
      X
  X   X       X
  X   X   X   X
  X   X   X   X   X
21  22  23  24  25
```

**3.** mean _____

| stem | leaf |
|------|------|
| 0 | 7 7 8 |
| 1 | 0 1 3 8 9 9 |
| 2 | 0 0 1 1 4 6 9 |
| 3 | 0 2 |

**4.** mean _____

| stem | leaf |
|------|------|
| 3 | 4 7 8 |
| 4 | 0 1 3 3 7 9 |
| 5 | 1 1 4 6 |
| 6 | 0 1 |

Find the mean, median, and mode(s) of each data set.

**5.** 8, 10, 10, 12, 14, 18, 21, 35

mean _____

median _____

mode(s) _____

**6.** 23, 28, 36, 36, 42, 49, 64, 83, 94

mean _____

median _____

mode(s) _____

**7.** 41, 18, 63, 24, 37, 72, 84

mean _____

median _____

mode(s) _____

**8.** 6, 3, 8, 7, 5, 7, 6, 2, 9, 9, 4, 3, 9, 4

mean _____

median _____

mode(s) _____

**9.** Find the mean, median, and mode(s) of the data showing the number of members of local scout troops.

41, 75, 32, 115, 75, 68, 81, 93, 102, 53, 49, 71

mean _____ median _____ mode(s) _____

**10.** Find the mean, median, and mode(s) of the data showing the number of points scored by the Hooping Cranes basketball team in their last 12 games.

87, 112, 98, 93, 79, 80, 89, 83, 91, 93, 86, 101

mean _____ median _____ mode(s) _____

Name _____

# The Effects of Outliers

Identify the outlier in each data set.

**1.** _____

23, 32, 21, 36, 84, 27, 32, 29

**2.** _____

90, 87, 112, 96, 11, 107, 93, 85

**3.** _____

| stem | leaf |
|------|------|
| 3 | 6 7 8 8 9 |
| 4 | 0 1 3 3 4 5 7 9 9 |
| 5 | 0 1 1 2 |
| 6 | 9 |

**4.** _____

| stem | leaf |
|------|------|
| 1 | 4 |
| 3 | 5 7 8 |
| 4 | 0 2 2 3 5 7 9 |
| 5 | 2 |

**5.** _____

| stem | leaf |
|------|------|
| 4 | 8 |
| 5 | 0 1 1 3 5 7 7 9 |
| 6 | 3 4 |
| 8 | 2 |

**6.** _____

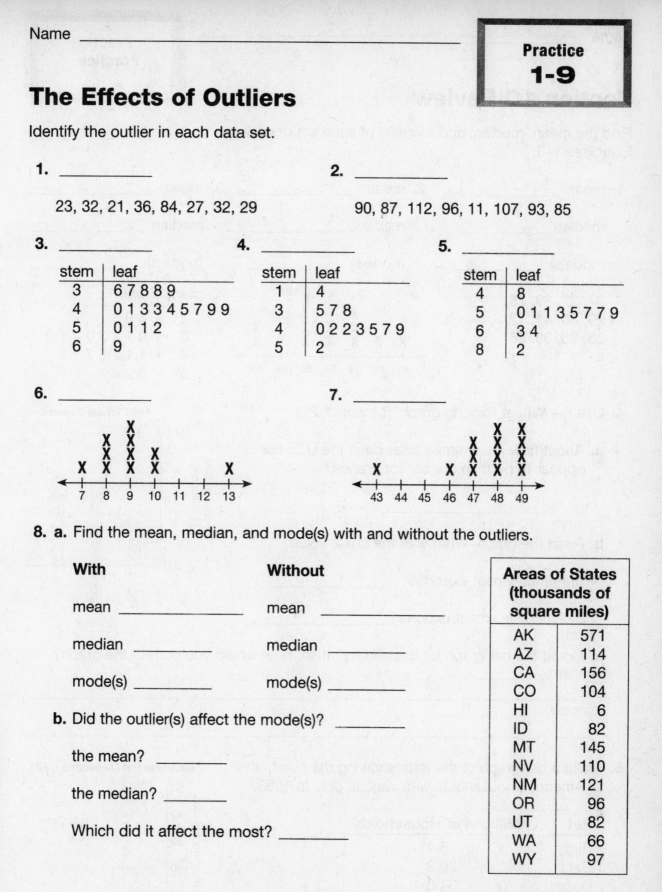

**7.** _____

**8. a.** Find the mean, median, and mode(s) with and without the outliers.

**With**

mean _____

median _____

mode(s) _____

**Without**

mean _____

median _____

mode(s) _____

| Areas of States (thousands of square miles) | |
|------|------|
| AK | 571 |
| AZ | 114 |
| CA | 156 |
| CO | 104 |
| HI | 6 |
| ID | 82 |
| MT | 145 |
| NV | 110 |
| NM | 121 |
| OR | 96 |
| UT | 82 |
| WA | 66 |
| WY | 97 |

**b.** Did the outlier(s) affect the mode(s)? _____

the mean? _____

the median? _____

Which did it affect the most? _____

Name _____

# Section 1C Review

Find the mean, median, and mode(s) of each set of data in Exercises 1–3.

**1.** mean _____

median _____

mode(s) _____

34, 27, 39, 25,
29, 30, 41, 12,
33, 25, 38, 26

**2.** mean _____

median _____

mode(s) _____

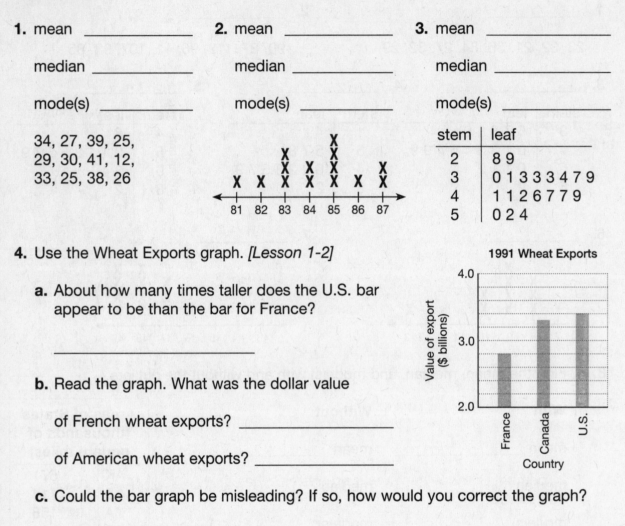

**3.** mean _____

median _____

mode(s) _____

| stem | leaf |
|------|------|
| 2 | 8 9 |
| 3 | 0 1 3 3 3 4 7 9 |
| 4 | 1 1 2 6 7 7 9 |
| 5 | 0 2 4 |

**4.** Use the Wheat Exports graph. *[Lesson 1-2]*

**a.** About how many times taller does the U.S. bar appear to be than the bar for France?

_____

**b.** Read the graph. What was the dollar value

of French wheat exports? _____

of American wheat exports? _____

**c.** Could the bar graph be misleading? If so, how would you correct the graph?

_____

_____

**1991 Wheat Exports**

**5.** Make a bar graph of the data showing the number of American households with various pets in 1993.

| Pet | Millions of Households |
|------|------|
| Birds | 5.4 |
| Cats | 29.2 |
| Dogs | 34.6 |
| Fish | 2.7 |
| Rabbits | 2.3 |

**American Pet Ownership, 1993**

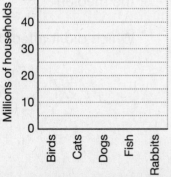

# Cumulative Review Chapter 1

Add, subtract, multiply, or divide. *[Previous Course]*

**1.**  3 8
     + 8 4

**2.**  8 3 7
     − 1 2 3

**3.**  3 8 7
     ×     3

**4.** 6)2322

**5.** 8)1552

**6.** 13)2171

**Social Science** Use the American Grandparents graph to answer each question. *[Lesson 1-8]*

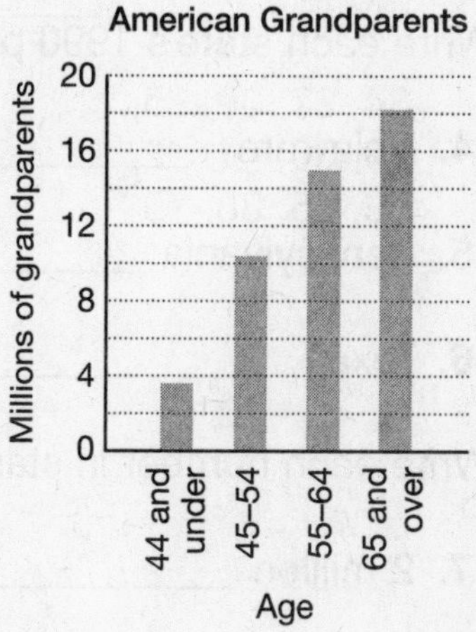

**American Grandparents**

**7.** Which age group includes

the most grandparents? _____

the fewest grandparents? _____

**8.** About how many are in the 45 to 54 age group?

_____

**9.** Estimate the total number of grandparents shown in the data. _____

The circle graph shows the results of a poll in which people were asked to name the most important factor in sleeping well. Use it to answer each question. *[Lesson 1-1]*

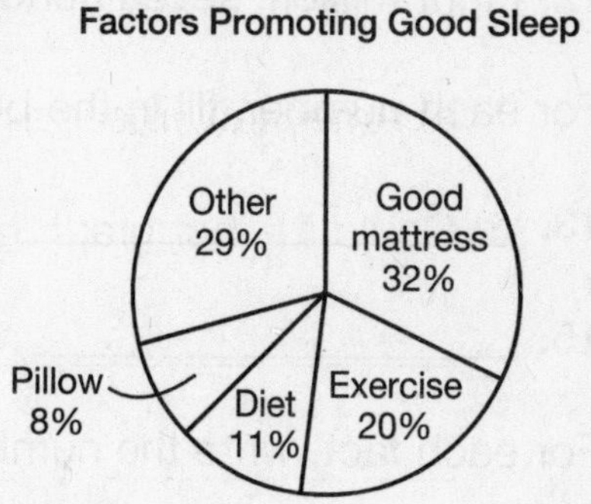

**Factors Promoting Good Sleep**

**10.** What percent of those surveyed said exercise was the most important factor?

_____

**11.** What was the most common response?

_____

Find the mean of each set of data. *[Lesson 1-8]*

**12.** mean _____

12, 17, 23, 42,
37, 21, 15, 45,
18, 31, 25, 38,
17, 24, 34, 29

**13.** mean _____

| stem | leaf |
|------|------|
| 3 | 4 7 7 8 |
| 4 | 0 0 2 3 3 4 7 8 |
| 5 | 1 3 3 5 9 |
| 6 | 2 5 |

**14.** mean _____

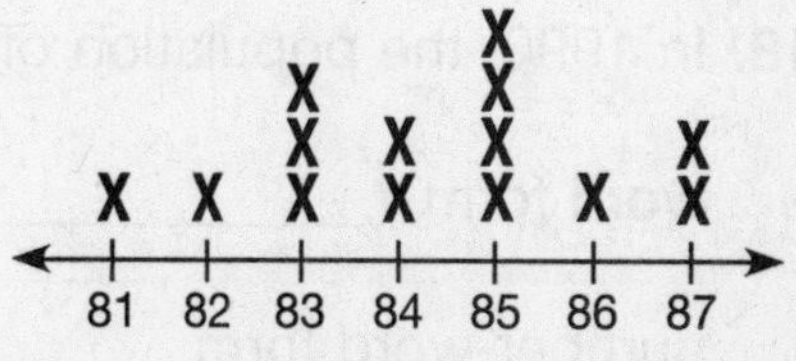

Name _____

# Reading and Writing Large Numbers

Write the number in words.

**1.** 3784 _____

**2.** 842,630 _____

**3.** 7,308,060 _____

Write each state's 1990 population in number-word form.

**4.** Delaware _____

**5.** Pennsylvania _____

**6.** Texas _____

| State | 1990 Population |
|-------|-----------------|
| Delaware | 700,000 |
| Pennsylvania | 12,000,000 |
| Texas | 18,000,000 |

Write each number in standard form.

**7.** 2 million _____   **8.** 63 thousand _____

**9.** 42 billion _____   **10.** 15 trillion _____

**11.** Five billion, six hundred fifty thousand, three hundred twenty _____

**12.** Eight million, seven hundred twenty thousand, two hundred five _____

For each number, fill in the blank. Give your answers in standard form.

**13.** _____ = 93 billion  **14.** _____ = 2 trillion

**15.** _____ = 23 million  **16.** _____ = 24 thousand

For each fact, write the number in word form and in number-word form.

**17.** In 1990, Pepsico had sales of $18,000,000,000.

word form _____

number-word form _____

**18.** In 1990, the population of New York City was 7,000,000.

word form _____

number-word form _____

# Rounding Large Numbers

Round to the given place.

**1.** 38,721,830, ten-millions

_____

**2.** 432,483, ten-thousands

_____

**3.** 1,387,216, tens

_____

**4.** 83,172,635,810, hundred-millions

_____

**5.** 392,621, hundred-thousands

_____

**6.** 471,832,103, millions

_____

**7.** 217,384,166,982,364, hundred-billions _____

**8.** 37,852,408,069,843, ten-thousands _____

**9.** 3,871,664,397,972, hundred-millions _____

**10.** 6,378,294,183,275, trillions _____

Major league baseball games were attended by 56,603,451 fans in 1990.

**11.** Write the number of fans in words. _____

_____

**12.** Round the number of fans to the given place.

**a.** hundreds _____

**b.** millions _____

**c.** ten-thousands _____

**d.** ten-millions _____

**e.** thousands _____

**f.** hundred-thousands _____

**13.** Thom's kitchen requires 33 feet of wallpaper border. He selects a
design that is available in a package containing a 10-foot length.
Since 33 rounds to 30, he buys 3 packages. Do you agree with his
reasoning? Explain.

_____

Name _____

# Comparing and Ordering Numbers

Order each group of numbers from least to greatest.

**1.** 3,000; 20,000; 400; 50 _____

**2.** 38,000; 37,940; 38,010 _____

**3.** 6,748; 6,847; 6,487; 6,874 _____

**4.** 3,333; 33,333; 33; 333 _____

**5.** 78,321; 873,210; 783,210 _____

**6.** 1,243; 1,342; 1,324; 1,234 _____

**7.** 99,909; 99,000; 99,900; 90,000 _____

**8.** 37,630; 37,628; 37,624; 37,700 _____

**9.** 82,270; 83,100; 82,200; 82,170 _____

**10.** 48,380; 48,376; 48,408; 48,480 _____

**11.** 63,821; 63,900; 63,800; 64,000 _____

**12.** 10 million; 1 billion; 10 thousand _____

**13.** 1,675; 15 hundred; 2 thousand _____

**14.** 19 million; 2 million; 30 thousand _____

**15.** 200 billion; 5 trillion; 990 million _____

**16.** 18 thousand; 18 million; 180,000 _____

**17.** In 1990, the Broadway show *Cats* grossed $22,941,820 and *Gypsy*
grossed $21,941,875. Compare these numbers using < or >.

_____

**18.** In 1990, 3,379,000 Americans were employed in food stores,
3,665,000 were employed in transportation, and 3,363,000 were
employed in finance. Rank these industries from the fewest
employees to the most employees.

_____

# Exponents

Write using exponents.

**1.** $3 \times 3 \times 3 \times 3$ _____

**2.** $364 \times 364$ _____

**3.** $2 \times 2 \times 2 \times 2 \times 2 \times 2 \times 2$ _____

**4.** $13 \times 13 \times 13$ _____

**5.** $8 \times 8 \times 8 \times 7 \times 7$ _____

**6.** $49$ _____

Write in expanded form.

**7.** $10^4$ _____

**8.** $6^5$ _____

**9.** $3^2$ _____

**10.** $7^3$ _____

**11.** $12^4$ _____

**12.** 5 cubed _____

Write in standard form.

**13.** $5^4$ _____

**14.** $2^6$ _____

**15.** 11 squared _____

**16.** $10^7$ _____

**17.** $12^2$ _____

**18.** 6 cubed _____

Compare using $<$, $>$, or $=$.

**19.** $4^2 \bigcirc 2^4$

**20.** $4^3 \bigcirc 3^4$

**21.** $5^8 \bigcirc 5^9$

**22.** $3^8 \bigcirc 3 \times 8$

**23.** $2^5 \bigcirc 5^2$

**24.** $10^3 \bigcirc 10 + 10 + 10$

**25.** $5^3 \bigcirc 5 \times 5 \times 5$

**26.** $7^3 \bigcirc 3^7$

**27.** $10^4 \bigcirc 4 \times 10$

For each number in exponential notation, identify the base, exponent, and power. Use a calculator to write each number in standard form.

**28.** A typical American kid watches about $18^4$ television advertisements between birth and high school graduation.

base _____          exponent _____

power _____          standard form _____

**29.** The highest point in Kentucky is Black Mountain. Its height is about $2^{12}$ feet.

base _____          exponent _____

power _____          standard form _____

# Section 2A Review

Write each number in standard form. Then round that number to the place indicated.

**1.** $3^4$; tens

standard form _____

rounded _____

**2.** $7^5$; thousands

standard form _____

rounded _____

**3.** $5^4$; hundreds

standard form _____

rounded _____

The table lists the 1990 populations of several American cities.

**4.** Order the populations from least to greatest.

_____

_____

| City | Population |
|------|-----------|
| Detroit, MI | 1,027,974 |
| St. Louis, MO | 396,685 |
| Cleveland, OH | 505,616 |
| Chattanooga, TN | 152,466 |
| Pittsburgh, PA | 369,879 |

**5.** Round each population to the nearest ten-thousand.

_____

Compare using $<$, $>$, or $=$.

**6.** 37,990 $\bigcirc$ 38,000

**7.** $4^5$ $\bigcirc$ $5^4$

**8.** 630,000 $\bigcirc$ six thousand, thirty

**9.** 8,000,000,000 $\bigcirc$ 8 trillion

**10.** $7 \times 3$ $\bigcirc$ $7^3$

**11.** 6580 $\bigcirc$ 64,800

**12.** The scatterplot shows the number of dogs and cats in several pet stores. *[Lesson 1-3]*

   **a.** Which point represents the store with the most dogs?

   _____

   How many dogs does this store have? _____

   **b.** Which two points represent stores with the same number of cats?

   _____

   How many cats does each of these stores have? _____

# Mental Math

Simplify.

**1.** $60 \times 70$ _____

**2.** $162 + 37$ _____

**3.** $142 + 321$ _____

**4.** $2 \times 21 \times 5$ _____

**5.** $3 \times 81$ _____

**6.** $2,700 \div 9$ _____

**7.** $162 + 17 + 38$ _____

**8.** $38 \times 7$ _____

**9.** $295 + 85$ _____

**10.** $28,000 \div 700$ _____

**11.** $37 + 42$ _____

**12.** $20 \times 50 \times 37$ _____

**13.** $100 \times 300$ _____

**14.** $62 \times 5$ _____

**15.** $875 + 627 + 125$ _____

**16.** $42 \times 9$ _____

**17.** $79 \times 4$ _____

**18.** $164 + 135$ _____

**19.** $8 \times 1,200$ _____

**20.** $173 - 98$ _____

**21.** $25 \times 40 \times 17$ _____

**22.** $38 + 87 + 62$ _____

**23.** $70 \times 3,000$ _____

**24.** $600 + 327 + 400$ _____

**25.** $87 \times 4$ _____

**26.** $3,800 \div 20$ _____

**27.** $3,143 + 222$ _____

**28.** $300 \times 160$ _____

**29.** $20 \times 21 \times 50$ _____

**30.** $387 - 295$ _____

**31.** $213 \times 2$ _____

**32.** $63,000 \div 700$ _____

**33.** $750,000 \div 2,500$ _____

**34.** $64 + 46$ _____

**35.** $12,387 - 4,387$ _____

**36.** $38,000 \div 190$ _____

**37.** $52 \times 40$ _____

**38.** $39 \times 90$ _____

**39.** $5 \times 37 \times 200$ _____

**40.** $6,700 + 1,200$ _____

**41.** $8,416 - 8,116$ _____

**42.** $83,725 - 300$ _____

**43.** $389 + 711$ _____

**44.** $100,000 \div 40$ _____

**45.** $320,000 \div 400$ _____

**46.** $310 \times 40$ _____

**47.** $56,000 \div 800$ _____

**48.** $185 + 32$ _____

**49.** $90,000 \div 300$ _____

**50.** $520,000 \div 130$ _____

**51.** $2,587 - 198$ _____

**52.** $64,107 - 304$ _____

**53.** $2,200 \times 30$ _____

**54.** $63,000 \div 90$ _____

**55.** It takes 300 gallons of water to produce one pound of synthetic rubber. How many gallons of water does it take to produce 8 pounds of synthetic rubber? _____

**56.** A typical box of personal bank checks contains 200 checks which have been assembled in 8 booklets. How many checks are in each booklet? _____

Name _____

# Estimating Sums and Differences

Estimate.

**1.** 38,624 + 83,102

_____

**2.** 47,623 − 12,385

_____

**3.** 37 + 42 + 43

_____

**4.** 387 + 410 + 405

_____

**5.** 824,368 + 217,638

_____

**6.** 847,167 − 382,208

_____

**7.** 6375 − 1890

_____

**8.** 7538 + 2317

_____

**9.** 163,462 + 3,210

_____

**10.** 6138 + 5963 + 6023 + 5874 + 6003 _____

**11.** 69 + 73 + 71 + 68 + 70 + 72 + 67 + 72 _____

**12.** 894 + 925 + 888 + 907 + 873 + 895 _____

**13.** 83,762 + 83,984 + 84,731 + 84,201 _____

**14.** 38,124 + 92,064 + 67,312 + 53,720 _____

**15.** 1632 + 3129 + 6473 + 3217 _____

**16.** 867,530 + 9,874 + 128,382 _____

**17.** 58,128 + 59,370 + 60,028 + 62,310 _____

**18.** 92,163 + 87,920 + 91,325 + 89,012 _____

**19.** A world record for dart throwing was set by the Broken Hill Darts Club, who achieved a score of 1,722,249 points in 24 hours. The record score for a women's team is 744,439, achieved by a British team. About how many more points were scored by the Broken Hill Darts Club than by the British team?

_____

**20.** In 1990, the population of Fresno, CA was 354,202, and the population of New Orleans, LA was 496,938. Estimate the combined population of these two cities.

_____

Name _____

# Estimating Products and Quotients

Estimate.

**1.** 38 × 47 _____   **2.** 58 × 72 _____   **3.** 867 × 12 _____

**4.** 163 ÷ 39 _____   **5.** 894 ÷ 293 _____   **6.** 37,183 ÷ 191 _____

**7.** 79 × 195 _____   **8.** 12,375 ÷ 29 _____   **9.** 5417 ÷ 59 _____

**10.** 83,921 ÷ 49 _____   **11.** 2414 ÷ 62 _____   **12.** 7398 ÷ 369 _____

**13.** 8700 ÷ 910 _____   **14.** 3972 ÷ 217 _____   **15.** 732 × 47 _____

**16.** 55,760 ÷ 692 _____   **17.** 64,900 ÷ 129 _____   **18.** 995 × 24 _____

**19.** 934 × 193 _____   **20.** 9583 ÷ 163 _____   **21.** 43,972 ÷ 493 _____

**22.** 72,389 ÷ 8888 _____   **23.** 29 × 817 _____   **24.** 447 ÷ 153 _____

**25.** 893 ÷ 61 _____   **26.** 95,831 ÷ 398 _____   **27.** 143,698 ÷ 119 _____

**28.** 7862 ÷ 101 _____   **29.** 869 ÷ 27 _____   **30.** 621,830 ÷ 7012 _____

**31.** 4982 × 61 _____   **32.** 350,123 ÷ 698 _____   **33.** 592 × 29 _____

**34.** 738 × 691 _____   **35.** 1284 × 691 _____

**36.** 94 × 83 × 41 _____   **37.** 37 × 61 × 59 _____

**38.** 872 × 6100 _____   **39.** 99 × 41 × 67 _____

**40.** 6843 × 592 _____   **41.** 13 × 61 × 8127 _____

**42.** 8397 × 1975 _____   **43.** 367 × 824 × 7 _____

**44.** 624 × 832 _____   **45.** 384 × 718 _____

**46.** Akira Matsushima rode a unicycle 3260 miles across the United
States in 44 days. Estimate how far he traveled every day.

_____

**47.** There are 60 minutes in an hour, 24 hours in a day, and 365 days
in a year. Estimate the number of minutes in a year.

_____

# Order of Operations

Evaluate each expression.

**1.** $6 \times 3 \div 2$ _____  **2.** $4 + 3 \times 7$ _____  **3.** $12 \div 4 + 2$ _____

**4.** $36 \div (6 + 3)$ _____  **5.** $8 \times 10 \div 5$ _____  **6.** $50 \div 10 + 15$ _____

**7.** $13 - 2 - 4$ _____  **8.** $25 - (12 - 10)$ _____  **9.** $(3 + 7^2) \div 4$ _____

**10.** $(9 - 4)^2$ _____  **11.** $6 \times 2^3$ _____  **12.** $(38 \div 19)^5$ _____

**13.** $8^2 - 5^2$ _____  **14.** $(21 - 15)^2 - 20$ _____  **15.** $600 \div 2 \div 3 \div 5$ _____

**16.** $125 \div (25 \div 5)$ _____  **17.** $6 \times 5 - 2^2$ _____  **18.** $128 \div 16 - 8 \div 2$ _____

**19.** $80,000 - 6 \times 5,000$ _____  **20.** $9000 + 7 \times 300$ _____

**21.** $21 + 39,000 \div 1,300$ _____  **22.** $700 - 300 \div 10$ _____

**23.** $20 \times 7 \div 5 + 11$ _____  **24.** $69,000 \div (1700 + 600)$ _____

Insert a pair of parentheses to make each statement true.

**25.** $3 \times 7 + 4 \times 8 = 264$  **26.** $18 \div 3 + 3 = 3$

**27.** $8 + 16 \div 4 = 6$  **28.** $500 \div 50 \div 2 \div 5 = 4$

**29.** $3 \times 2^2 - 1 = 35$  **30.** $48 \div 12 \times 2 = 2$

**31.** A store has 27 six-packs, 15 twelve-packs, and 34 single cans of soda. Write an expression using the numbers 27, 6, 15, 12, and 34 to show how many cans the store has all together. Do not use parentheses unless they are necessary. Then evaluate your expression to find the number of cans.

_____

**32.** Find an arithmetic expression equal to 25 that contains the following operations.

**a.** addition and multiplication  _____

**b.** subtraction and division  _____

**c.** addition and at least one exponent  _____

**d.** division and an exponent  _____

# Numerical Patterns

Write the number you must add or subtract to get the next number.

**1.** 3, 10, 17, 24, 31, … _____

**2.** 88, 87, 86, 85, 84, … _____

**3.** 91, 86, 81, 76, 71, … _____

**4.** 5, 8, 11, 14, 17, … _____

**5.** 47, 43, 39, 35, 31, … _____

**6.** 21, 30, 39, 48, 57, … _____

**7.** 225, 240, 255, 270, … _____

**8.** 144, 132, 120, 108, … _____

**9.** 681, 660, 639, 618, … _____

**10.** 318, 355, 392, 429, … _____

Find the next three numbers in the pattern.

**11.** 6, 14, 22, 30, 38, _____ , _____ , _____ , …

**12.** 100, 92, 84, 76, 68, _____ , _____ , _____ , …

**13.** 20, 30, 35, 45, 50, _____ , _____ , _____ , …

**14.** 123, 110, 97, 84, 71, _____ , _____ , _____ , …

**15.** 217, 302, 387, 472, _____ , _____ , _____ , …

**16.** 5, 11, 23, 47, 95, _____ , _____ , _____ , …

**17.** 1, 2, 4, 8, 16, _____ , _____ , _____ , …

**18.** 294, 276, 258, 240, _____ , _____ , _____ , …

**19.** 20, 24, 30, 38, 48, _____ , _____ , _____ , …

**20.** 1, 4, 9, 16, 25, _____ , _____ , _____ , …

**21.** 21, 26, 24, 29, 27, _____ , _____ , _____ , …

**22.** In 1996, it cost 32¢ to mail a 1-oz letter, 55¢ to mail a 2-oz letter, 78¢ to mail a 3-oz letter, and $1.01 to mail a 4-oz letter. If the pattern continues, how much did it cost to send a 7-oz letter? _____

**23. Science** Kris is conducting a science experiment with bacteria. She begins with 15 organisms. If the number of organisms triples every day, how many organisms will she have after 4 days? _____

# Section 2B Review

Simplify using mental math.

**1.** $8 \times 7 \times 25$ _____    **2.** $127 + 311$ _____    **3.** $60{,}000 \div 300$ _____

**4.** $40 \times 5{,}000$ _____    **5.** $97 + 387$ _____    **6.** $450{,}000 \div 150$ _____

Estimate.

**7.** $3{,}827 + 1{,}789$ _____    **8.** $364 \times 738$ _____    **9.** $58 + 62 + 57 + 61$ ____

**10.** $5{,}394 - 1{,}286$ _____    **11.** $3{,}842 + 9{,}169$ _____    **12.** $71{,}835 \div 5981$ _____

In Exercises 13–16, match the problem and the operation needed to solve it. Each operation is used exactly once.

Sherry's class has 35 students. Carrie's class has 28 students.

**13.** Sherry's class is split into five equal groups. How _____ many students are in each group?

**14.** How much larger is Sherry's class than Carrie's? _____

**15.** Everyone in Sherry's class shook hands with _____ everyone in Carrie's class. How many handshakes took place?

**16.** Sherry's class and Carrie's class went on a field trip _____ together. How many students went on the trip?

(A) addition

(B) subtraction

(C) multiplication

(D) division

Use the Channel Capacity of U.S. Televisions graph to answer each question. *[Lesson 1-1]*

**Channel Capacity of U.S. Televisions, 1993**

**17.** What percent of U.S. televisions had 49 or more channels?

_____

**18.** Which category included exactly 25% of the televisions?

_____

37-48 channels 25%

49 or more channels 45%

12-36 channels 30%

**19.** Cedina needs to give a 1293-kilobyte computer file to her friend. Since the capacity of her floppy disk, 1440 kilobytes, rounds to 1000 kilobytes, she is worried that the file might not fit on the disk. Should she be concerned? Explain.

_____

Name _____

# Variables and Expressions

**1.** Complete the table by evaluating each expression for $x = 2, 3,$ and $4$.

| $x$ | $x + 5$ | $17 - x$ | $9x$ | $\frac{144}{x}$ | $x \times 7$ | $x^2$ | $5x$ |
|-----|---------|----------|------|-----------------|--------------|-------|------|
| 2 | | | | | | | |
| 3 | | | | | | | |
| 4 | | | | | | | |

**2.** Complete the table by evaluating each expression for $x = 3, 5,$ and $9$.

| $x$ | $16 + x$ | $x - 3$ | $12 \times x$ | $90 \div x$ | $20x$ | $100 - x$ | $x \div x$ |
|-----|----------|---------|---------------|-------------|-------|-----------|------------|
| 3 | | | | | | | |
| 5 | | | | | | | |
| 9 | | | | | | | |

**3.** Complete the table by evaluating each expression for $x = 2, 4,$ and $7$.

| $x$ | $x + 43$ | $30 - x$ | $x \times x$ | $x \times 10$ | $2x$ | $\frac{112}{x}$ | $x^3$ |
|-----|----------|----------|--------------|---------------|------|-----------------|-------|
| 2 | | | | | | | |
| 4 | | | | | | | |
| 7 | | | | | | | |

Complete the table.

**4.** Americans as a whole consume 90 acres of pizza every day.

| Number of days | Number of acres of pizza |
|----------------|--------------------------|
| 1 | |
| 2 | |
| 3 | |
| 4 | |
| d | |

**5.** Tennis balls are sold in packages of three balls.

| Number of balls | Number of packages |
|-----------------|--------------------|
| 30 | |
| 72 | |
| 378 | |
| 999 | |
| t | |

# Writing Expressions

Write the phrase as an expression.

**1.** 12 more than *x* _____

**2.** *x* less than 36 _____

**3.** one-third of *a* _____

**4.** 17 times *s* _____

**5.** *b* multiplied by 5 _____

**6.** *y* to the fourth power _____

**7.** 64 plus *k* _____

**8.** *u* tripled _____

**9.** *p* cubed _____

**10.** 18 minus *x* _____

**11.** 4 less than *k* _____

**12.** *z* increased by 12 _____

Write an expression to answer each question.

**13.** What is the product of 82 and *g*? _____

**14.** What is the difference between *n* and 7? _____

**15.** What is the quotient of 32 and *x*? _____

**16.** What is the sum of *h* and 7? _____

**17.** What is 31 less than *c*? _____

**18.** What is the fifth power of *t*? _____

**19.** What is one-eighth of *r*? _____

**20.** Carolyn made *t* batches of 12 cookies. How many cookies did she make? _____

**21.** A jar holds *n* ounces of jam. How many jars are needed for 200 ounces of jam? _____

Write the problem as an expression.

**22. History** Thomas Jefferson was born in 1801. George Washington was born *y* years earlier. In what year was George Washington born? _____

**23. Science** A spider has 8 legs. How many legs do *s* spiders have? _____

Name _____

# Using Equations

Is the equation true for the given value of the variable?

**1.** $x + 5 = 17$, $x = 22$ _____

**2.** $3 - y = 1$, $y = 2$ _____

**3.** $4x = 24$, $x = 6$ _____

**4.** $g - 7 = 11$, $g = 18$ _____

**5.** $s \div 7 = 3$, $s = 21$ _____

**6.** $u + 12 = 31$, $u = 20$ _____

**7.** $h - 13 = 21$, $h = 34$ _____

**8.** $64 \div n = 16$, $n = 8$ _____

**9.** $20 \times t = 300$, $t = 160$ _____

**10.** $18 - c = 10$, $c = 8$ _____

**11.** $m + 40 = 92$, $m = 50$ _____

**12.** $x \div 5 = 15$, $x = 75$ _____

**13.** $3k = 27$, $k = 9$ _____

**14.** $z - 9 = 61$, $z = 52$ _____

**15.** $12 + v = 21$, $v = 7$ _____

**16.** $5w = 20$, $w = 4$ _____

**17.** $n - 6 = 24$, $n = 18$ _____

**18.** $k \div 8 = 9$, $k = 56$ _____

**19.** $m + 12 = 61$, $m = 49$ _____

**20.** $j + 17 = 86$, $j = 79$ _____

Write an equation for each situation.

**21.** Jim had 18 CDs. He bought $x$ more. Then he had 21 CDs. _____

**22.** Rolando baked 4 loaves of bread, each weighing $w$ oz. The total weight was 80 oz. _____

**23.** Veronica had $m$ marbles. She gave 5 to Marco. She had 12 marbles left. _____

**24.** The lunch period at Eisenhower School is normally 35 minutes. On Thursday, students were given an extra $t$ minutes, so they had 55 minutes for lunch. _____

**25.** Stella dealt an entire deck of 52 cards to make $h$ hands. Each hand had 13 cards. _____

**26. Careers** The average executive burns an average of 105 calories per hour at work. This is $c$ calories more than the average secretary, who burns 88 calories per hour. _____

**27. Social Studies** Each of the 50 United States has $s$ U.S. Senators. There are 100 U.S. Senators all together. _____

# Solving Equations

Find the given value of $x$ that makes the equation true.

**1.** $\frac{x}{7} = 4$; $x = 28, 35, 42,$ or $49$

_____

**2.** $x - 6 = 13$; $x = 18, 19, 20,$ or $21$

_____

**3.** $5x = 45$; $x = 6, 7, 8,$ or $9$

_____

**4.** $x + 8 = 17$; $x = 8, 9, 10,$ or $11$

_____

Find the values for the variable that will provide the given values for the expressions.

**5.**

| $u$ | $u + 16$ |
|---|---|
| | 18 |
| | 31 |
| | 64 |
| | 100 |

**6.**

| $k$ | $6k$ |
|---|---|
| | 24 |
| | 42 |
| | 60 |
| | 90 |

Solve the equation.

**7.** $x + 7 = 30$ _____

**8.** $m - 10 = 7$ _____

**9.** $\frac{s}{8} = 13$ _____

**10.** $11t = 88$ _____

**11.** $d - 12 = 69$ _____

**12.** $21 + g = 42$ _____

**13.** $7u = 35$ _____

**14.** $n \div 7 = 8$ _____

**15.** $b - 7 = 24$ _____

Write an equation for each situation and then solve the equation.

**16.** The top three best-selling albums of all time are Michael Jackson's
*Thriller* (24 million copies), Fleetwood Mac's *Rumours* (17 million
copies), and Boston's *Boston* (*b* million copies). The three albums
sold a combined total of 56 million copies. How many million
copies of *Boston* were sold?

_____

**17.** The main audience section of the Mel Mello Center for the Arts has
9 rows of *c* chairs. There are 126 chairs all together. How many
chairs are in each row?

_____

# Section 2C Review

State whether the quantity should be represented as a variable or a constant.

**1.** the time it takes you to run 500 yards _____

**2.** the number of seconds in a week _____

Write the phrase as an expression.

**3.** x minus 5 _____          **4.** 12 more than p _____

**5.** the product of 11 and g _____          **6.** 16 divided by d _____

Write an expression to answer each question.

**7.** Rhonda has u CDs and each of her CDs has 10 songs. What is the total number of songs in her collection? _____

**8.** Max is 48 in. tall. Nell is n in. shorter than Max. How tall is Nell? _____

Is the equation true for the given value of the variable?

**9.** $x + 17 = 23, x = 4$ _____          **10.** $15p = 105, p = 7$ _____

**11.** $42 - k = 19, k = 23$ _____          **12.** $\frac{12}{m} = 3, m = 36$ _____

Solve.

**13.** $p - 11 = 38$ _____          **14.** $16z = 48$ _____          **15.** $u + 9 = 64$ _____

**16.** $7j = 84$ _____          **17.** $\frac{t}{5} = 7$ _____          **18.** $6r = 150$ _____

**19.** Make a stem-and-leaf diagram of the data showing the estimated earnings of the ten highest-paid actors and actresses of 1990.
*[Lesson 1-6]*

| Star | $ millions |
|------|-----------|
| Sean Connery | 28 |
| Tom Cruise | 18 |
| Harrison Ford | 13 |
| Michael J. Fox | 22 |
| Mel Gibson | 9 |

| Star | $ millions |
|------|-----------|
| Eddie Murphy | 25 |
| Arnold Schwarzenegger | 30 |
| Sylvester Stallone | 24 |
| Meryl Streep | 9 |
| Bruce Willis | 28 |

| stem | leaf |
|------|------|
|  |  |

Name _____

# Cumulative Review Chapters 1–2

For each plot, determine if there is a trend. If there is, describe the pattern of the data. *[Lesson 1-3]*

1. _____

2. _____

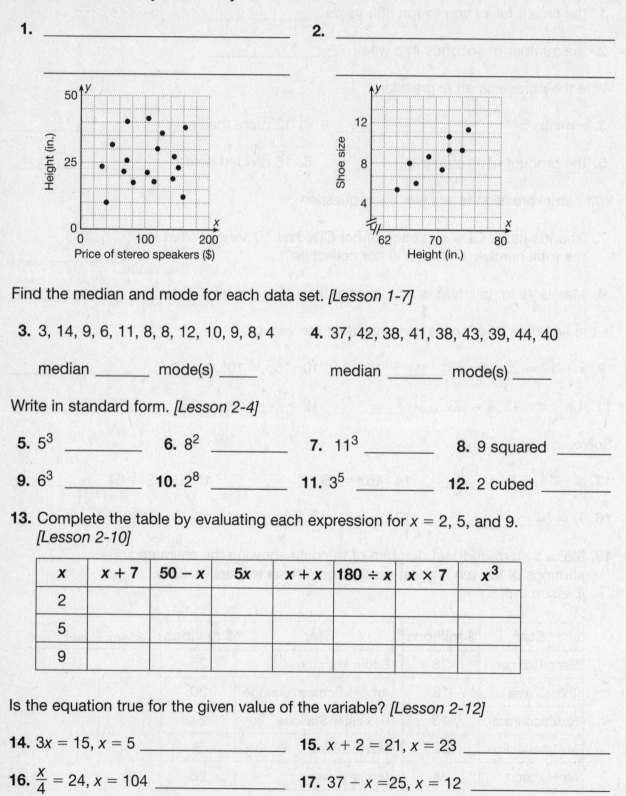

Find the median and mode for each data set. *[Lesson 1-7]*

**3.** 3, 14, 9, 6, 11, 8, 8, 12, 10, 9, 8, 4

median _____ mode(s) _____

**4.** 37, 42, 38, 41, 38, 43, 39, 44, 40

median _____ mode(s) _____

Write in standard form. *[Lesson 2-4]*

**5.** $5^3$ _____

**6.** $8^2$ _____

**7.** $11^3$ _____

**8.** 9 squared _____

**9.** $6^3$ _____

**10.** $2^8$ _____

**11.** $3^5$ _____

**12.** 2 cubed _____

**13.** Complete the table by evaluating each expression for $x = 2$, 5, and 9. *[Lesson 2-10]*

| x | x + 7 | 50 − x | 5x | x + x | 180 ÷ x | x × 7 | $x^3$ |
|---|-------|--------|-----|-------|---------|-------|-------|
| 2 |       |        |     |       |         |       |       |
| 5 |       |        |     |       |         |       |       |
| 9 |       |        |     |       |         |       |       |

Is the equation true for the given value of the variable? *[Lesson 2-12]*

**14.** $3x = 15$, $x = 5$ _____

**15.** $x + 2 = 21$, $x = 23$ _____

**16.** $\frac{x}{4} = 24$, $x = 104$ _____

**17.** $37 - x = 25$, $x = 12$ _____

# Decimal Notation

What decimal number does each grid represent?

**1.** _____

**2.** _____

**3.** _____

Fill in the grid to represent the decimal.

**4.** 0.9

**5.** 0.35

**6.** 0.72

For Exercises 7–9, write the number as a decimal.

**7.** six tenths

**8.** seventeen hundredths

**9.** two and six hundredths

_____    _____    _____

For Exercises 10–13, write the decimal in word form.

**10.** 0.63

**11.** 7.8

_____    _____

**12.** 0.012

**13.** 0.09

_____    _____

**14.** The average American eats three and thirty-six hundredths pounds
of peanut butter each year. Write this number as a decimal. _____

**15.** A 150-pound person contains 97.5 pounds of oxygen and 0.165 pounds
of sodium. Write both decimal numbers in word form.

_____

# Rounding Decimals

Round to the underlined place value.

**1.** 42.4

**2.** 7.7961

**3.** 96.08

**4.** 13.2093

_____

_____

_____

_____

**5.** 1.88

**6.** 3.292

**7.** 27.27

**8.** 191.8

_____

_____

_____

_____

**9.** 796.84

**10.** 8.465

**11.** 59.305

**12.** 8.094

_____

_____

_____

_____

Estimate each object's length to the nearest centimeter and tenth of a centimeter.

**13.** nearest cm: _____    nearest tenth: _____

**14.** nearest cm: _____    nearest tenth: _____

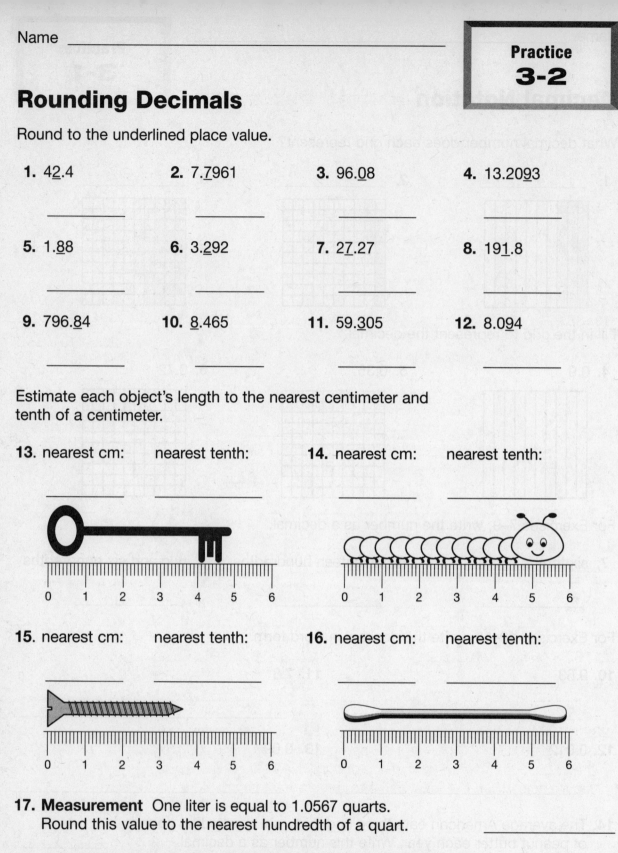

**15.** nearest cm: _____    nearest tenth: _____

**16.** nearest cm: _____    nearest tenth: _____

**17. Measurement** One liter is equal to 1.0567 quarts.
Round this value to the nearest hundredth of a quart. _____

**18.** Colleen's house is made of bricks measuring about 20.955 cm
long, and she guesses that each row in one wall is about
60 bricks long. Estimate the length of the wall.

_____

# Comparing and Ordering Decimals

For Exercises 1–15, compare using $>$ , $<$ , or $=$.

**1.** 0.387 ◯ 0.378     **2.** 4.8 ◯ 4.83     **3.** 12.75 ◯ 12.749

**4.** 8.32 ◯ 8.23     **5.** 23.65 ◯ 22.66     **6.** 7.382 ◯ 7.823

**7.** 32.8 ◯ 32.80     **8.** 61.23 ◯ 63.21     **9.** 89.6 ◯ 89.06

**10.** 5.36 ◯ 6.35     **11.** 2.75 ◯ 2.750     **12.** 11.53 ◯ 11.503

**13.** 38.97 ◯ 39.87     **14.** 64.381 ◯ 64.38     **15.** 12.46 ◯ 12.48

Use the graph for Exercises 16–18.

**16.** Which month has the most rainfall? _____

**17.** Which month has the least rainfall? _____

**18.** Which months have the same amount of rainfall?

_____

**Monthly Rainfall in London
United Kingdom**

Order from least to greatest.

**19.** 21.600, 21.006, 21.060          **20.** 38.88, 38.888, 38.8

_____          _____

**21.** 8.23, 8.132, 8.123, 8.213          **22.** 6.578, 5.687, 5.678, 5.876

_____          _____

**23.** In 1994, a Greek drachma was worth $0.0041220, an Italian lira was worth $0.0006207, a Mexican peso was worth $0.0002963, and a South Korean won was worth $0.0012447. Order these currencies from the least value to the greatest value.

_____

**24. Science** An egg laid by a vervain hummingbird weighs 0.0132 oz, and one laid by a Costa hummingbird weighs 0.017 oz. Which egg is smaller?

_____

Name _____

# Scientific Notation

For exercises 1–13, write the number in standard form.

**1.** $2.87 \times 10^2$         **2.** $3.982 \times 10^4$         **3.** $5.843 \times 10^5$         **4.** $8.95 \times 10^3$

_____         _____         _____         _____

**5.** $5.47 \times 10^6$         **6.** $4.638 \times 10^4$         **7.** $7.140 \times 10^3$         **8.** $1.457 \times 10^5$

_____         _____         _____         _____

**9.** $8.292 \times 10^7$         **10.** $1.419 \times 10^9$         **11.** $9.47 \times 10^5$

_____         _____         _____

**12.** $4.5185 \times 10^{11}$              **13.** $6.09577 \times 10^{13}$

_____              _____

**14. Geography** The area of Saudi Arabia is about $7.57 \times 10^5$
square miles. Write this number in standard form.         _____

For exercises 15–29, write the number in scientific notation.

**15.** 38,700              **16.** 16 billion              **17.** 8 million

_____         _____         _____

**18.** 6,540              **19.** 60,000              **20.** 43,950

_____         _____         _____

**21.** 85 trillion              **22.** 682,300              **23.** 2,137,000

_____         _____         _____

**24.** 238,000,000              **25.** 560,000,000              **26.** 341,700,000

_____         _____         _____

**27.** 4,382,000,000,000              **28.** 5,863,000,000,000              **29.** 493,000,000,000

_____         _____         _____

**30. Astronomy** The sun is about 149,597,900 km away
from Earth. Write this number in scientific notation.         _____

Name _____

Practice

# Section 3A Review

Write as a decimal.

**1.** $\dfrac{27}{100}$    **2.** $\dfrac{63}{1000}$    **3.** eight and seven tenths

_____    _____    _____

Measure each object to the nearest centimeter.

**4.** _____    **5.** _____

SIZE AA    1.5
BATTERY    VOLTS

0  1  2  3  4  5  6        0  1  2  3  4  5  6

Round to the underlined place value.

**6.** 3.8$\underline{7}$5    **7.** $\underline{6}$.241    **8.** 9.3$\underline{1}$6    **9.** 2.$\underline{1}$49

_____    _____    _____    _____

**10. Health** The average person produces enough
saliva in a lifetime to fill a swimming pool, about
$1.2 \times 10^6$ fl oz. Write this number in standard form.    _____

Write the number in standard form.

**11.** $3.89 \times 10^4$ _____    **12.** $7.13 \times 10^2$ _____    **13.** $8.3 \times 10^5$ _____

Write the number in scientific notation.

**14.** 7 billion _____    **15.** 6,510,000 _____

**16. Science** The line plot shows the duration (in days) of each space
shuttle mission conducted by any nation from 1988–1990. *[Lesson 1-9]*

  **a.** Find the mean, median, and mode(s) of the data.

    mean _____ median _____ mode(s) _____

  **b.** Did the outlier affect the mean? _____

3  4  5  6  7  8  9  10  152

**17.** Lance earns $80 per day at his job. If he worked
200 days last year, how much did he earn? *[Lesson 2-5]*    _____

# Estimating with Decimals

Estimate each sum, difference, product, or quotient.

**1.** 3.68 + 1.75      **2.** 38.73 × 7.9      **3.** 12.837 − 2.14      **4.** 63.917 ÷ 7.6

_____     _____     _____     _____

**5.** 13.6875 + 7.94    **6.** 18.374 − 8.47    **7.** 31.27 × 5.837    **8.** 75.59 ÷ 4.23

_____     _____     _____     _____

**9.** 81.238 + 61.59    **10.** 163.94 − 39.4    **11.** $8.47 × 7.31    **12.** 15.83 ÷ 3.57

_____     _____     _____     _____

**13.** 8.743 + 9.14    **14.** 28.6 − 13.14    **15.** 8.138 × 7.2    **16.** 39.61 ÷ 4.83

_____     _____     _____     _____

**17.** 3.941 + 14.83    **18.** 68.1 − 15.23    **19.** 3.6 × 5.12    **20.** 96.3 ÷ 6.41

_____     _____     _____     _____

**21.** 1.09 + 3.06    **22.** $53.82 − $16.24    **23.** 18.39 × 1.94    **24.** 56.43 ÷ 13.8

_____     _____     _____     _____

**25.** 8.3 + 12.741    **26.** 38.89 − 15.63    **27.** 21.4 × 5.2    **28.** 196.4 ÷ 6.9

_____     _____     _____     _____

**29.** 37.14 + 9.3    **30.** 103.45 − 23.2    **31.** 9.74 × 39.1    **32.** 35.74 ÷ 5.63

_____     _____     _____     _____

**33.** You go to a garage sale where all books are priced at $0.35.

     **a.** About how many books could you buy for $10.00? _____

     **b.** Miguel bought 18 books. About how much did he pay? _____

**34.** Tonja has 3 dogs which are all about the same size. If the
dogs weigh a total of 83.4 lb, estimate the weight of each dog. _____

**35.** Fred wants to buy a $15.95 CD and a $9.35 book. He has
$24.00. Does he have enough money for the two items? _____

# Adding and Subtracting Decimal Numbers

Simplify.

**1.** 2.84 + 1.9     **2.** 3.824 − 1.73     **3.** 9.876 + 1.349     **4.** 8.67 − 4.21

_____     _____     _____     _____

**5.** $3.87 + $12.43     **6.** 21.874 − 3.69     **7.** 5.3 + 8.49     **8.** 24.3 − 7.631

_____     _____     _____     _____

**9.** 5.87 + 9.321     **10.** 8.743 − 2.38     **11.** 5.61 + 21.379     **12.** 5.3 − 2.1483

_____     _____     _____     _____

**13.** 9.6413 − 2.14     **14.** 8.365 + 9.3     **15.** 12.67 − 10     **16.** 43 + 5.374

_____     _____     _____     _____

**17.** 39.74 − 5.678     **18.** 21.473 + 8.2     **19.** 193.8 − 21.73     **20.** $84.67 + $91.49

_____     _____     _____     _____

**21.** 36.04 + 9.87     **22.** 56.583 − 39.42     **23.** $48.43 − $27.62     **24.** 394.2 + 7.165

_____     _____     _____     _____

**25.** 2.375 + 6.841 + 9.3894     **26.** 8.23 + 12.7 + 6.74 + 9.32

_____     _____

**27.** 7.124 + 8.1 + 9.32 + 7     **28.** 9.45 + 6.38 + 7.42 + 21.63

_____     _____

**29.** Three lizards weighing 1.57 oz, 1.438 oz, and 1.6412 oz
are in a cage. What is their combined weight?     _____

**30. Science** Jupiter rotates once every 9.925 hr,
and Saturn rotates once every 10.673 hr. Saturn's
rotation is how much longer than Jupiter's rotation?     _____

Name _____

# Solving Decimal Equations: Addition and Subtraction

Solve.

**1.** $h + 3.6 = 8.6$

$h =$ _____

**2.** $b - 7 = 12.3$

$b =$ _____

**3.** $9 + t = 12.4$

$t =$ _____

**4.** $10 - a = 3.4$

$a =$ _____

**5.** $r + 2.2 = 5.7$

$r =$ _____

**6.** $n - 6.2 = 11.4$

$n =$ _____

**7.** $8 + j = 15.34$

$j =$ _____

**8.** $14.3 - g = 6.3$

$g =$ _____

**9.** $m + 7.3 = 9.1$

$m =$ _____

**10.** $d - 10.3 = 1.8$

$d =$ _____

**11.** $6.3 + f = 10.5$

$f =$ _____

**12.** $3.9 - c = 3.1$

$c =$ _____

**13.** $q + \$18.3 = \$20$

$q =$ _____

**14.** $k - 5.1 = 2.9$

$k =$ _____

**15.** $3.89 + x = 5.2$

$x =$ _____

**16.** $18.4 - u = 9.6$

$u =$ _____

**17.** $e + 2.7 = 10$

$e =$ _____

**18.** $r - 7.5 = 3.1$

$r =$ _____

**19.** $5.62 + p = 5.99$

$p =$ _____

**20.** $8.3 - y = 2.7$

$y =$ _____

**Geometry** Given the distance around the shape, find the length of the unknown side.

**21.** Total distance: 31.9 cm

$w =$ _____

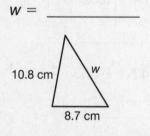

10.8 cm    w

8.7 cm

**22.** Total distance: 62.5 m

$v =$ _____

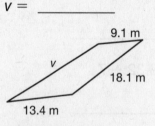

9.1 m

v

18.1 m

13.4 m

**23.** Yesterday Stephanie spent $38.72 on new shoes and $23.19 on computer software. When she was finished, she had $31.18. How much money did she have before she went shopping?

_____

**24.** The owner of a used music store bought a compact disc for $4.70 and sold it for $9.45. Write and solve an equation to find the profit.

_____

# Section 3B Review

Estimate the length to the nearest tenth of a centimeter.

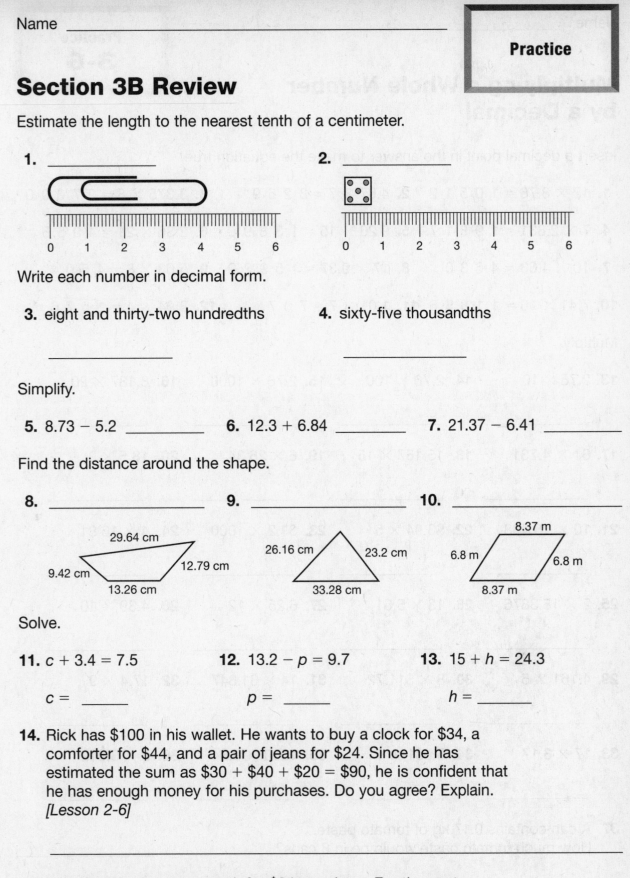

**1.** _____

**2.** _____

Write each number in decimal form.

**3.** eight and thirty-two hundredths

_____

**4.** sixty-five thousandths

_____

Simplify.

**5.** $8.73 - 5.2$ _____  **6.** $12.3 + 6.84$ _____  **7.** $21.37 - 6.41$ _____

Find the distance around the shape.

**8.** _____

29.64 cm
9.42 cm
12.79 cm
13.26 cm

**9.** _____

26.16 cm   23.2 cm
33.28 cm

**10.** _____

8.37 m
6.8 m   6.8 m
8.37 m

Solve.

**11.** $c + 3.4 = 7.5$

$c =$ _____

**12.** $13.2 - p = 9.7$

$p =$ _____

**13.** $15 + h = 24.3$

$h =$ _____

**14.** Rick has $100 in his wallet. He wants to buy a clock for $34, a comforter for $44, and a pair of jeans for $24. Since he has estimated the sum as $30 + $40 + $20 = $90, he is confident that he has enough money for his purchases. Do you agree? Explain. *[Lesson 2-6]*

_____

**15.** Jennifer bought some stock for $24 per share. For the next 6 months, the stock increased in value each month by $3 per share. How much was each share worth 6 months after she bought it? *[Lesson 2-9]*

_____

Name _____

# Multiplying a Whole Number by a Decimal

Insert a decimal point in the answer to make the equation true.

**1.** 12 × 8.76 = 1 0 5 1 2  **2.** 4.67 × 7 = 3 2 6 9  **3.** 3.375 × 8 = 2 7 0 0 0

**4.** 7 × 2.831 = 1 9 8 1 7  **5.** 9.26 × 15 = 1 3 8 9 0  **6.** 2.36 × 21 = 4 9 5 6

**7.** 10 × 4.63 = 4 6 3 0  **8.** 17 × 9.37 = 1 5 9 2 9  **9.** 5.63 × 8 = 4 5 0 4

**10.** 7.41 × 16 = 1 1 8 5 6  **11.** 1.01 × 7 = 7 0 7  **12.** 3.94 × 4 = 1 5 7 6

Multiply.

**13.** 2.76 × 10  **14.** 2.76 × 100  **15.** 2.76 × 1000  **16.** 8.137 × 20

_____  _____  _____  _____

**17.** 61 × 4.731  **18.** 15.167 × 15  **19.** 6 × 26.34  **20.** 18.5 × 3

_____  _____  _____  _____

**21.** 10 × 18.438  **22.** $3.94 × 5  **23.** 31.2 × 1000  **24.** 4 × 16.81

_____  _____  _____  _____

**25.** 2 × 18.3876  **26.** 13 × 5.61  **27.** 6.25 × 12  **28.** 4.39 × 10

_____  _____  _____  _____

**29.** 4.161 × 5  **30.** 8 × $11.72  **31.** 14 × 31.347  **32.** 17.4 × 9

_____  _____  _____  _____

**33.** 17 × 3.17  **34.** 5.631 × 11  **35.** 1000 × 9.34  **36.** 8 × 3.812

_____  _____  _____  _____

**37.** A can contains 0.17 kg of tomato paste.
How much tomato paste would be in 8 cans?  _____

**38.** In a typical day, Cheryl works for 8 hours at the rate
of $7.61 per hour. She also buys lunch for $5.43.
How much does she have at the end of the day?  _____

# Multiplying a Decimal by a Decimal

Insert a decimal point in the answer to make the equation true.

**1.** 3.7 × 19.8 = 7 3 2 6      **2.** 5.7 × 19.9 = 1 1 3 4 3

**3.** 2.9 × 13.82 = 4 0 0 7 8      **4.** 10.2 × 9.49 = 9 6 7 9 8

**5.** 12.14 × 8 = 9 7 1 2      **6.** 16.6 × 7.1 = 1 1 7 8 6

**7.** 3.0 × 5.18 = 1 5 5 4      **8.** 10.9 × 10.611 = 1 1 5 6 5 9 9

Multiply.

**9.** 9.031 × 0.5    **10.** 0.01 × 9.1    **11.** 50.9 × 0.9    **12.** 0.6 × 0.07

**13.** 0.2 × 0.278    **14.** 9.2 × 0.25    **15.** 5.6 × 4.8    **16.** 0.02 × 0.3

**17.** 0.6 × 0.005    **18.** 55.5 × 0.07    **19.** 0.3 × 38.8    **20.** 0.5 × 2.1

**21.** 0.01 × 7.3    **22.** 52.62 × 0.8    **23.** 0.42 × 0.2    **24.** 7.07 × 4.9

**25.** A health food store sells granola for $1.80 per
pound. How much would 1.3 pounds of granola cost? _____

**26. Health** Raw broccoli has 0.78 mg of iron per cup.
How much iron is in 2.3 cups of broccoli? _____

Compare using < , > , or =.

**27.** 6.14 × 0.25 ◯ 61.4 × 2.5      **28.** 0.03 × 12.4 ◯ 0.3 × 1.24

**29.** 5.2 × 62.9 ◯ 0.52 × 6.29      **30.** 4.7 × 8.17 ◯ 4.7 × 81.7

**31.** 7.0 × 1.72 ◯ 0.07 × 172.0      **32.** 8.54 × 27.0 ◯ 85.4 × 2.7

**33. Consumer** If gasoline costs $1.539 per gallon, how much
would you pay for 12.64 gallons? (Round your answer to
the nearest cent.) _____

Name _____

# Dividing by a Whole Number

Insert a decimal point in the answer to make the equation true.

**1.** 37.164 ÷ 76 = 0 4 8 9   **2.** 110.24 ÷ 32 = 3 4 4 5   **3.** 41.34 ÷ 6 = 6 8 9

**4.** 320.662 ÷ 67 = 4 7 8 6   **5.** 143.68 ÷ 20 = 7 1 8 4   **6.** 15.9 ÷ 3 = 5 3

**7.** 6.3 ÷ 7 = 0 9           **8.** 17.505 ÷ 3 = 5 8 3 5   **9.** 6.532 ÷ 4 = 1 6 3 3

Divide.

**10.** 33.628 ÷ 14      **11.** 111.618 ÷ 39      **12.** 22.8 ÷ 19       **13.** 257.24 ÷ 59

_____      _____      _____      _____

**14.** 162.5 ÷ 65      **15.** 27.23 ÷ 7       **16.** 16.668 ÷ 3      **17.** 23.94 ÷ 63

_____      _____      _____      _____

**18.** 190.4 ÷ 28      **19.** 23.58 ÷ 20      **20.** 20.305 ÷ 5      **21.** 0.931 ÷ 19

_____      _____      _____      _____

**22.** 90.034 ÷ 59     **23.** 385.92 ÷ 48     **24.** 179.8 ÷ 58      **25.** 5.337 ÷ 3

_____      _____      _____      _____

**26.** 36.11 ÷ 23      **27.** 244.29 ÷ 51     **28.** 150.92 ÷ 49     **29.** 15.98 ÷ 47

_____      _____      _____      _____

**30.** 503.7 ÷ 69      **31.** 12.6 ÷ 42       **32.** 4.14 ÷ 9        **33.** 113.26 ÷ 14

_____      _____      _____      _____

**34.** 465.272 ÷ 76    **35.** 469.7 ÷ 61      **36.** 8.6 ÷ 86        **37.** 13.425 ÷ 15

_____      _____      _____      _____

**38.** Keith paid $24.57 for 9 blank videotapes.
How much did each tape cost?          _____

**39.** In 1988, a team of 32 divers set a record by pedaling
a tricycle 116.66 miles underwater. Find the mean
distance pedaled by each diver.          _____

Name _____

# Dividing by a Decimal

Insert a decimal point in the answer to make the equation true.

**1.** 7.4096 ÷ 1.1 = 6 7 3 6   **2.** 22.3443 ÷ 5.49 = 4 0 7   **3.** 3.1515 ÷ 1.5 = 2 1 0 1

**4.** 4.8225 ÷ 2.5 = 1 9 2 9   **5.** 17.22 ÷ 4.1 = 4 2 0   **6.** 12.576 ÷ 2.4 = 5 2 4

Divide.

**7.** 11.5213 ÷ 0.7     **8.** 5.18 ÷ 0.7     **9.** 8.7 ÷ 4.35     **10.** 37.014 ÷ 5.97

_____    _____    _____    _____

**11.** 0.3798 ÷ 0.18   **12.** 0.65232 ÷ 13.59 **13.** 100.859 ÷ 8.65   **14.** 0.51272 ÷ 0.754

_____    _____    _____    _____

**15.** 1.8136 ÷ 0.2    **16.** 46.2 ÷ 16.5    **17.** 3.915 ÷ 13.05    **18.** 1.44 ÷ 1.6

_____    _____    _____    _____

**19.** 20.013 ÷ 2.1    **20.** 0.65355 ÷ 0.15  **21.** 1.265 ÷ 0.23    **22.** 19.76 ÷ 2.6

_____    _____    _____    _____

**23.** 2.2242 ÷ 0.33   **24.** 46.02 ÷ 3.9    **25.** 1.512 ÷ 0.672   **26.** 0.061 ÷ 0.1

_____    _____    _____    _____

**27.** 3.86 ÷ 3.86    **28.** 7.896 ÷ 3.29    **29.** 9.8072 ÷ 5.33   **30.** 3.0768 ÷ 0.8

_____    _____    _____    _____

**31.** 0.908 ÷ 4.54   **32.** 0.056 ÷ 1.4    **33.** 9.57 ÷ 2.9     **34.** 0.414 ÷ 4.6

_____    _____    _____    _____

**35.** 92.7 ÷ 12.36   **36.** 1.9312 ÷ 1.136  **37.** 18.65 ÷ 2.5    **38.** 132.16 ÷ 11.2

_____    _____    _____    _____

**39. Science** Jupiter revolves around the Sun once every
11.86 years. How many times does it revolve in 40.324 years?

_____

**40. Health** 4.7 oz of pistachio nuts contain 1.786 mg
of zinc. How much zinc is in 1 oz of pistachios?

_____

Name _____

# Solving Decimal Equations: Multiplication and Division

Solve.

**1.** $4n = 1.72$

$n =$ _____

**2.** $\dfrac{d}{2.5} = 1.263$

$d =$ _____

**3.** $0.9g = 9.99$

$g =$ _____

**4.** $1.9v = 9.025$

$v =$ _____

**5.** $\dfrac{r}{0.8} = 11.279$

$r =$ _____

**6.** $\dfrac{n}{0.5} = 1.537$

$n =$ _____

**7.** $1.2k = 7.968$

$k =$ _____

**8.** $\dfrac{s}{0.85} = 2.4$

$s =$ _____

**9.** $8.3y = 28.967$

$y =$ _____

**10.** $\dfrac{a}{5.5} = 6.25$

$a =$ _____

**11.** $5.9c = 8.555$

$c =$ _____

**12.** $\dfrac{x}{8.1} = 6.31$

$x =$ _____

**13.** $8.5t = 77.18$

$t =$ _____

**14.** $\dfrac{b}{3.5} = 6.5$

$b =$ _____

**15.** $1.1s = 0.726$

$s =$ _____

**16.** $\dfrac{w}{13} = 0.12$

$w =$ _____

**17.** $0.1t = 1.1$

$t =$ _____

**18.** $\dfrac{m}{6.7} = 1.57$

$m =$ _____

**19.** $3.59p = 4.308$

$p =$ _____

**20.** $\dfrac{k}{4.67} = 10.8$

$k =$ _____

**21.** $0.15n = 1.3575$

$n =$ _____

**22.** $\dfrac{d}{0.243} = 0.1$

$d =$ _____

**23.** $0.65p = 0.5395$

$p =$ _____

**24.** $\dfrac{m}{3.902} = 5$

$m =$ _____

**25.** $\dfrac{r}{0.35} = 2.76$

$r =$ _____

**26.** $\dfrac{c}{4.1} = 5.48$

$c =$ _____

**27.** $\dfrac{u}{6.9} = 10.3$

$u =$ _____

**28.** $8.77m = 6.139$

$m =$ _____

**29.** $2.94q = 7.35$

$q =$ _____

**30.** $5.6t = 58.8$

$t =$ _____

**31.** $0.8d = 9.816$

$d =$ _____

**32.** $13.41w = 17.433$

$w =$ _____

For Exercises 33 and 34, set up an equation and solve.

**33.** Yesterday Helen used one-seventh of the vegetable oil in her kitchen. If she used 2.43 oz, how much did she have originally? _____

**34.** **Consumer** In 1994, the Louisiana sales tax on an item was 0.04 times the price of the item. If Tom paid $1.09 in sales tax when he bought a shirt, what was the price of the shirt? _____

# Section 3C Review

Simplify.

**1.** 3 × 0.63　　　**2.** 0.016 × 0.02　　　**3.** 205.65 ÷ 15　　　**4.** 26 × 0.009

_____　　　　_____　　　　_____　　　　_____

**5.** 16.936 ÷ 73　　　**6.** 36 × 0.11　　　**7.** 0.05 × 4.9　　　**8.** 245.49 ÷ 30

_____　　　　_____　　　　_____　　　　_____

**9.** 7 × 0.05　　　**10.** 0.07 × 0.845　　　**11.** 140.6 ÷ 37　　　**12.** 27.216 ÷ 17.01

_____　　　　_____　　　　_____　　　　_____

Write the number in standard form.

**13.** $3.84 \times 10^3$　　　**14.** $1.789 \times 10^5$　　　**15.** $6.4432 \times 10^6$

_____　　　　_____　　　　_____

**16.** $6.387 \times 10^9$　　　**17.** $8.3764 \times 10^4$　　　**18.** $4.3857 \times 10^{10}$

_____　　　　_____　　　　_____

Solve.

**19.** $4.63a = 12.964$　**20.** $\dfrac{d}{6.21} = 8.9$　**21.** $5w = 15.05$　**22.** $\dfrac{k}{0.81} = 7.39$

$a =$ _____　　$d =$ _____　　$w =$ _____　　$k =$ _____

**23.** $1.4f = 0.0882$　**24.** $0.9w = 0.5634$　**25.** $10.6g = 1.166$　**26.** $\dfrac{t}{4.61} = 6.7$

$f =$ _____　　$w =$ _____　　$g =$ _____　　$t =$ _____

**27.** Five bunches of broccoli weigh 0.94 lb, 1.27 lb, 0.83 lb, 1.07 lb, and 0.98 lb. What is the average of these weights? _____

**28. Science** A goat typically lives 4 times as long as a rat. A rat's lifetime lasts *t* years. Write an expression to show how long a goat lives. _____

**29.** In 1974, the federal minimum wage was $2.00 per hour. Use mental math to determine how much a worker earning minimum wage would be paid for working 38 hours. *[Lesson 2-5]* _____

Name _____

# Cumulative Review Chapters 1–3

Use the 1992 Election Results graph to answer each question. *[Lesson 1-1]*

**1.** Who had the most votes? _____

**2.** About how many people voted for Ross Perot?

_____

**3.** Estimate the total number of votes shown in the data.

_____

**1992 Presidential Election Results**

Round to the given place. *[Lesson 2-2]*

**4.** 27,341, thousands

_____

**5.** 3,137,621, hundred-thousands

_____

For Exercises 6–11, compare using <, >, or =. *[Lesson 3-3]*

**6.** 3.9 ◯ 3.87

**7.** 7.03 ◯ 7.30

**8.** 9.26 ◯ 9.62

**9.** 3.4 ◯ 4.3

**10.** 8.64 ◯ 8.640

**11.** 12.75 ◯ 12.7499

Estimate each sum, difference, product, or quotient. *[Lesson 3-5]*

**12.** 12.63 + 4.07

**13.** 3.96 − 1.24

**14.** $9.14 × 7.2

**15.** 26.64 ÷ 8.73

_____ _____ _____ _____

**16.** $3.84 + $5.62

**17.** 11.49 − 2.36

**18.** 9.1 × 4.873

**19.** 119.6 × 20.4

_____ _____ _____ _____

Solve using inverse operations. *[Lesson 3-12]*

**20.** $0.6p = 3.12$

**21.** $\frac{m}{6.9} = 0.47$

**22.** $6.18v = 3.0282$

**23.** $1.6t = 13.344$

$p =$ _____

$m =$ _____

$v =$ _____

$t =$ _____

**24.** $\frac{w}{1.61} = 4.3$

**25.** $\frac{x}{8.7} = 0.25$

**26.** $0.39a = 3.276$

**27.** $\frac{a}{1.8} = 5.87$

$w =$ _____

$x =$ _____

$a =$ _____

$a =$ _____

# Perimeter

Find the perimeter.

1. _____   2. _____   3. _____

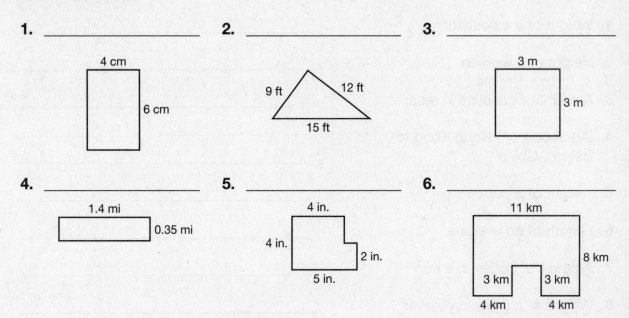

4. _____   5. _____   6. _____

Find the lengths of each unknown side.

7. a = _____  b = _____   8. c = _____  d = _____   9. x = _____  y = _____

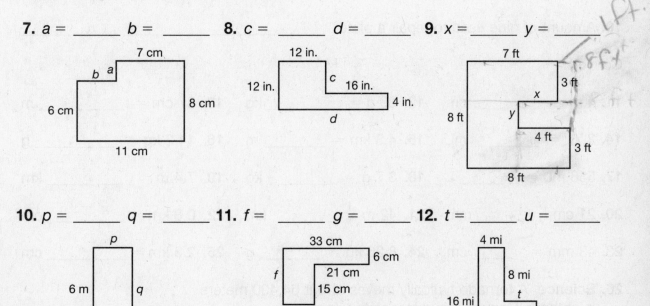

10. p = _____  q = _____   11. f = _____  g = _____   12. t = _____  u = _____

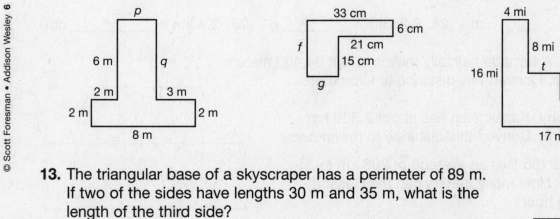

13. The triangular base of a skyscraper has a perimeter of 89 m.
If two of the sides have lengths 30 m and 35 m, what is the
length of the third side?

_____

Name _____

# Converting in the Metric System

For Exercises 1–10, name an appropriate metric unit of measure.

**1.** Weight of a calculator _____

**2.** Height of a woman _____

**3.** Amount of gasoline in a car _____

**4.** Distance from Hong Kong to
   Beijing, China _____

**5.** Weight of a paper clip _____

**6.** Length of an airplane _____

**7.** Amount of coffee in a cup _____

**8.** Weight of a golden retriever _____

**9.** Width of a playing card _____

**10.** Amount of glue used to repair a plate _____

Convert.

**11.** 4 m = _____ cm  **12.** 39 g = _____ kg  **13.** 87 cm = _____ m

**14.** 2.7 L = _____ mL  **15.** 4.3 km = _____ m  **16.** 14.2 kg = _____ g

**17.** 538 mL = _____ L  **18.** 3.7 g = _____ kg  **19.** 7.4 m = _____ km

**20.** 21 cm = _____ mm  **21.** 42 m = _____ km  **22.** 0.8 km = _____ cm

**23.** 43 mm = _____ cm  **24.** 8.26 kg = _____ g  **25.** 2.3 km = _____ cm

**26. Science** A tornado typically moves about 64,400 meters
   in an hour. Convert this distance to kilometers. _____

**27. Geography** Kazakhstan has about 2,320 km
   of coastline. Convert this distance to millimeters. _____

**28.** A Cessna 185 flies an average of 208 km in
   one hour. How many meters can the Cessna
   fly in one hour? _____

# Using Conversion Factors

Convert.

**1.** 21 feet = _____ inches

**2.** 21 feet = _____ yards

**3.** 4 miles = _____ feet

**4.** 15 pounds = _____ ounces

**5.** 36 quarts = _____ gallons

**6.** 252 inches = _____ feet

**7.** 48 ounces = _____ pounds

**8.** 31 gallons = _____ quarts

**9.** 35 yards = _____ feet

**10.** 8 quarts = _____ gallons

**11.** 21,120 feet = _____ miles

**12.** 80 ounces = _____ pounds

**13.** 63 gallons = _____ quarts

**14.** 32 quarts = _____ gallons

**15.** 39 feet = _____ yards

**16.** 18 miles = _____ feet

**17.** 23 gallons = _____ quarts

**18.** 96 ounces = _____ pounds

**19.** 132 inches = _____ feet

**20.** 71 yards = _____ feet

**21.** 60 quarts = _____ gallons

**22.** 31 pounds = _____ ounces

**23.** 63,360 feet = _____ miles

**24.** 47 feet = _____ inches

**25.** 23 gallons = _____ quarts

**26.** 42 feet = _____ yards

**27.** 288 ounces = _____ pounds

**28.** 73 miles = _____ feet

**29.** 84 quarts = _____ gallons

**30.** 46 pounds = _____ ounces

**31.** 276 inches = _____ feet

**32.** 51 yards = _____ feet

**33.** 7 gallons = _____ quarts

**34.** 656 ounces = _____ pounds

**35.** 79,200 feet = _____ miles

**36.** 53 feet = _____ inches

**37.** 26 pounds = _____ ounces

**38.** 127 miles = _____ feet

**39. Science** A gray whale can be up to 540 inches in length.
How many feet is that? How many yards?

**40.** In 1986, G. Graham of Edmond, Oklahoma, grew a
pumpkin weighing 7.75 lb. How many ounces is that? _____

Name _____

# Section 4A Review

For Exercises 1–5, find the perimeter and give the answer in meters.

1. _____  2. _____  3. _____

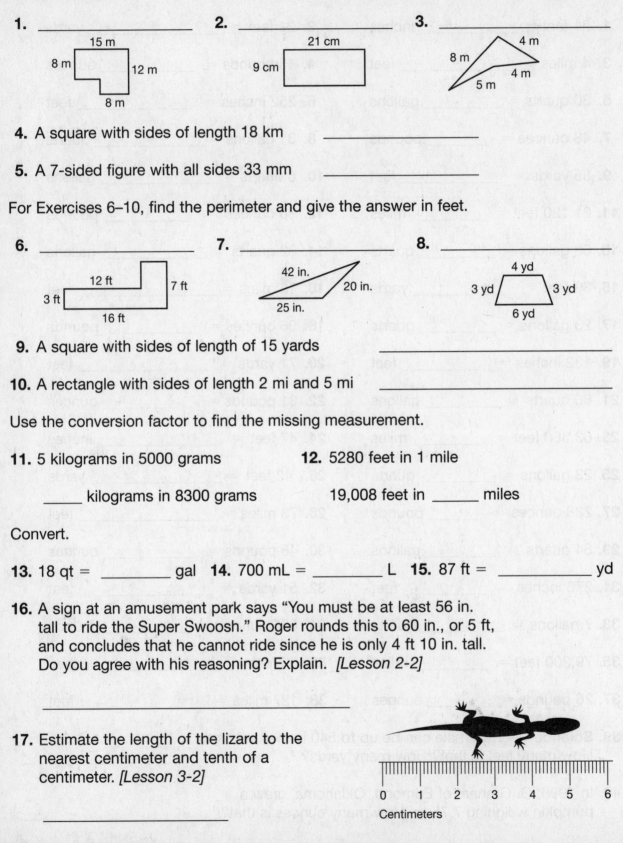

4. A square with sides of length 18 km    _____

5. A 7-sided figure with all sides 33 mm    _____

For Exercises 6–10, find the perimeter and give the answer in feet.

6. _____  7. _____  8. _____

9. A square with sides of length of 15 yards    _____

10. A rectangle with sides of length 2 mi and 5 mi    _____

Use the conversion factor to find the missing measurement.

11. 5 kilograms in 5000 grams          12. 5280 feet in 1 mile

_____ kilograms in 8300 grams          19,008 feet in _____ miles

Convert.

13. 18 qt = _____ gal   14. 700 mL = _____ L   15. 87 ft = _____ yd

16. A sign at an amusement park says "You must be at least 56 in. tall to ride the Super Swoosh." Roger rounds this to 60 in., or 5 ft, and concludes that he cannot ride since he is only 4 ft 10 in. tall. Do you agree with his reasoning? Explain. *[Lesson 2-2]*

_____

17. Estimate the length of the lizard to the nearest centimeter and tenth of a centimeter. *[Lesson 3-2]*

Centimeters

_____

Name _____

# Area of Squares and Rectangles

Find the missing measurement for each rectangle.

1. Area = _____

   Base = 7 ft

   Height = 9 ft

2. Area = 24 cm²

   Base = _____

   Height = 6 cm

3. Area = 84 in²

   Base = 7 in.

   Height = _____

4. Area = 11.5 m²

   Base = 5 m

   Height = _____

5. Area = _____

   Base = 5.875 in.

   Height = 4 in.

6. Area = 12.46 cm²

   Base = _____

   Height = 7 cm

Find the area of each figure.

7. Square with sides of length 8 ft  _____

8. Rectangle with sides 4.7 m and 7.3 m  _____

9. Square with sides of length 21 cm  _____

10. Rectangle with sides 8.3 m and 5.2 m  _____

11. Rectangle with sides 9 in. and 4 in.  _____

Use the scatterplot for Exercises 12–14.

12. What is the area of each rectangle?

    R _____  S _____  T _____

    U _____  V _____  W_____

13. Which rectangle is also a square?  _____

14. What is the area of the rectangle
    with the greatest height?  _____

**Rectangles R–W**

15. Shelly plans to paint a wall in her bedroom. The wall is 11 ft long
    and 8 ft high. She needs enough paint to cover how much area? _____

16. In 1993, the Food Bank for Monterey County (California) set
    a record by baking a lasagne with an area of 490 ft². If the
    lasagne was 70 ft long, how wide was it?  _____

Name _____

# Area of Parallelograms

Find each area. The dashed line is a height.

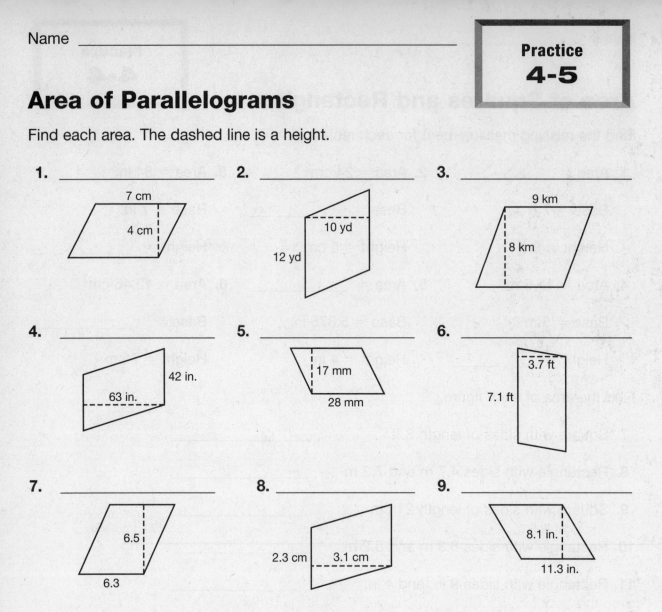

1. _____

7 cm

4 cm

2. _____

10 yd

12 yd

3. _____

9 km

8 km

4. _____

42 in.

63 in.

5. _____

17 mm

28 mm

6. _____

3.7 ft

7.1 ft

7. _____

6.5

6.3

8. _____

2.3 cm    3.1 cm

9. _____

8.1 in.

11.3 in.

Find the area if *b* is the base and *h* is the height of the parallelogram.

**10.** $b = 5$ cm, $h = 7$ cm

**11.** $b = 8.6$ m, $h = 12.0$ m

**12.** $b = 8.4$ m, $h = 5.3$ m

_____    _____    _____

**13.** $h = 83$ in., $b = 104$ in.

**14.** $b = 23$ cm, $h = 8.7$ cm

**15.** $h = 2.1$ mi, $b = 2.5$ mi

_____    _____    _____

**16.** A woodworker built a table whose top was inlaid with
a parallelogram with base 8 in. and height 9.5 in.
What was the area of the inlay?

_____

**17.** An unusual tabletop has the shape of a parallelogram with
base 147 cm and height 136 cm. What is the area of the
tabletop?

_____

# Area of Triangles

Find the area of each triangle. The dashed line is a height.

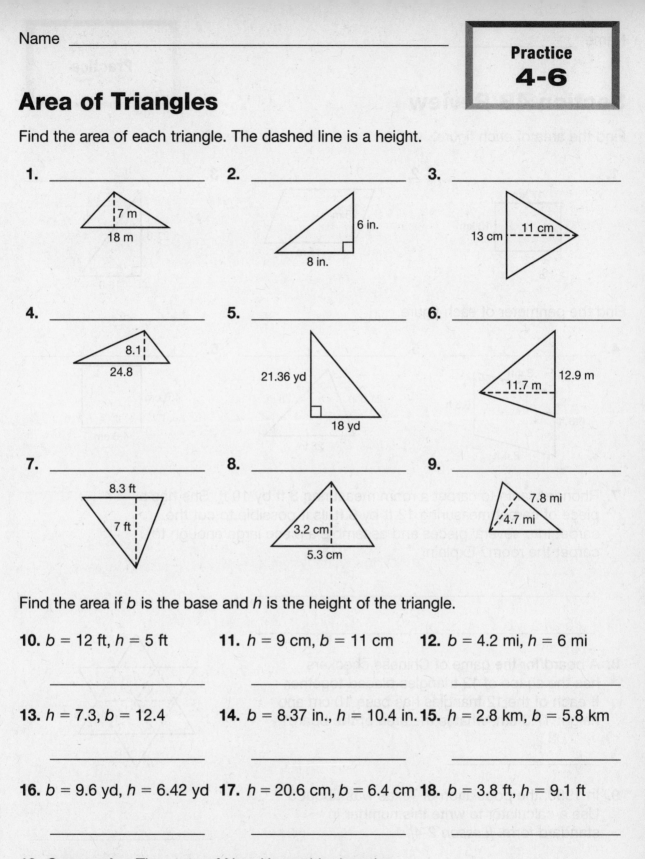

1. _____

7 m
18 m

2. _____

6 in.
8 in.

3. _____

13 cm    11 cm

4. _____

8.1
24.8

5. _____

21.36 yd
18 yd

6. _____

12.9 m
11.7 m

7. _____

8.3 ft
7 ft

8. _____

3.2 cm
5.3 cm

9. _____

7.8 mi
4.7 mi

Find the area if *b* is the base and *h* is the height of the triangle.

**10.** *b* = 12 ft, *h* = 5 ft      **11.** *h* = 9 cm, *b* = 11 cm      **12.** *b* = 4.2 mi, *h* = 6 mi

_____      _____      _____

**13.** *h* = 7.3, *b* = 12.4      **14.** *b* = 8.37 in., *h* = 10.4 in. **15.** *h* = 2.8 km, *b* = 5.8 km

_____      _____      _____

**16.** *b* = 9.6 yd, *h* = 6.42 yd  **17.** *h* = 20.6 cm, *b* = 6.4 cm **18.** *b* = 3.8 ft, *h* = 9.1 ft

_____      _____      _____

**19. Geography** The state of New Hampshire has the
approximate shape of a triangle with base 90 mi and
height 180 mi. Estimate the area of New Hampshire.  _____

# Section 4B Review

Find the area of each figure.

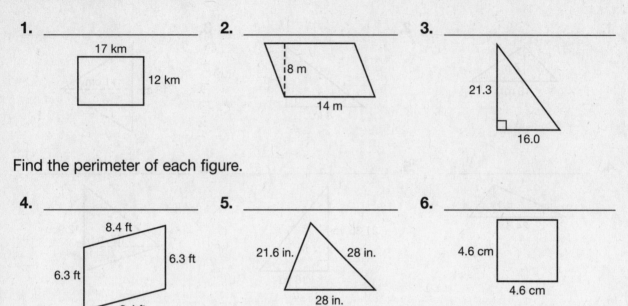

1. _____

17 km

12 km

2. _____

8 m

14 m

3. _____

21.3

16.0

Find the perimeter of each figure.

4. _____

8.4 ft

6.3 ft

6.3 ft

8.4 ft

5. _____

21.6 in.    28 in.

28 in.

6. _____

4.6 cm

4.6 cm

7. Rhonda wants to carpet a room measuring 8 ft by 10 ft. She has a piece of carpet measuring 12 ft by 6 ft. Is it possible to cut the carpet into several pieces and assemble a piece large enough to carpet the room? Explain.

_____

_____

8. A board for the game of Chinese checkers has the shape of 12 triangles placed together. If each of the 12 triangles has base 10 cm and height 17.3 cm, what is the area of the board?

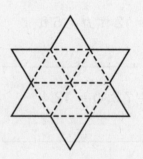

_____

9. In 1980, the population of Texas was about $3^{15}$. Use a calculator to write this number in standard form. *[Lesson 2-4]*

10. There are about 4,014,500,000 square inches in a square mile. Write this number in scientific notation. *[Lesson 3-4]*

_____

# Discovering π

Find the circumference. Use 3.14 for π.

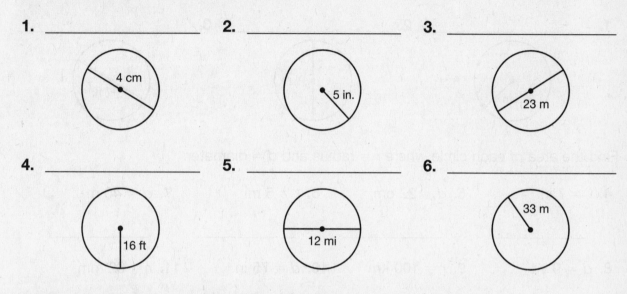

1. _____

2. _____

3. _____

4 cm

5 in.

23 m

4. _____

5. _____

6. _____

16 ft

12 mi

33 m

Find the missing measurements for each circle where $r$ = radius,
$d$ = diameter, and $c$ = circumference.

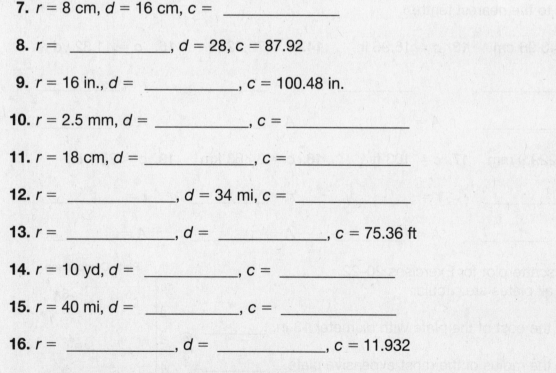

7. $r$ = 8 cm, $d$ = 16 cm, $c$ = _____

8. $r$ = _____, $d$ = 28, $c$ = 87.92

9. $r$ = 16 in., $d$ = _____, $c$ = 100.48 in.

10. $r$ = 2.5 mm, $d$ = _____, $c$ = _____

11. $r$ = 18 cm, $d$ = _____, $c$ = _____

12. $r$ = _____, $d$ = 34 mi, $c$ = _____

13. $r$ = _____, $d$ = _____, $c$ = 75.36 ft

14. $r$ = 10 yd, $d$ = _____, $c$ = _____

15. $r$ = 40 mi, $d$ = _____, $c$ = _____

16. $r$ = _____, $d$ = _____, $c$ = 11.932

17. A circular track has a circumference of
    0.4082 km. Find the diameter of the track. _____

18. **Geometry** The radius of the earth is about 3960 mi.
    Estimate the length of the equator. _____

# Area of Circles

Find the area. Use 3.14 for π.

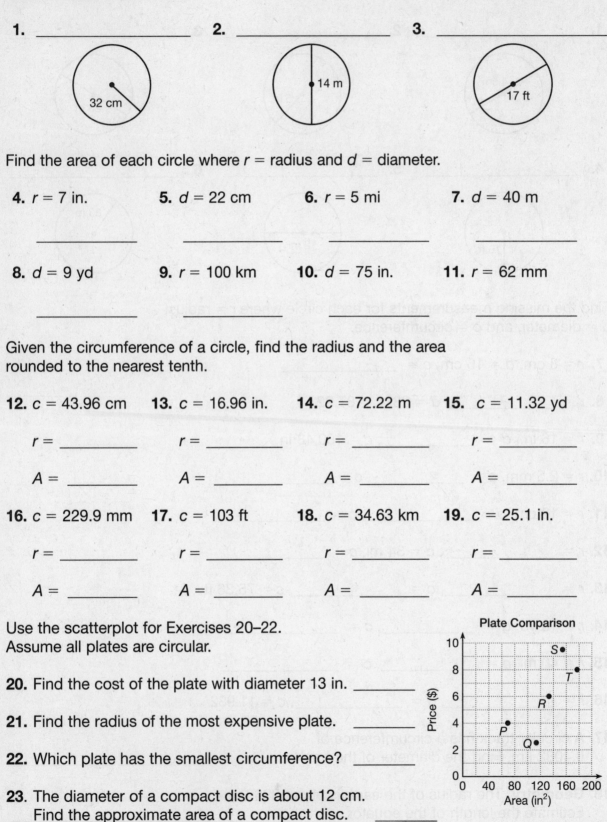

1. _____ 2. _____ 3. _____

(32 cm)     (14 m)     (17 ft)

Find the area of each circle where r = radius and d = diameter.

**4.** r = 7 in.    **5.** d = 22 cm    **6.** r = 5 mi    **7.** d = 40 m

_____    _____    _____    _____

**8.** d = 9 yd    **9.** r = 100 km    **10.** d = 75 in.    **11.** r = 62 mm

_____    _____    _____    _____

Given the circumference of a circle, find the radius and the area rounded to the nearest tenth.

**12.** c = 43.96 cm    **13.** c = 16.96 in.    **14.** c = 72.22 m    **15.** c = 11.32 yd

r = _____    r = _____    r = _____    r = _____

A = _____    A = _____    A = _____    A = _____

**16.** c = 229.9 mm    **17.** c = 103 ft    **18.** c = 34.63 km    **19.** c = 25.1 in.

r = _____    r = _____    r = _____    r = _____

A = _____    A = _____    A = _____    A = _____

Use the scatterplot for Exercises 20–22.
Assume all plates are circular.

**20.** Find the cost of the plate with diameter 13 in. _____

**21.** Find the radius of the most expensive plate. _____

**22.** Which plate has the smallest circumference? _____

**23.** The diameter of a compact disc is about 12 cm.
Find the approximate area of a compact disc. _____

**Plate Comparison**

Price ($) vs Area (in²)

# Area of Irregular Shapes

Find the area of each irregular figure. Use 3.14 for π.

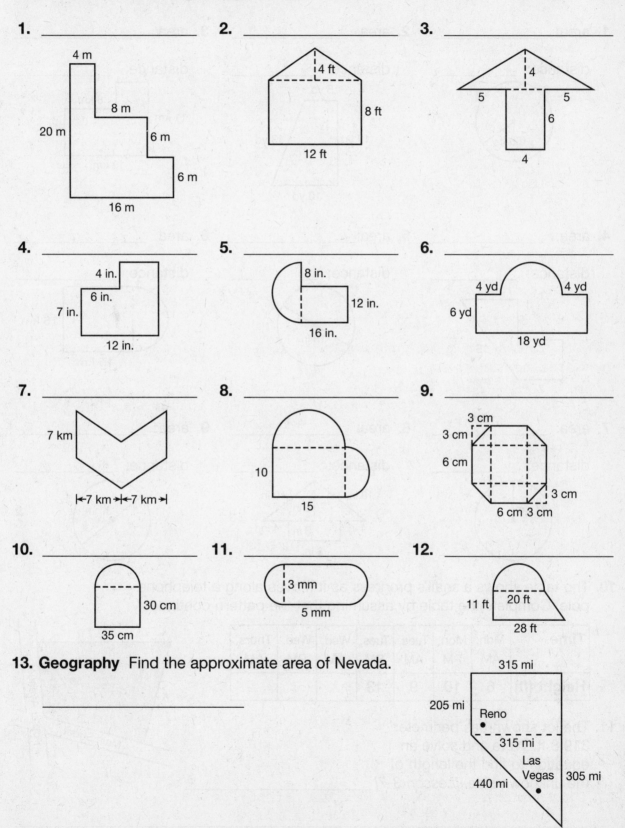

1. _____

4 m
8 m
20 m
6 m
6 m
16 m

2. _____

4 ft
8 ft
12 ft

3. _____

4
5    5
6
4

4. _____

4 in.
6 in.
7 in.
12 in.

5. _____

8 in.
12 in.
16 in.

6. _____

4 yd    4 yd
6 yd
18 yd

7. _____

7 km
|←7 km→|←7 km→|

8. _____

10
15

9. _____

3 cm
3 cm
6 cm
3 cm
6 cm   3 cm

10. _____

30 cm
35 cm

11. _____

3 mm
5 mm

12. _____

20 ft
11 ft
28 ft

**13. Geography** Find the approximate area of Nevada.

_____

315 mi
205 mi
Reno
315 mi
440 mi
Las Vegas
305 mi

**Practice**

# Section 4C Review

Find the area and the distance around the shape.

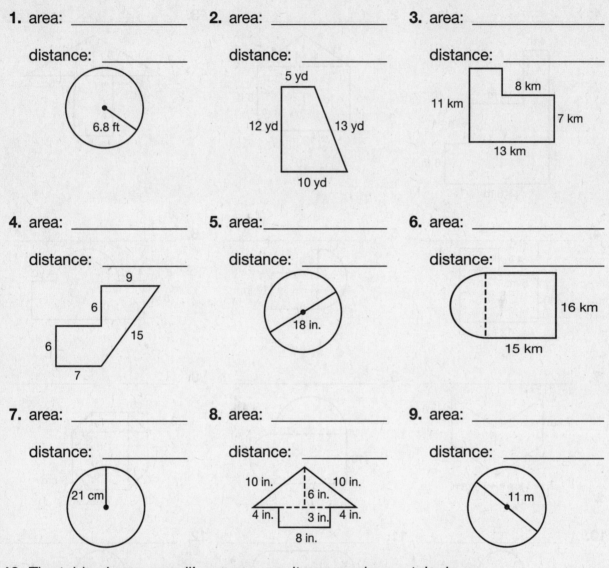

**1.** area: _____

distance: _____

6.8 ft

**2.** area: _____

distance: _____

5 yd

12 yd          13 yd

10 yd

**3.** area: _____

distance: _____

8 km

11 km

7 km

13 km

**4.** area: _____

distance: _____

9

6

6        15

6

7

**5.** area: _____

distance: _____

18 in.

**6.** area: _____

distance: _____

16 km

15 km

**7.** area: _____

distance: _____

21 cm

**8.** area: _____

distance: _____

10 in.        10 in.

6 in.

4 in.    3 in.    4 in.

8 in.

**9.** area: _____

distance: _____

11 m

**10.** The table shows a snail's progress as it moves along a telephone pole. Complete the table by assuming that the pattern continues.

| Time | Mon. AM | Mon. PM | Tues. AM | Tues. PM | Wed. AM | Wed. PM | Thurs. AM |
|------|---------|---------|----------|----------|---------|---------|-----------|
| **Height (ft)** | 6 | 10 | 9 | 13 | | | |

**11.** The lot shown has perimeter 319.8 ft. Write and solve an equation to find the length of the unknown side. *[Lesson 3-7]* _____

103.7 ft

56.2 ft

*x*

81.3 ft

Main Street

Poplar Avenue

# Cumulative Review Chapters 1–4

Find the mean of each set of data. *[Lesson 1-8]*

**1.** 37, 43, 64, 53, 39, 28

_____

**2.** 635, 842, 963, 612, 385

_____

**3.** 8, 5, 8, 3, 9, 8, 8, 4, 3, 7

_____

**4.** 8.6, 12.4, 7.3, 11.2, 13.1, 14.2, 13.0

_____

Estimate. *[Lesson 2-6]*

**5.** 286 + 541

_____

**6.** 8,912 − 4,371

_____

**7.** 305 + 290 + 310 + 286

_____

**8.** 914 − 352

_____

**9.** 2,165 + 891

_____

**10.** 6,140 + 5,912 + 6,041

_____

Round to the underlined place value. *[Lesson 3-2]*

**11.** 38.4$\underline{6}$5

_____

**12.** 5.$\underline{8}$364

_____

**13.** 2.1$\underline{7}$59

_____

**14.** 14.3$\underline{7}$55

_____

**15.** 5.8$\underline{1}$49

_____

**16.** 6.74$\underline{3}$1

_____

**17.** 2.$\underline{8}$65

_____

**18.** 56.4$\underline{1}$3

_____

Convert. *[Lesson 4-3]*

**19.** 17 feet = _____ inches

**20.** 32 pounds = _____ ounces

**21.** 14 miles = _____ feet

**22.** 136 quarts = _____ gallons

Find the area. *[Lesson 4-5]*

**23.** _____

**24.** _____

**25.** _____

# Divisibility

Tell whether the number is divisible by 2, 3, 5, 6, 9, or 10.

**1.** 75

**2.** 532

**3.** 625

**4.** 39

_____    _____    _____    _____

**5.** 118

**6.** 354

**7.** 585

**8.** 408

_____    _____    _____    _____

**9.** 235

**10.** 105

**11.** 186

**12.** 73

_____    _____    _____    _____

**13.** 69

**14.** 317

**15.** 200

**16.** 366

_____    _____    _____    _____

**17.** 306

**18.** 645

**19.** 223

**20.** 326

_____    _____    _____    _____

Tell whether the first number is divisible by the second.

**21.** 46, 7 _____   **22.** 65, 2 _____   **23.** 43, 10 _____   **24.** 165, 3 _____

**25.** 133, 5 _____   **26.** 66, 11 _____   **27.** 85, 3 _____   **28.** 185, 5 _____

**29.** 99, 6 _____   **30.** 106, 7 _____   **31.** 150, 3 _____   **32.** 196, 2 _____

**33.** 99, 5 _____   **34.** 128, 4 _____   **35.** 39, 6 _____   **36.** 33, 3 _____

**37.** 110, 6 _____   **38.** 129, 9 _____   **39.** 37, 5 _____   **40.** 126, 7 _____

**41.** 117, 8 _____   **42.** 96, 8 _____   **43.** 63, 2 _____   **44.** 192, 10 _____

**45.** 74, 4 _____   **46.** 55, 5 _____   **47.** 171, 8 _____   **48.** 165, 11 _____

**49.** There are 365 days in a non-leap year.
Test 365 for divisibility by 2, 3, 5, 6, and 10.   _____

**50. Social Science** During an election year, the
U.S. President is chosen by 538 electoral votes.
Test 538 for divisibility by 2, 3, 5, 6, and 10.   _____

# Prime Factorization

Given the number and its factors, tell whether it is prime or composite.

**1.** 92: 1, 2, 4, 23, 46, 92     **2.** 121: 1, 11, 121     **3.** 83: 1, 83

_____     _____     _____

**4.** 129: 1, 3, 43, 129     **5.** 52: 1, 2, 4, 13, 26, 52     **6.** 55: 1, 5, 11, 55

_____     _____     _____

**7.** 29: 1, 29     **8.** 57: 1, 3, 19, 57     **9.** 63: 1, 3, 7, 9, 21, 63

_____     _____     _____

Find the prime factorization.

**10.** 12     **11.** 40     **12.** 64

_____     _____     _____

**13.** 36     **14.** 60     **15.** 65

_____     _____     _____

**16.** 20     **17.** 30     **18.** 56

_____     _____     _____

**19.** 21     **20.** 18     **21.** 16

_____     _____     _____

**22.** 630     **23.** 1001     **24.** 625

_____     _____     _____

**25.** The prime factorization of a number is
$2 \times 2 \times 3 \times 3 \times 3 \times 5 \times 5 \times 5 \times 5 \times 5$.
What is the number?

**26. Social Science** The House of Representatives has
435 members. If a committee has a prime number of
members, and that number is a factor of 435, then how
many members can be on the committee?          _____

# Least Common Multiples

List the first three common multiples of the given numbers.

**1.** 3, 2

**2.** 3, 4

**3.** 5, 4

**4.** 2, 8

_____

_____

_____

_____

**5.** 3, 5

**6.** 2, 7

**7.** 6, 5

**8.** 13, 2

_____

_____

_____

_____

Find the LCM of each pair.

**9.** 6, 23 _____

**10.** 3, 21 _____

**11.** 9, 5 _____

**12.** 17, 3 _____

**13.** 7, 5 _____

**14.** 21, 7 _____

**15.** 2, 12 _____

**16.** 15, 11 _____

**17.** 4, 19 _____

**18.** 6, 28 _____

**19.** 14, 18 _____

**20.** 23, 2 _____

**21.** 15, 14 _____

**22.** 11, 33 _____

**23.** 5, 15 _____

**24.** 8, 5 _____

**25.** 26, 22 _____

**26.** 3, 22 _____

**27.** 2, 34 _____

**28.** 15, 8 _____

**29.** 10, 15 _____

**30.** 12, 4 _____

**31.** 6, 10 _____

**32.** 43, 13 _____

**33.** 24, 3 _____

**34.** 36, 45 _____

**35.** 17, 2 _____

**36.** 24, 7 _____

**37.** 29, 5 _____

**38.** 27, 2 _____

**39.** 9, 10 _____

**40.** 31, 5 _____

**41.** 62, 9 _____

**42.** 2, 7 _____

**43.** 6, 4 _____

**44.** 10, 2 _____

**45.** 4, 10 _____

**46.** 6, 11 _____

**47.** 11, 2 _____

**48.** 7, 12 _____

**49.** 7, 16 _____

**50.** 16, 6 _____

**51.** 10, 14 _____

**52.** 22, 4 _____

**53.** Marti works Monday through Saturday, so she has a day off once every 7 days. She needs to give her dog some medicine every 5 days. How often does she give her dog medicine on her day off?

_____

**54.** The traffic signal at 4th and Main turns green every 6 minutes. The signal at 5th and Broadway turns green every 4 minutes. If both turned green at 12:15 P.M., when are the next three times that both will turn green at the same time?

_____

Name _____

# Section 5A Review

Tell whether the first number is divisible by the second.

**1.** 95, 5 _____     **2.** 72, 6 _____     **3.** 38, 4 _____     **4.** 48, 9 _____

Find the prime factorization.

**5.** 85 _____     **6.** 72 _____     **7.** 220 _____

**8.** 231 _____     **9.** 128 _____     **10.** 148 _____

List the first seven multiples of the number.

**11.** 3     **12.** 11

_____     _____

**13.** 8     **14.** 60

_____     _____

Find the LCM of each pair.

**15.** 2, 9 _____     **16.** 15, 10 _____     **17.** 7, 63 _____     **18.** 22, 4 _____

**19.** A certain city holds elections for mayor in years divisible by 3. These elections will be held in which years between 1996 and 2015?

_____

**20.** Margo's locker combination consists of the first three even multiples of 9, in order. What is her combination?     _____

**21.** The prime factorization of a number is $5 \times 7 \times 7 \times 17$. What is the number?     _____

**22.** **Health** A serving of stir fried mung bean sprouts has 3 times as much iron as a serving of boiled mung bean sprouts. The stir fried sprouts have 2.4 mg of iron. Write and solve an equation to find the amount of iron in a serving of boiled bean sprouts.
*[Lesson 3-12]*

_____

**23.** A certain brand of washing machine uses 140 liters of water to do a load of laundry. Convert this amount to milliliters. *[Lesson 4-2]*     _____

# Understanding Fractions

For each fraction, draw a model and name an equivalent fraction.

1. $\frac{1}{3}$ _____

2. $\frac{3}{5}$ _____

3. $\frac{8}{12}$ _____

4. $\frac{5}{7}$ _____

5. $\frac{5}{9}$ _____

6. $\frac{8}{20}$ _____

7. $\frac{15}{25}$ _____

8. $\frac{2}{5}$ _____

9. $\frac{1}{6}$ _____

10. $\frac{5}{6}$ _____

11. $\frac{1}{10}$ _____

12. $\frac{3}{6}$ _____

The picture shows how to set up the game of backgammon.
The 24 triangular-shaped spaces on the board are called points.

13. What fraction of the points have
white playing pieces?            _____

14. What fraction of the points have
five black playing pieces?            _____

15. What fraction of the white playing
pieces are on the point shown at
the upper left corner of the board?            _____

16. Arturo has 3 dogs and 5 cats. What
fraction of his pets are dogs?

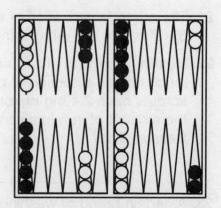

# Fractions in Lowest Terms

Find two fractions equivalent to each fraction.

1. $\frac{8}{10}$ _____  2. $\frac{3}{4}$ _____  3. $\frac{8}{24}$ _____

4. $\frac{4}{7}$ _____  5. $\frac{18}{21}$ _____  6. $\frac{6}{8}$ _____

7. $\frac{12}{14}$ _____  8. $\frac{5}{9}$ _____  9. $\frac{6}{9}$ _____

10. $\frac{6}{14}$ _____  11. $\frac{12}{30}$ _____  12. $\frac{4}{13}$ _____

Write in lowest terms.

13. $\frac{12}{24}$ _____  14. $\frac{6}{9}$ _____  15. $\frac{9}{21}$ _____  16. $\frac{8}{10}$ _____

17. $\frac{6}{28}$ _____  18. $\frac{18}{20}$ _____  19. $\frac{30}{38}$ _____  20. $\frac{8}{20}$ _____

21. $\frac{12}{18}$ _____  22. $\frac{14}{32}$ _____  23. $\frac{8}{12}$ _____  24. $\frac{12}{16}$ _____

25. $\frac{12}{30}$ _____  26. $\frac{9}{15}$ _____  27. $\frac{6}{42}$ _____  28. $\frac{9}{12}$ _____

29. $\frac{6}{15}$ _____  30. $\frac{6}{10}$ _____  31. $\frac{6}{12}$ _____  32. $\frac{24}{30}$ _____

Find the GCF of each pair.

33. 16, 10 _____  34. 11, 18 _____  35. 15, 6 _____  36. 8, 6 _____

37. 3, 6 _____  38. 20, 15 _____  39. 12, 18 _____  40. 3, 14 _____

41. 8, 12 _____  42. 10, 14 _____  43. 21, 15 _____  44. 49, 70 _____

45. 36, 60 _____  46. 70, 42 _____  47. 32, 76 _____  48. 64, 4 _____

49. 15, 75 _____  50. 63, 42 _____  51. 30, 65 _____  52. 32, 24 _____

53. **Measurement** A kilometer is about $\frac{6}{10}$ of a mile.
Write this distance in lowest terms. _____

54. $\frac{25}{30}$ of the students in Mrs. Lim's class went on last
week's field trip. Write this fraction in lowest terms. _____

Name _____

**Practice
5-6**

# Improper Fractions and Mixed Numbers

Write each mixed number as an improper fraction.

1. $2\frac{1}{6}$ _____
2. $5\frac{1}{5}$ _____
3. $1\frac{2}{5}$ _____
4. $13\frac{1}{2}$ _____

5. $8\frac{3}{4}$ _____
6. $3\frac{2}{3}$ _____
7. $1\frac{3}{5}$ _____
8. $4\frac{1}{2}$ _____

9. $14\frac{2}{9}$ _____
10. $12\frac{2}{3}$ _____
11. $3\frac{5}{8}$ _____
12. $9\frac{1}{9}$ _____

13. $5\frac{2}{3}$ _____
14. $7\frac{4}{5}$ _____
15. $8\frac{1}{3}$ _____
16. $4\frac{3}{4}$ _____

Write each improper fraction as a mixed number.

17. $\frac{17}{4}$ _____
18. $\frac{19}{2}$ _____
19. $\frac{37}{3}$ _____
20. $\frac{16}{7}$ _____

21. $\frac{32}{3}$ _____
22. $\frac{77}{8}$ _____
23. $\frac{101}{7}$ _____
24. $\frac{33}{4}$ _____

25. $\frac{27}{2}$ _____
26. $\frac{19}{3}$ _____
27. $\frac{41}{9}$ _____
28. $\frac{61}{6}$ _____

29. $\frac{59}{10}$ _____
30. $\frac{19}{4}$ _____
31. $\frac{5}{3}$ _____
32. $\frac{26}{5}$ _____

**Science** Write the mixed number as an improper fraction or the improper fraction as a mixed number.

33. A geranosaurus was $1\frac{1}{5}$ m long. _____

34. Each arm of a deinocherius was $\frac{17}{2}$ ft long. _____

35. A hypsilophodon was $\frac{23}{10}$ m long. _____

36. A protoceratops was $\frac{9}{5}$ m long. _____

37. An anatosaurus was $13\frac{2}{3}$ m long. _____

38. Heidi built a fort with a ceiling that was $\frac{21}{4}$ ft high. Marvin is $5\frac{3}{4}$ ft tall. Can Marvin stand up straight in Heidi's fort? _____

© Scott Foresman • Addison Wesley 6

**66** Use with pages 298–301.

# Converting Fractions and Decimals

Rewrite using bar notation.

**1.** 0.77777777 ... _____   **2.** 0.58585858 ... _____   **3.** 2.65656565 ... _____

**4.** 3.008008008 ... _____   **5.** 4.876767676 ... _____   **6.** 12.12121212 ... _____

**7.** 4.93333333 ... _____   **8.** 7.50505050 ... _____   **9.** 6.80888888 ... _____

Write each fraction as a decimal. State whether the decimal terminates or repeats.

**10.** $\frac{2}{3}$ _____   **11.** $\frac{7}{10}$ _____   **12.** $\frac{3}{5}$ _____   **13.** $\frac{15}{6}$ _____

_____   _____   _____   _____

**14.** $\frac{23}{33}$ _____   **15.** $\frac{1}{8}$ _____   **16.** $\frac{5}{11}$ _____   **17.** $\frac{36}{25}$ _____

_____   _____   _____   _____

**18.** $\frac{41}{100}$ _____   **19.** $\frac{5}{6}$ _____   **20.** $\frac{21}{40}$ _____   **21.** $\frac{49}{50}$ _____

_____   _____   _____   _____

Write each decimal as a fraction in lowest terms.

**22.** 0.25 _____   **23.** 0.74 _____   **24.** 0.5 _____   **25.** 0.47 _____

**26.** 0.8 _____   **27.** 0.375 _____   **28.** 0.515 _____   **29.** 0.863 _____

**30.** 0.28 _____   **31.** 0.45 _____   **32.** 0.7 _____   **33.** 0.186 _____

**34.** 0.504 _____   **35.** 0.84 _____   **36.** 0.775 _____   **37.** 0.868 _____

**38. Measurement** Gilbert is using a set of drill bits that came in the
following sizes: 0.0625 in., 0.125 in., 0.1875 in., 0.25 in., and
0.375 in. Write each drill bit size as a fraction in lowest terms.

_____

**39. Technology** A computer word processing program allows users to
select a font size of 8 pt, 10 pt, 12 pt, or 16 pt. These sizes are
equivalent to $\frac{1}{9}$ in., $\frac{5}{36}$ in., $\frac{1}{6}$ in., and $\frac{2}{9}$ in., respectively. Write each
font size as a decimal.

_____

# Comparing and Ordering

Compare using < , > , or =.

1. $\dfrac{1}{4} \bigcirc \dfrac{4}{13}$   2. $\dfrac{2}{4} \bigcirc \dfrac{10}{20}$   3. $\dfrac{5}{7} \bigcirc \dfrac{6}{7}$   4. $\dfrac{5}{12} \bigcirc \dfrac{3}{5}$

5. $\dfrac{2}{9} \bigcirc \dfrac{1}{5}$   6. $\dfrac{1}{7} \bigcirc \dfrac{3}{18}$   7. $\dfrac{4}{9} \bigcirc \dfrac{3}{7}$   8. $\dfrac{12}{18} \bigcirc \dfrac{10}{14}$

9. $\dfrac{12}{16} \bigcirc \dfrac{4}{6}$   10. $\dfrac{7}{20} \bigcirc \dfrac{1}{3}$   11. $\dfrac{2}{8} \bigcirc \dfrac{3}{15}$   12. $\dfrac{2}{6} \bigcirc \dfrac{4}{12}$

13. $\dfrac{2}{5} \bigcirc \dfrac{5}{11}$   14. $\dfrac{10}{16} \bigcirc \dfrac{3}{4}$   15. $\dfrac{7}{11} \bigcirc \dfrac{9}{13}$   16. $\dfrac{2}{7} \bigcirc \dfrac{2}{9}$

Order from smallest to largest.

17. $\dfrac{3}{8}, \dfrac{3}{9}, \dfrac{3}{10}$   18. $\dfrac{4}{5}, \dfrac{5}{4}, \dfrac{4}{4}$   19. $\dfrac{7}{10}, \dfrac{18}{25}, \dfrac{3}{5}$

_____   _____   _____

20. $\dfrac{3}{4}, \dfrac{2}{5}, \dfrac{11}{20}$   21. $\dfrac{2}{3}, \dfrac{3}{4}, \dfrac{5}{6}$   22. $\dfrac{7}{15}, \dfrac{1}{3}, \dfrac{2}{5}$

_____   _____   _____

23. $\dfrac{1}{5}, \dfrac{1}{6}, \dfrac{7}{30}$   24. $\dfrac{6}{11}, \dfrac{3}{7}, \dfrac{4}{9}$   25. $\dfrac{1}{2}, \dfrac{2}{5}, \dfrac{1}{3}$

_____   _____   _____

26. $\dfrac{5}{8}, \dfrac{3}{4}, \dfrac{7}{10}$   27. $\dfrac{33}{100}, \dfrac{3}{10}, \dfrac{33}{1000}$   28. $\dfrac{40}{49}, \dfrac{13}{28}, \dfrac{3}{14}$

_____   _____   _____

29. **Measurement** Ralph has $2\dfrac{1}{3}$ cups of milk. Does
he have enough to prepare a recipe that uses $2\dfrac{1}{2}$ cups?   _____

30. **Measurement** Jody's Hardware stocks wooden dowels in
the following widths: $\dfrac{3}{16}$ in., $\dfrac{1}{8}$ in., $\dfrac{3}{8}$ in., $\dfrac{1}{4}$ in., $\dfrac{1}{2}$ in. Write these
widths in order from the least to the greatest.

_____

# Section 5B Review

Determine what fraction the shaded part represents.
Identify the numerator and denominator of each fraction.

**1.** fraction: _____

numerator: _____

denominator: _____

**2.** fraction: _____

numerator: _____

denominator: _____

**3.** fraction: _____

numerator: _____

denominator: _____

**4.** fraction: _____

numerator: _____

denominator: _____

Write each fraction in lowest terms and as a decimal.

**5.** $\frac{16}{20}$

**6.** $\frac{6}{16}$

**7.** $\frac{8}{24}$

**8.** $\frac{21}{42}$

_____   _____   _____   _____

**9.** $\frac{84}{100}$

**10.** $\frac{9}{36}$

**11.** $\frac{10}{12}$

**12.** $\frac{45}{72}$

_____   _____   _____   _____

Write each mixed number as an improper fraction or the improper
fraction as a mixed number.

**13.** $3\frac{5}{6}$ _____

**14.** $\frac{23}{5}$ _____

**15.** $7\frac{3}{8}$ _____

**16.** $\frac{47}{10}$ _____

**17.** Fred and Gina are baking cookies. Fred puts chocolate
icing on every eighth cookie, and Gina puts colored
sprinkles on every fifth cookie. Which cookies have
both chocolate icing and colored sprinkles? _____

**18.** Bill correctly answered $\frac{3}{14}$ of the problems on an algebra
test. Cheryl correctly answered $\frac{1}{7}$ of the problems, and
Dana correctly answered $\frac{1}{4}$ of the problems. Order these
students from the fewest correct answers to the most. _____

**19.** A store owner obtained a compact stereo system for $86.72
and sold it for $97.95. What was the profit? *[Lesson 3-1]* _____

**20. Science** A king salmon can weigh up to 100 pounds
or more. How many ounces is that? *[Lesson 4-3]* _____

# Cumulative Review Chapters 1–5

Order each group of numbers from least to greatest.
*[Lesson 2-3]*

**1.** 3,333; 33,333; 333

_____

**2.** 60,660; 60,606; 66,006

_____

**3.** 7,000; 7,010; 7,009; 6,999

_____

**4.** 5 billion; 4 million; 6 hundred

_____

Simplify. *[Lessons 3-6 and 3-11]*

**5.** 8.37 + 21

_____

**6.** 5.43 − 1.9

_____

**7.** 6.98 + 7.47

_____

**8.** 12 − 5.63

_____

**9.** 24.893 ÷ 3.1

_____

**10.** 4.36 + 8.9

_____

**11.** 1.4535 ÷ 0.085

_____

**12.** 0.828 ÷ 3.6

_____

Find the missing measurement for each rectangle. *[Lesson 4-4]*

**13.** Area = 66 in$^2$

   Base = _____

   Height= 6 in.

**14.** Area = _____

   Base = 6 ft

   Height = 15 ft

**15.** Area = 35 m$^2$

   Base = 5 m

   Height = _____

**16.** Area = 48 km$^2$

   Base = 12 km

   Height = _____

**17.** Area = _____

   Base = 6.5 yd

   Height = 4.1 yd

**18.** Area = 9.25 mm$^2$

   Base = _____

   Height = 2.5 mm

Find the prime factorization. *[Lesson 5-2]*

**19.** 350 _____

**20.** 135 _____

**21.** 616 _____

**22.** 180 _____

Write as a fraction in lowest terms *[Lesson 5-7]*

**23.** 0.625 _____

**24.** 0.47 _____

**25.** 0.775 _____

**26.** 0.42 _____

Name _____

# Adding and Subtracting Fractions with Like Denominators

Simplify. Write each answer in lowest terms.

**1.** $\frac{3}{20} - \frac{1}{20}$ _____

**2.** $\frac{6}{15} + \frac{4}{15}$ _____

**3.** $\frac{3}{4} + \frac{3}{4}$ _____

**4.** $\frac{6}{8} + \frac{3}{8}$ _____

**5.** $\frac{2}{13} + \frac{3}{13}$ _____

**6.** $\frac{6}{8} - \frac{5}{8}$ _____

**7.** $\frac{3}{15} + \frac{10}{15}$ _____

**8.** $\frac{8}{10} - \frac{4}{10}$ _____

**9.** $\frac{7}{14} - \frac{3}{14}$ _____

**10.** $\frac{1}{4} + \frac{1}{4}$ _____

**11.** $\frac{6}{7} - \frac{1}{7}$ _____

**12.** $\frac{14}{19} - \frac{5}{19}$ _____

**13.** $\frac{5}{6} + \frac{5}{6}$ _____

**14.** $\frac{2}{3} + \frac{1}{3}$ _____

**15.** $\frac{15}{18} + \frac{4}{18}$ _____

**16.** $\frac{10}{15} - \frac{6}{15}$ _____

State whether the answer is greater than, less than, or equal to 1.

**17.** $\frac{7}{11} - \frac{3}{11}$

**18.** $\frac{4}{10} + \frac{6}{10}$

**19.** $\frac{2}{4} + \frac{3}{4}$

_____

_____

_____

**20.** $\frac{1}{4} + \frac{2}{4}$

**21.** $\frac{5}{6} - \frac{1}{6}$

**22.** $\frac{2}{5} + \frac{4}{5}$

_____

_____

_____

Each guest at Tony's 8th birthday party brought one gift or a card. The bar graph shows the gifts that Tony received. Use the graph for Exercises 23–25.

**23.** What fraction of the gifts were books or games? _____

**24.** What fraction of the gifts were clothing, games, or toys? _____

**25.** There were 18 guests at the party. What fraction brought cards only? _____

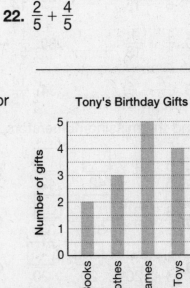

**Tony's Birthday Gifts**

**26.** In 1990, about $\frac{1}{8}$ of the American population was of age 65 or older. What fraction of the population was under 65? _____

**27.** In 1993, $\frac{11}{20}$ of America's electricity was produced using coal, and $\frac{4}{20}$ of America's electricity was produced using nuclear power. What fraction was produced using other means such as natural gas or hydroelectric power? _____

# Adding and Subtracting Fractions with Unlike Denominators

Simplify. Write each answer in lowest terms.

**1.** $\frac{3}{5} - \frac{1}{3}$ _____

**2.** $\frac{1}{2} + \frac{7}{22}$ _____

**3.** $\frac{9}{16} - \frac{1}{8}$ _____

**4.** $\frac{3}{5} - \frac{4}{9}$ _____

**5.** $\frac{1}{5} - \frac{1}{7}$ _____

**6.** $\frac{11}{24} + \frac{1}{3}$ _____

**7.** $\frac{1}{3} - \frac{1}{10}$ _____

**8.** $\frac{7}{10} - \frac{3}{5}$ _____

**9.** $\frac{8}{9} - \frac{7}{12}$ _____

**10.** $\frac{5}{6} - \frac{1}{2}$ _____

**11.** $\frac{7}{10} + \frac{2}{25}$ _____

**12.** $\frac{4}{5} + \frac{1}{10}$ _____

**13.** $\frac{5}{8} - \frac{1}{3}$ _____

**14.** $\frac{1}{6} + \frac{9}{16}$ _____

**15.** $\frac{1}{2} + \frac{5}{11}$ _____

**16.** $\frac{1}{6} + \frac{17}{24}$ _____

**17.** $\frac{1}{7} + \frac{2}{3}$ _____

**18.** $\frac{1}{5} + \frac{3}{5}$ _____

**19.** $\frac{1}{7} - \frac{1}{9}$ _____

**20.** $\frac{5}{7} - \frac{1}{2}$ _____

**21.** $\frac{1}{2} - \frac{5}{11}$ _____

**22.** $\frac{1}{9} + \frac{2}{3}$ _____

**23.** $\frac{1}{4} - \frac{1}{11}$ _____

**24.** $\frac{5}{13} + \frac{2}{5}$ _____

**25.** $\frac{5}{6} - \frac{4}{15}$ _____

**26.** $\frac{13}{14} - \frac{1}{2}$ _____

**27.** $\frac{7}{8} - \frac{1}{2}$ _____

**28.** $\frac{1}{4} + \frac{3}{10}$ _____

**29.** $\frac{1}{5} - \frac{1}{13}$ _____

**30.** $\frac{1}{5} + \frac{1}{6}$ _____

**31.** $\frac{2}{7} + \frac{1}{3}$ _____

**32.** $\frac{6}{25} - \frac{1}{10}$ _____

**33.** $\frac{14}{15} - \frac{2}{3}$ _____

**34.** $\frac{14}{15} - \frac{7}{10}$ _____

**35.** $\frac{4}{5} + \frac{1}{25}$ _____

**36.** $\frac{1}{6} + \frac{3}{10}$ _____

Find the missing numerators.

**37.** $\frac{5}{6} + \frac{4}{7} = \frac{\boxed{\phantom{0}}}{42} + \frac{\boxed{\phantom{0}}}{42}$

**38.** $\frac{1}{5} - \frac{1}{14} = \frac{\boxed{\phantom{0}}}{70} - \frac{\boxed{\phantom{0}}}{70}$

**39.** $\frac{3}{4} - \frac{5}{9} = \frac{\boxed{\phantom{0}}}{36} - \frac{\boxed{\phantom{0}}}{36}$

**40.** $\frac{3}{5} + \frac{3}{7} = \frac{\boxed{\phantom{0}}}{35} + \frac{\boxed{\phantom{0}}}{35}$

**41.** $\frac{4}{9} - \frac{2}{5} = \frac{\boxed{\phantom{0}}}{45} - \frac{\boxed{\phantom{0}}}{45}$

**42.** $\frac{1}{8} + \frac{5}{6} = \frac{\boxed{\phantom{0}}}{24} + \frac{\boxed{\phantom{0}}}{24}$

**43.** $\frac{4}{5} - \frac{3}{20} = \frac{\boxed{\phantom{0}}}{20} - \frac{\boxed{\phantom{0}}}{20}$

**44.** $\frac{2}{3} - \frac{1}{15} = \frac{\boxed{\phantom{0}}}{15} - \frac{\boxed{\phantom{0}}}{15}$

**45.** $\frac{4}{9} + \frac{1}{3} = \frac{\boxed{\phantom{0}}}{9} + \frac{\boxed{\phantom{0}}}{9}$

**46.** $\frac{5}{6} - \frac{2}{15} = \frac{\boxed{\phantom{0}}}{30} - \frac{\boxed{\phantom{0}}}{30}$

**47.** $\frac{1}{4} + \frac{3}{7} = \frac{\boxed{\phantom{0}}}{28} + \frac{\boxed{\phantom{0}}}{28}$

**48.** $\frac{5}{6} - \frac{3}{4} = \frac{\boxed{\phantom{0}}}{12} - \frac{\boxed{\phantom{0}}}{12}$

**49.** Randy spends $\frac{1}{3}$ of his week sleeping and $\frac{5}{21}$ of his week working. What fraction of the week is left for other activities? _____

**50. Geography** The three states with the largest areas are Alaska ($\frac{4}{25}$ of U.S. area), Texas ($\frac{2}{27}$ of U.S. area), and California ($\frac{2}{45}$ of U.S. area). What fraction of U.S. area do these states make up altogether? _____

# Solving Fraction Equations: Addition and Subtraction

Solve. Write each answer in lowest terms.

**1.** $\dfrac{5}{17} + a = \dfrac{8}{17}$  **2.** $\dfrac{2}{7} + g = \dfrac{5}{7}$  **3.** $u - \dfrac{1}{2} = \dfrac{1}{10}$  **4.** $\dfrac{7}{8} - v = \dfrac{13}{16}$

$a =$ _____  $g =$ _____  $u =$ _____  $v =$ _____

**5.** $\dfrac{4}{7} - w = \dfrac{6}{35}$  **6.** $n - \dfrac{1}{5} = \dfrac{3}{10}$  **7.** $f + \dfrac{7}{22} = \dfrac{13}{22}$  **8.** $\dfrac{7}{9} - a = \dfrac{1}{36}$

$w =$ _____  $n =$ _____  $f =$ _____  $a =$ _____

**9.** $z - \dfrac{1}{6} = \dfrac{1}{6}$  **10.** $g + \dfrac{1}{4} = \dfrac{7}{16}$  **11.** $\dfrac{5}{6} + w = \dfrac{17}{18}$  **12.** $\dfrac{3}{8} - f = \dfrac{1}{24}$

$z =$ _____  $g =$ _____  $w =$ _____  $f =$ _____

Write a true equation using the fractions given.

**13.** $\dfrac{3}{5}, \dfrac{1}{3}, \dfrac{14}{15}$  **14.** $\dfrac{12}{35}, \dfrac{1}{7}, \dfrac{1}{5}$  **15.** $\dfrac{5}{8}, \dfrac{3}{4}, \dfrac{1}{8}$  **16.** $\dfrac{1}{12}, \dfrac{3}{20}, \dfrac{1}{15}$

_____  _____  _____  _____

**17.** $\dfrac{3}{8}, \dfrac{15}{16}, \dfrac{9}{16}$  **18.** $\dfrac{6}{7}, \dfrac{5}{7}, \dfrac{1}{7}$  **19.** $\dfrac{2}{3}, \dfrac{1}{7}, \dfrac{17}{21}$  **20.** $\dfrac{5}{12}, \dfrac{1}{4}, \dfrac{2}{3}$

_____  _____  _____  _____

**21.** $\dfrac{3}{5}, \dfrac{1}{2}, \dfrac{1}{10}$  **22.** $\dfrac{1}{7}, \dfrac{3}{4}, \dfrac{25}{28}$  **23.** $\dfrac{13}{15}, \dfrac{1}{5}, \dfrac{2}{3}$  **24.** $\dfrac{7}{10}, \dfrac{9}{20}, \dfrac{1}{4}$

_____  _____  _____  _____

Write and solve an equation for the given situation.

**25.** Lori and Fraz ate $\dfrac{7}{12}$ of a pizza. If Lori ate $\dfrac{1}{3}$ of the pizza, how much of it did Fraz eat?

_____

**26.** Irene's gas tank was $\dfrac{9}{10}$ full when she left her house, and it was $\dfrac{7}{15}$ full when she arrived for her vacation. What fraction of a tank of gas did she use driving there?

_____

# Section 6A Review

Simplify. Write each answer in lowest terms.

1. $\frac{12}{15} - \frac{1}{15}$ _____

2. $\frac{11}{20} + \frac{7}{20}$ _____

3. $\frac{2}{3} - \frac{1}{3}$ _____

4. $\frac{4}{6} - \frac{2}{6}$ _____

5. $\frac{6}{11} - \frac{2}{11}$ _____

6. $\frac{4}{7} - \frac{1}{7}$ _____

7. $\frac{12}{13} + \frac{6}{13}$ _____

8. $\frac{18}{20} - \frac{3}{20}$ _____

9. $\frac{1}{3} + \frac{3}{7}$ _____

10. $\frac{1}{10} + \frac{1}{2}$ _____

11. $\frac{1}{2} + \frac{1}{3}$ _____

12. $\frac{21}{25} - \frac{1}{2}$ _____

13. $\frac{6}{7} - \frac{3}{4}$ _____

14. $\frac{5}{7} - \frac{1}{3}$ _____

15. $\frac{1}{2} + \frac{3}{8}$ _____

16. $\frac{3}{10} - \frac{1}{8}$ _____

17. $\frac{2}{3} - \frac{1}{6}$ _____

18. $\frac{3}{5} + \frac{1}{3}$ _____

19. $\frac{1}{2} + \frac{1}{6}$ _____

20. $\frac{2}{3} + \frac{1}{8}$ _____

21. **Career** Lorenzo's job consists of filing, typing, and answering telephones. He spends $\frac{1}{6}$ of his time filing and $\frac{5}{8}$ of his time typing. What fraction of his time does he spend answering telephones?

_____

22. About $\frac{1}{6}$ of Rhode Island's population lives in Providence, and $\frac{1}{12}$ of the state's population lives in Warwick. What fraction of the state's population lives in these two cities combined?

_____

Solve.

23. $k - \frac{5}{11} = \frac{1}{22}$

24. $\frac{7}{10} - s = \frac{1}{30}$

25. $f - \frac{3}{4} = \frac{1}{36}$

26. $c + \frac{2}{3} = \frac{23}{30}$

$k =$ _____

$s =$ _____

$f =$ _____

$c =$ _____

27. $\frac{5}{7} - d = \frac{13}{21}$

28. $\frac{1}{6} + p = \frac{13}{30}$

29. $\frac{1}{5} + c = \frac{2}{5}$

30. $w + \frac{17}{20} = \frac{14}{15}$

$d =$ _____

$p =$ _____

$c =$ _____

$w =$ _____

31. The largest maze ever created had the shape of a rectangle with base 500 ft and height 252 ft. Find the area of the maze. *[Lesson 4-4]*

_____

32. Beth and Carlos are riding on two different Ferris wheels at the park. Beth's Ferris wheel rotates once every 90 seconds, and Carlos' Ferris wheel rotates once every 75 seconds. If Beth and Carlos are both at the bottom of the wheel now, when is the next time they will both be at the bottom?

_____

# Estimation: Sums and Differences of Mixed Numbers

Round to the nearest whole number.

1. $2\frac{4}{5}$ _____    2. $11\frac{13}{24}$ _____    3. $19\frac{19}{36}$ _____    4. $9\frac{21}{34}$ _____

5. $2\frac{1}{9}$ _____    6. $8\frac{4}{11}$ _____    7. $15\frac{1}{2}$ _____    8. $17\frac{5}{21}$ _____

9. $9\frac{5}{9}$ _____    10. $4\frac{4}{5}$ _____    11. $5\frac{7}{20}$ _____    12. $2\frac{2}{9}$ _____

13. $6\frac{8}{23}$ _____    14. $3\frac{1}{7}$ _____    15. $6\frac{1}{2}$ _____    16. $13\frac{6}{7}$ _____

Estimate.

17. $1\frac{1}{7} + 6\frac{5}{6}$ _____    18. $9\frac{7}{24} - 7\frac{5}{6}$ _____    19. $19\frac{4}{7} + 7\frac{1}{3}$ _____

20. $14\frac{4}{5} + 1\frac{3}{8}$ _____    21. $20\frac{1}{15} - 15\frac{2}{5}$ _____    22. $4\frac{1}{30} + 2\frac{5}{6} + 3\frac{5}{7}$ _____

23. $7\frac{1}{2} + 6\frac{5}{6}$ _____    24. $4\frac{2}{5} + 2\frac{7}{10}$ _____    25. $12\frac{17}{18} - 1\frac{1}{2}$ _____

26. $16\frac{5}{8} - 2\frac{1}{2}$ _____    27. $9\frac{2}{3} + 3\frac{7}{8} + 4\frac{1}{3}$ _____    28. $6\frac{8}{15} - 1\frac{1}{3}$ _____

29. $11\frac{7}{24} + 10\frac{1}{12}$ _____    30. $5\frac{3}{8} + 1\frac{11}{24}$ _____    31. $11\frac{2}{9} + 4\frac{4}{9} + 8\frac{1}{7}$ _____

32. $3\frac{1}{2} + 9\frac{10}{17}$ _____    33. $3\frac{23}{24} - 1\frac{1}{3}$ _____    34. $12\frac{22}{25} - 11\frac{4}{5}$ _____

35. $7\frac{1}{20} - 4\frac{9}{20}$ _____    36. $1\frac{1}{3} + 14\frac{2}{3}$ _____    37. $9\frac{5}{18} - 4\frac{1}{2}$ _____

38. $23\frac{23}{24} - 21\frac{3}{8}$ _____    39. $1\frac{7}{12} + 9\frac{1}{6}$ _____    40. $11\frac{5}{16} + 11\frac{1}{2}$ _____

41. $6\frac{8}{23} + 5\frac{2}{23}$ _____    42. $9\frac{1}{2} + 8\frac{10}{11}$ _____    43. $5\frac{5}{9} + 5\frac{1}{2}$ _____

44. $20\frac{23}{30} - 8\frac{3}{5}$ _____    45. $24\frac{3}{5} - 17\frac{17}{20}$ _____    46. $12\frac{1}{2} + 3\frac{3}{7} + 2\frac{8}{9}$ _____

47. $15\frac{7}{12} + 11\frac{5}{8}$ _____    48. $2\frac{2}{7} + 1\frac{5}{6}$ _____    49. $19\frac{2}{5} + 5\frac{7}{9}$ _____

50. Bob's punch bowl holds 9 cups. He plans to make a punch using $7\frac{1}{3}$ cups of water and $2\frac{1}{2}$ cups of juice concentrate. Does he need a larger bowl? _____

51. On Monday, Stephanie bought some stock for $\$36\frac{5}{8}$ per share. Her stock went up 2 on Tuesday, up $1\frac{1}{4}$ on Wednesday, up $3\frac{9}{16}$ on Thursday, and was unchanged on Friday. Estimate the price on Friday. _____

Name _____

# Adding Mixed Numbers

Add. Write the answer as a whole or mixed number in lowest terms.

**1.** $13\frac{1}{5} + 5\frac{3}{5}$ _____

**2.** $7\frac{2}{5} + 1\frac{2}{3}$ _____

**3.** $9\frac{20}{23} + 14$ _____

**4.** $6 + 14\frac{1}{2}$ _____

**5.** $4 + 9\frac{5}{17}$ _____

**6.** $3\frac{16}{19} + 7$ _____

**7.** $10\frac{13}{15} + 4\frac{13}{15}$ _____

**8.** $2 + 16\frac{5}{19}$ _____

**9.** $6\frac{1}{7} + 19\frac{2}{5}$ _____

**10.** $15\frac{1}{2} + 17\frac{1}{7}$ _____

**11.** $22\frac{1}{6} + 10\frac{4}{5}$ _____

**12.** $10\frac{1}{4} + 7\frac{3}{4}$ _____

**13.** $1\frac{4}{5} + 3\frac{5}{6}$ _____

**14.** $11\frac{10}{11} + 5$ _____

**15.** $11\frac{3}{8} + 16\frac{3}{4}$ _____

**16.** $11\frac{4}{5} + 2\frac{13}{15}$ _____

**17.** $16\frac{4}{15} + 8\frac{13}{15}$ _____

**18.** $3\frac{7}{12} + 6\frac{17}{24}$ _____

**19.** $3\frac{1}{15} + 4\frac{3}{5}$ _____

**20.** $4\frac{1}{3} + 7\frac{5}{13}$ _____

**21.** $1\frac{3}{8} + 10$ _____

**22.** $12\frac{1}{8} + 1\frac{1}{3}$ _____

**23.** $8\frac{7}{15} + 3\frac{5}{9}$ _____

**24.** $2\frac{21}{22} + 5\frac{1}{2}$ _____

**25.** $5\frac{5}{12} + 10\frac{11}{24}$ _____

**26.** $18 + 8\frac{11}{13}$ _____

**27.** $3\frac{3}{7} + 1\frac{1}{2}$ _____

Use the table for Exercises 28–30.

| U.S. Immigrants, 1820–1993 (millions) | | | | |
|---|---|---|---|---|
| Europe | Asia | North America, Central America | South America | Africa, Oceania, Other |
| $37\frac{11}{20}$ | $7\frac{1}{20}$ | $13\frac{11}{20}$ | $1\frac{4}{10}$ | $1\frac{1}{50}$ |

**28.** How many people immigrated from Europe? _____

**29.** How many people immigrated from Asia and South America combined? _____

**30.** What was the total number of immigrants? _____

**31.** A cake recipe calls for $2\frac{1}{3}$ cups of milk plus enough water to make $3\frac{1}{4}$ cups of liquid. How much water is used in the recipe? _____

Name _____

# Subtracting Mixed Numbers

Subtract. Write the answer as a whole or mixed number in lowest terms.

**1.** $5\frac{2}{7} - 4\frac{2}{3}$

**2.** $15\frac{7}{10} - 12\frac{2}{5}$

**3.** $7\frac{1}{3} - 4\frac{1}{18}$

**4.** $2\frac{3}{8} - 2\frac{5}{16}$

_____

**5.** $8\frac{5}{8} - 4\frac{7}{24}$

**6.** $10\frac{1}{3} - 4\frac{5}{6}$

**7.** $9\frac{2}{3} - 1\frac{1}{10}$

**8.** $12\frac{3}{11} - 8\frac{5}{11}$

_____

**9.** $5\frac{1}{6} - 2\frac{5}{6}$

**10.** $9\frac{4}{5} - 7\frac{2}{5}$

**11.** $6 - 1\frac{2}{19}$

**12.** $3\frac{2}{3} - 1\frac{8}{15}$

_____

**13.** $10\frac{4}{5} - 1\frac{14}{25}$

**14.** $8\frac{4}{7} - 1\frac{1}{2}$

**15.** $2\frac{1}{2} - 1\frac{19}{21}$

**16.** $12\frac{3}{4} - 5\frac{1}{7}$

_____

**17.** $7\frac{4}{5} - 2\frac{5}{8}$

**18.** $10\frac{17}{21} - 1\frac{5}{7}$

**19.** $10\frac{7}{18} - 4\frac{1}{3}$

**20.** $15\frac{11}{14} - 14\frac{1}{7}$

_____

**21.** $3\frac{5}{8} - 1\frac{9}{10}$

**22.** $7\frac{5}{6} - 6\frac{5}{7}$

**23.** $5\frac{1}{9} - 1\frac{4}{9}$

**24.** $8\frac{4}{5} - 3\frac{13}{20}$

_____

Use the circle graph for Exercises 25–27.

**25.** What fraction of U.S. public schools are elementary schools? _____

**26.** What fraction of U.S. schools are colleges, universities, or in the "other" category?

**27.** What fraction of U.S. schools are secondary schools?

**28.** Jessie baked $6\frac{1}{2}$ dozen cookies for a bake sale, and $4\frac{2}{3}$ dozen of the cookies were sold. How many dozen cookies were left over?

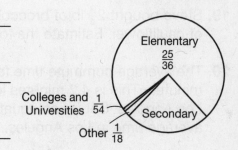

**U.S. Public Schools**

Elementary $\frac{25}{36}$

Colleges and Universities $\frac{1}{54}$

Secondary

Other $\frac{1}{18}$

Name _____

# Section 6B Review

Simplify. Write each answer in lowest terms.

**1.** $6 - 1\frac{3}{14}$

**2.** $3\frac{1}{6} - 1\frac{7}{9}$

**3.** $3 + 5\frac{7}{16}$

**4.** $10\frac{1}{4} + 17\frac{1}{4}$

_____ _____ _____ _____

**5.** $7 + 4\frac{2}{5}$

**6.** $8\frac{5}{17} + 1\frac{2}{17}$

**7.** $23\frac{3}{5} - 13\frac{2}{7}$

**8.** $10 - 7\frac{13}{16}$

_____ _____ _____ _____

**9.** $12\frac{3}{7} + 3\frac{2}{3}$

**10.** $9\frac{1}{2} - 6\frac{4}{9}$

**11.** $2\frac{2}{3} + 5\frac{1}{12}$

**12.** $3\frac{1}{5} + 1\frac{7}{8}$

_____ _____ _____ _____

**13.** $2\frac{1}{9} + 10$

**14.** $2\frac{4}{5} + 4\frac{4}{7}$

**15.** $6\frac{11}{20} - 4\frac{9}{10}$

**16.** $20\frac{5}{6} + 6\frac{2}{7}$

_____ _____ _____ _____

**17.** At Paul's Pet Palace, $\frac{3}{16}$ of the animals are dogs and $\frac{5}{24}$ of the animals are cats. What fraction of the animals are neither dogs nor cats?

_____

**18.** At a school music festival, Judy played saxophone for $2\frac{2}{3}$ hours, Carol sang for $1\frac{3}{4}$ hours, Bob played saxophone for $1\frac{1}{4}$ hours, and Ross sang for $2\frac{3}{8}$ hours.

**a.** Who had more time, the saxophone players or the singers? _____

**b.** How much more? _____

**19.** Steve bought $2\frac{3}{4}$ lb of broccoli, $1\frac{1}{3}$ lb of carrots, and $\frac{7}{8}$ lb of cauliflower. Estimate the total amount of vegetables. _____

**20.** The average commute time for workers in New York is 30.6 minutes. This is 4.2 minutes longer than the average time in Los Angeles. Set up an equation and solve to find the average time in Los Angeles. *[Lesson 3-12]*

_____

**21.** A typical drink coaster is about 0.045 inches thick. Write this amount as a fraction in lowest terms. *[Lesson 5-7]* _____

Name _____

# Cumulative Review Chapters 1–6

Evaluate each expression. *[Lesson 2-8]*

**1.** $7 - 12 \div 3$ _____   **2.** $7 \times 4 + 8$ _____   **3.** $16 \div 2 \times 4$ _____

**4.** $5 \times (3 - 1)$ _____   **5.** $18 - (5 - 2)$ _____   **6.** $(7 - 4)^2$ _____

**7.** $6 + 4 \times 5$ _____   **8.** $10 - 2^2$ _____   **9.** $21 \div 3 + 4$ _____

**10.** $8 - 2 \times 3$ _____   **11.** $(7 + 2) \times 5$ _____   **12.** $2 \times (6 - 1)^2$ _____

Write each number in scientific notation. *[Lesson 3-4]*

**13.** 38,600       **14.** 1,420       **15.** 3,800,000       **16.** 41,500,000

_____     _____     _____       _____

**17.** 6,700,000,000    **18.** 17 million    **19.** 128 thousand    **20.** 7 billion

_____     _____     _____       _____

Find the perimeter. *[Lesson 4-1]*

**21.** _____   **22.** _____   **23.** _____   **24.** _____

Find the LCM of each pair. *[Lesson 5-3]*

**25.** 5, 12 _____   **26.** 40, 30 _____   **27.** 8, 7 _____   **28.** 18, 30 _____

**29.** 10, 8 _____   **30.** 6, 3 _____   **31.** 18, 21 _____   **32.** 36, 18 _____

Simplify. *[Lesson 6-2]*

**33.** $\dfrac{2}{3} + \dfrac{1}{8}$ _____   **34.** $\dfrac{1}{6} + \dfrac{1}{5}$ _____   **35.** $\dfrac{4}{5} - \dfrac{4}{7}$ _____

**36.** $\dfrac{7}{13} + \dfrac{1}{3}$ _____   **37.** $\dfrac{5}{8} + \dfrac{1}{12}$ _____   **38.** $\dfrac{2}{3} - \dfrac{1}{5}$ _____

**39.** $\dfrac{13}{20} + \dfrac{1}{10}$ _____   **40.** $\dfrac{7}{9} - \dfrac{5}{7}$ _____   **41.** $\dfrac{1}{2} - \dfrac{1}{16}$ _____

Name _____

# Estimation: Products and Quotients of Fractions

Estimate.

1. $6\frac{1}{3} \times 12\frac{1}{7}$ _____

2. $7\frac{9}{10} \div 3\frac{1}{3}$ _____

3. $4\frac{2}{3} \times 3\frac{3}{4}$ _____

4. $7\frac{2}{5} \div 2\frac{2}{3}$ _____

5. $3\frac{1}{3} \times 5\frac{1}{7}$ _____

6. $12\frac{3}{5} \div 7\frac{1}{5}$ _____

7. $7\frac{5}{8} \times 9\frac{3}{5}$ _____

8. $8\frac{2}{9} \div 3\frac{3}{5}$ _____

9. $7\frac{1}{4} \times 13\frac{4}{5}$ _____

10. $9\frac{1}{4} \div 3\frac{3}{4}$ _____

11. $2\frac{1}{2} \times 3\frac{4}{9}$ _____

12. $8\frac{7}{8} \div 3\frac{2}{9}$ _____

13. $4\frac{4}{5} \times 5\frac{1}{2}$ _____

14. $8\frac{2}{3} \div 4\frac{1}{3}$ _____

15. $7\frac{2}{5} \times 7\frac{1}{2}$ _____

16. $6\frac{1}{7} \div 2\frac{2}{5}$ _____

17. $9\frac{3}{4} \times 13\frac{5}{6}$ _____

18. $10\frac{1}{9} \div 5\frac{1}{6}$ _____

19. $11\frac{5}{7} \times 4\frac{2}{3}$ _____

20. $8\frac{3}{7} \div 4\frac{1}{6}$ _____

21. $7\frac{2}{3} \times 6\frac{1}{3}$ _____

22. $11\frac{2}{3} \div 6\frac{3}{7}$ _____

23. $3\frac{7}{10} \times 11\frac{1}{8}$ _____

24. $12\frac{4}{5} \div 6\frac{1}{2}$ _____

25. $8\frac{2}{3} \times 9\frac{8}{9}$ _____

26. $10\frac{3}{8} \div 5\frac{2}{5}$ _____

27. $4\frac{2}{5} \times 6\frac{1}{2}$ _____

28. $10\frac{4}{9} \div 5\frac{5}{6}$ _____

29. $11\frac{3}{4} \times 10\frac{5}{7}$ _____

30. $10\frac{1}{6} \div 6\frac{1}{3}$ _____

31. $3\frac{2}{3} \times 10\frac{2}{5}$ _____

32. $11\frac{1}{8} \div 6\frac{1}{4}$ _____

33. $12\frac{1}{3} \times 7\frac{1}{2}$ _____

34. $8\frac{3}{5} \div 4\frac{1}{10}$ _____

35. $3\frac{3}{4} \times 3\frac{7}{10}$ _____

36. $13\frac{3}{4} \div 7\frac{1}{2}$ _____

37. $9\frac{4}{7} \times 12\frac{5}{7}$ _____

38. $9\frac{2}{5} \div 4\frac{1}{3}$ _____

39. $8\frac{7}{9} \times 9\frac{4}{9}$ _____

40. A CD box measures $5\frac{5}{8}$ inches across. A music
store manager wants to display 7 CDs
side-by-side on a 42-inch shelf. Is there enough
room for the display?

_____

41. Computer sales to dealers increased from about
$2\frac{2}{5}$ billion in 1984 to about $8\frac{1}{2}$ billion in 1995.
About how many times larger was the dollar
amount of sales in 1995?

_____

# Multiplying by a Whole Number

Simplify.

**1.** $5\frac{1}{2} \times 3$ _____

**2.** $3 \times 4\frac{5}{6}$ _____

**3.** $4 \times 5\frac{2}{3}$ _____

**4.** $10 \times 3\frac{5}{6}$ _____

**5.** $12\frac{4}{7} \times 4$ _____

**6.** $10 \times 2\frac{1}{3}$ _____

**7.** $6 \times 6\frac{1}{7}$ _____

**8.** $4\frac{1}{2} \times 2$ _____

**9.** $3\frac{4}{7} \times 8$ _____

**10.** $12 \times 3\frac{1}{4}$ _____

**11.** $5 \times 5\frac{1}{3}$ _____

**12.** $14 \times 3\frac{1}{2}$ _____

**13.** $3\frac{3}{4} \times 2$ _____

**14.** $4 \times 9\frac{5}{9}$ _____

**15.** $3 \times 6\frac{2}{3}$ _____

**16.** $8 \times 5\frac{3}{5}$ _____

**17.** $10 \times 4\frac{1}{2}$ _____

**18.** $4 \times 12\frac{2}{3}$ _____

**19.** $8\frac{1}{6} \times 4$ _____

**20.** $11 \times 4\frac{1}{3}$ _____

**21.** $10\frac{1}{2} \times 5$ _____

**22.** $14 \times 3\frac{1}{5}$ _____

**23.** $2\frac{1}{2} \times 5$ _____

**24.** $7 \times 7\frac{5}{9}$ _____

**25.** $10\frac{1}{2} \times 2$ _____

**26.** $7\frac{1}{5} \times 6$ _____

**27.** $13 \times 2\frac{1}{2}$ _____

**28.** $6\frac{5}{6} \times 4$ _____

**29.** $4\frac{1}{5} \times 4$ _____

**30.** $12\frac{5}{7} \times 4$ _____

**31.** $4 \times 10\frac{1}{2}$ _____

**32.** $11\frac{7}{10} \times 4$ _____

**33.** $2 \times 13\frac{1}{4}$ _____

**34.** $12 \times 2\frac{4}{7}$ _____

**35.** $4 \times 11\frac{2}{3}$ _____

**36.** $8\frac{1}{7} \times 4$ _____

**37.** $4 \times 12\frac{1}{2}$ _____

**38.** $10\frac{3}{4} \times 4$ _____

**39.** $3 \times 12\frac{1}{5}$ _____

**40. Health** Complete the table for calories in a certain brand of granola cereal.

| Servings | $\frac{1}{2}$ | $\frac{2}{3}$ | $\frac{3}{4}$ | 1 | $1\frac{1}{3}$ | $2\frac{1}{2}$ |
|---|---|---|---|---|---|---|
| **Ounces** | | | | 2 | | |
| **Calories** | | | | 240 | | |

**41. Science** The longest recorded jump by a kangaroo covered a distance of 45 feet. This is $3\frac{3}{4}$ times the longest jump from a standing position by a human. Find the length of the longest jump from a standing position by a human.

_____

Name _____

# Multiplying by a Fraction

Find each product.

**1.** $5\frac{1}{2} \times \frac{1}{2}$ _____

**2.** $\frac{2}{3} \times \frac{9}{10}$ _____

**3.** $\frac{1}{4} \times \frac{3}{5}$ _____

**4.** $8\frac{1}{4} \times \frac{1}{2}$ _____

**5.** $\frac{5}{6} \times \frac{2}{3}$ _____

**6.** $\frac{5}{8} \times \frac{1}{9}$ _____

**7.** $\frac{1}{7} \times \frac{1}{2}$ _____

**8.** $\frac{2}{3} \times \frac{4}{9}$ _____

**9.** $\frac{5}{8} \times \frac{3}{8}$ _____

**10.** $\frac{1}{2} \times \frac{4}{13}$ _____

**11.** $\frac{1}{3} \times \frac{2}{7}$ _____

**12.** $\frac{13}{15} \times \frac{1}{4}$ _____

**13.** $\frac{2}{5} \times \frac{4}{5}$ _____

**14.** $\frac{1}{11} \times \frac{2}{5}$ _____

**15.** $\frac{7}{9} \times \frac{2}{11}$ _____

**16.** $\frac{3}{4} \times \frac{1}{2}$ _____

**17.** $\frac{1}{2} \times \frac{14}{15}$ _____

**18.** $\frac{1}{5} \times \frac{1}{3}$ _____

**19.** $\frac{11}{15} \times \frac{1}{10}$ _____

**20.** $\frac{8}{9} \times \frac{2}{7}$ _____

**21.** $\frac{7}{8} \times \frac{11}{14}$ _____

**22.** $\frac{1}{2} \times \frac{5}{7}$ _____

**23.** $\frac{3}{4} \times \frac{1}{3}$ _____

**24.** $\frac{1}{2} \times \frac{7}{8}$ _____

**25.** $\frac{2}{15} \times \frac{1}{2}$ _____

**26.** $\frac{1}{3} \times \frac{4}{5}$ _____

**27.** $\frac{10}{11} \times 5\frac{2}{3}$ _____

**28.** $\frac{10}{11} \times \frac{5}{6}$ _____

**29.** $\frac{1}{5} \times \frac{1}{2}$ _____

**30.** $\frac{3}{10} \times 2\frac{1}{2}$ _____

**31.** $\frac{12}{13} \times \frac{3}{10}$ _____

**32.** $\frac{2}{3} \times \frac{1}{3}$ _____

**33.** $\frac{2}{3} \times \frac{7}{9}$ _____

**34.** $\frac{5}{12} \times 3\frac{7}{12}$ _____

**35.** $\frac{1}{6} \times \frac{2}{7}$ _____

**36.** $\frac{3}{5} \times \frac{7}{11}$ _____

**37.** $\frac{1}{2} \times 7\frac{9}{13}$ _____

**38.** $\frac{2}{3} \times \frac{2}{5}$ _____

**39.** $\frac{2}{7} \times \frac{1}{10}$ _____

**40. Science** The total weight of all of the insects in the world is about $\frac{7}{20}$ of a billion tons. The total weight of all humans is about $\frac{1}{3}$ of this amount. Find the total weight of all humans. _____

**41.** A recipe for minestrone soup calls for $3\frac{1}{2}$ cups of vegetable stock. How much stock would you use to make $\frac{2}{3}$ of the amount of soup in the original recipe? _____

Name _____

# Section 7A Review

Estimate each product or quotient.

**1.** $4\frac{5}{6} \times 12\frac{2}{5}$ _____

**2.** $7\frac{3}{4} \div 2\frac{2}{3}$ _____

**3.** $3\frac{4}{9} \times 10\frac{2}{7}$ _____

**4.** $9\frac{1}{4} \div 4\frac{4}{7}$ _____

**5.** $11\frac{1}{2} \times 13\frac{2}{5}$ _____

**6.** $8\frac{4}{7} \div 3\frac{5}{9}$ _____

Simplify.

**7.** $4\frac{1}{9} \times 4$ _____

**8.** $8 \times 3\frac{1}{2}$ _____

**9.** $1\frac{1}{3} \times 2\frac{1}{2}$ _____

**10.** $4\frac{1}{10} \times 8$ _____

**11.** $\frac{1}{2} \times 4$ _____

**12.** $5 \times 2\frac{3}{8}$ _____

**13.** The table shows the ingredients in a recipe for papaya ice cream from *Kathy Cooks Naturally*. Complete the table to show how much of each ingredient you would use to make 4 times or 6 times the amount of the original recipe.

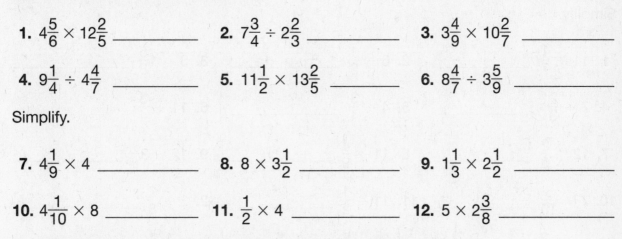

| Ingredient | Ripe papaya | Orange juice | Lemon juice | Whipping cream | Honey |
|---|---|---|---|---|---|
| **Original recipe** | $1\frac{1}{2}$cups | $\frac{1}{2}$ cup | $\frac{3}{16}$ cup | $1\frac{1}{2}$ cups | $\frac{1}{2}$ cup |
| **4 times** | | | | | |
| **6 times** | | | | | |

**14.** Fancy tomatoes are selling for $1.95 per pound. Can you buy $2\frac{1}{4}$ pounds if you only have $4.00? _____

**15.** Mrs. Gonzales bought $3\frac{1}{8}$ pounds of candy for Halloween. She gave away $\frac{3}{5}$ of the candy. How much candy was left over? _____

**16. Fine Arts** Rodney is making a macramé belt that is to be $1\frac{1}{4}$ meters long. If $\frac{1}{3}$ of the belt has been completed, how many meters of the belt have been completed? _____

**17.** Some giant dump trucks use tires with a diameter of 12.5 feet. Find the area of a wheel with this tire. *[Lesson 4-8]* _____

**18.** Rick had $\frac{7}{8}$ of a cup of lemon juice. After making a pie, he had $\frac{1}{2}$ cup of lemon juice left. How much lemon juice did he use in the pie? *[Lesson 6-3]* _____

# Dividing Whole Numbers
# by Fractions

Simplify.

**1.** $11 \div \frac{1}{7}$ _____

**2.** $6 \div \frac{1}{3}$ _____

**3.** $3 \div 1\frac{5}{8}$ _____

**4.** $7 \div \frac{2}{3}$ _____

**5.** $4 \div \frac{3}{4}$ _____

**6.** $11 \div \frac{3}{4}$ _____

**7.** $12 \div \frac{2}{5}$ _____

**8.** $11 \div \frac{4}{9}$ _____

**9.** $12 \div 3\frac{1}{2}$ _____

**10.** $7 \div \frac{3}{10}$ _____

**11.** $11 \div \frac{1}{2}$ _____

**12.** $3 \div \frac{2}{5}$ _____

**13.** $5 \div 2\frac{2}{9}$ _____

**14.** $7 \div 2\frac{8}{9}$ _____

**15.** $8 \div \frac{1}{3}$ _____

**16.** $8 \div 1\frac{1}{4}$ _____

**17.** $8 \div 1\frac{5}{6}$ _____

**18.** $10 \div 1\frac{7}{9}$ _____

**19.** $7 \div 1\frac{1}{5}$ _____

**20.** $4 \div 4\frac{1}{3}$ _____

**21.** $3 \div 4\frac{1}{5}$ _____

**22.** $10 \div 1\frac{1}{2}$ _____

**23.** $6 \div \frac{1}{2}$ _____

**24.** $7 \div \frac{2}{9}$ _____

**25.** $3 \div 2\frac{3}{5}$ _____

**26.** $11 \div 1\frac{3}{10}$ _____

**27.** $10 \div 1\frac{5}{9}$ _____

**28.** $7 \div 2\frac{4}{7}$ _____

**29.** $8 \div 1\frac{1}{3}$ _____

**30.** $8 \div 1\frac{1}{2}$ _____

**31.** $12 \div 1\frac{1}{3}$ _____

**32.** $8 \div \frac{3}{7}$ _____

**33.** $5 \div 2\frac{2}{5}$ _____

**34.** $8 \div \frac{1}{7}$ _____

**35.** $8 \div 2\frac{1}{3}$ _____

**36.** $5 \div \frac{2}{3}$ _____

**37.** $7 \div 2\frac{5}{9}$ _____

**38.** $3 \div \frac{1}{3}$ _____

**39.** $11 \div 2\frac{2}{3}$ _____

**40.** $3 \div 2\frac{1}{3}$ _____

**41.** $5 \div 1\frac{1}{5}$ _____

**42.** $4 \div \frac{2}{5}$ _____

**43. Science** A baby walrus is 4 feet long. This is $\frac{2}{5}$ of the length of an adult male. What is the length of an adult male walrus? _____

**44. Measurement** One yard (36 inches) is equal to $\frac{2}{11}$ of a rod. How many inches are in a rod? _____

Name _____

# Dividing Fractions by Fractions

Simplify.

1. $1\frac{4}{5} \div \frac{1}{3}$ _____

2. $1\frac{2}{3} \div \frac{1}{8}$ _____

3. $3\frac{4}{7} \div 3\frac{1}{2}$ _____

4. $3\frac{4}{5} \div 1\frac{5}{7}$ _____

5. $\frac{2}{5} \div 4\frac{3}{5}$ _____

6. $4\frac{1}{8} \div \frac{3}{7}$ _____

7. $\frac{1}{2} \div \frac{2}{5}$ _____

8. $2\frac{4}{5} \div 4\frac{3}{4}$ _____

9. $\frac{5}{6} \div 1\frac{3}{4}$ _____

10. $1\frac{5}{7} \div 1\frac{2}{3}$ _____

11. $\frac{8}{9} \div \frac{1}{2}$ _____

12. $\frac{1}{4} \div \frac{2}{5}$ _____

13. $\frac{1}{3} \div 2\frac{1}{6}$ _____

14. $1\frac{4}{9} \div \frac{6}{7}$ _____

15. $1\frac{3}{4} \div \frac{4}{5}$ _____

16. $\frac{1}{3} \div \frac{2}{5}$ _____

17. $1\frac{1}{3} \div 1\frac{3}{4}$ _____

18. $\frac{1}{3} \div \frac{2}{7}$ _____

19. $\frac{1}{2} \div 3\frac{1}{4}$ _____

20. $2\frac{1}{4} \div 3\frac{4}{9}$ _____

21. $4\frac{2}{7} \div 1\frac{1}{6}$ _____

22. $\frac{4}{5} \div 3\frac{2}{5}$ _____

23. $1\frac{1}{5} \div \frac{1}{3}$ _____

24. $\frac{4}{5} \div \frac{1}{6}$ _____

25. $\frac{8}{9} \div 2\frac{5}{7}$ _____

26. $1\frac{1}{4} \div 2\frac{2}{3}$ _____

27. $\frac{1}{4} \div 1\frac{5}{9}$ _____

28. $\frac{1}{4} \div \frac{1}{4}$ _____

29. $1\frac{7}{8} \div 1\frac{1}{4}$ _____

30. $1\frac{3}{4} \div \frac{1}{5}$ _____

31. $4\frac{2}{7} \div 1\frac{1}{2}$ _____

32. $5\frac{1}{7} \div 2\frac{1}{2}$ _____

33. $1\frac{1}{9} \div \frac{1}{5}$ _____

34. $1\frac{1}{2} \div 1\frac{2}{3}$ _____

35. $\frac{7}{8} \div \frac{2}{7}$ _____

36. $1\frac{5}{8} \div \frac{5}{9}$ _____

37. $\frac{1}{4} \div \frac{4}{5}$ _____

38. $1\frac{1}{2} \div 3\frac{1}{2}$ _____

39. $1\frac{3}{5} \div \frac{1}{3}$ _____

40. $\frac{1}{2} \div 3\frac{5}{7}$ _____

41. $1\frac{1}{3} \div 1\frac{2}{3}$ _____

42. $1\frac{1}{2} \div 2\frac{3}{4}$ _____

43. **Measurement** A cake recipe calls for $\frac{5}{8}$ of a cup of butter. One tablespoon equals $\frac{1}{16}$ of a cup. How many tablespoons of butter are used to make the cake? _____

44. **Geography** One square mile equals $\frac{1}{36}$ of a township. The area of Austin, Texas, is $6\frac{4}{9}$ townships. Find the area in square miles. _____

# Solving Fraction Equations: Multiplication and Division

Solve.

**1.** $n \div 4\frac{1}{3} = \frac{1}{2}$     **2.** $2\frac{6}{7}f = \frac{1}{3}$     **3.** $f \div 2\frac{5}{7} = \frac{1}{2}$     **4.** $n \div 3\frac{3}{5} = 2\frac{1}{3}$

$n =$ _____     $f =$ _____     $f =$ _____     $n =$ _____

**5.** $n \div 1\frac{3}{5} = 1$     **6.** $\frac{1}{2}u = 5\frac{3}{5}$     **7.** $q \div 2\frac{1}{3} = \frac{3}{8}$     **8.** $c \div 2\frac{4}{5} = \frac{1}{2}$

$n =$ _____     $u =$ _____     $q =$ _____     $c =$ _____

**9.** $b \div \frac{2}{3} = 2\frac{6}{7}$     **10.** $\frac{1}{4}n = 2$     **11.** $t \div 1\frac{1}{7} = 3$     **12.** $h \div 2\frac{2}{5} = \frac{3}{5}$

$b =$ _____     $n =$ _____     $t =$ _____     $h =$ _____

**13.** $2f = \frac{1}{4}$     **14.** $2z = 3\frac{2}{3}$     **15.** $2\frac{1}{4}v = \frac{1}{4}$     **16.** $h \div 3\frac{1}{8} = 2$

$f =$ _____     $z =$ _____     $v =$ _____     $h =$ _____

**17.** $v \div \frac{1}{3} = \frac{2}{5}$     **18.** $3\frac{7}{10}q = 1$     **19.** $h \div \frac{7}{10} = \frac{1}{2}$     **20.** $1c = 1\frac{1}{3}$

$v =$ _____     $q =$ _____     $h =$ _____     $c =$ _____

**21.** $w \div 1\frac{1}{2} = 3\frac{1}{4}$     **22.** $d \div 2\frac{1}{8} = 2\frac{1}{3}$     **23.** $v \div \frac{2}{3} = 1\frac{1}{2}$     **24.** $z \div \frac{1}{3} = 1$

$w =$ _____     $d =$ _____     $v =$ _____     $z =$ _____

**25.** $t \div 2 = 2$     **26.** $b \div 1 = 1\frac{2}{5}$     **27.** $\frac{5}{9}z = \frac{1}{3}$     **28.** $1\frac{7}{10}m = 4$

$t =$ _____     $b =$ _____     $z =$ _____     $m =$ _____

**29.** The largest U.S. standard postage stamp ever issued has a width of $1\frac{1}{11}$ inches, which was $\frac{3}{4}$ of the height of the stamp. Write and solve an equation to find the height of the stamp.

_____

**30.** Candace said, "I'm thinking of a fraction. If I divide it by $2\frac{1}{2}$, I get $\frac{3}{11}$." What fraction was Candace thinking of? _____

# Section 7B Review

Simplify.

**1.** $1\frac{7}{8} \div 1\frac{5}{7}$ _____  **2.** $7 \div 3\frac{3}{5}$ _____  **3.** $1\frac{5}{6} \times 5\frac{2}{3}$ _____  **4.** $3 \div 2\frac{1}{2}$ _____

**5.** $3\frac{1}{3} \times 7\frac{1}{2}$ _____  **6.** $3\frac{3}{5} \div \frac{1}{3}$ _____  **7.** $2\frac{1}{2} \div 7\frac{2}{3}$ _____  **8.** $2\frac{3}{5} \times 8$ _____

**9. Measurement** One teaspoon is $\frac{1}{3}$ of a tablespoon. A bread recipe calls for 2 tablespoons of yeast. How many teaspoons is this? _____

**10. Measurement** There are $1\frac{3}{25}$ American tons in one British ton (long ton). How many British tons are in 7 American tons? _____

Solve.

**11.** $1\frac{2}{7}g = \frac{1}{2}$  **12.** $x \div \frac{1}{2} = 1\frac{1}{3}$  **13.** $\frac{7}{8}f = \frac{3}{5}$  **14.** $s \div 3 = \frac{3}{4}$

$g =$ _____  $x =$ _____  $f =$ _____  $s =$ _____

**15.** Write and solve an equation to find the number of furlongs in 12 rods. (1 rod $= \frac{1}{40}$ furlong)

_____

**16.** Write and solve an equation to find the number of pounds in 8 kilograms. (1 kilogram $\approx 2\frac{1}{5}$ pounds)

_____

**17.** The road distance from Toledo, Ohio, to Detroit, Michigan, is 4720 chains. One mile = 80 chains. Explain how you could use either multiplication or division to find the number of miles from Toledo to Detroit.

_____

**18. Science** The largest birds' egg ever measured was laid by an ostrich in 1988 and had a mass of 2.32 kilograms. A typical albatross egg has about one fourth of this mass. Find the mass of an albatross egg. *[Lesson 3-12]* _____

**19. Fine Arts** Rodin's bronze sculpture of Jules Dalov is $20\frac{3}{4}$ inches tall. His marble *Hand of God* is $15\frac{7}{8}$ inches taller. Find the height of the *Hand of God*. _____

Name _____

# Cumulative Review Chapters 1–7

Write the phrase as an expression. *[Lesson 2-11]*

**1.** *y* divided by 7 _____

**2.** *m* times 5 _____

**3.** 15 less than *u* _____

**4.** one-third of *k* _____

**5.** *d* increased by 12 _____

**6.** *c* doubled _____

**7.** half of *g* _____

**8.** *p* cubed _____

Multiply. *[Lesson 3-9]*

**9.** $0.01 \times 6.45$ _____

**10.** $895 \times 0.001$ _____

**11.** $2.83 \times 9.7$ _____

**12.** $0.38 \times 0.08$ _____

**13.** $12.7 \times 0.85$ _____

**14.** $2.3 \times 18$ _____

**15.** $0.43 \times 0.7$ _____

**16.** $8.41 \times 0.03$ _____

**17.** $34.8 \times 1.2$ _____

Convert. *[Lesson 4-2]*

**18.** 85 g = _____ kg

**19.** 42 kg = _____ g

**20.** 3.82 mL = _____ L

**21.** 73 cm = _____ m

**22.** 6.2 L = _____ mL

**23.** 9.4 m = _____ mm

**24.** 183 m = _____ km

**25.** 31 mm = _____ m

**26.** 2.9 km = _____ cm

Simplify. *[Lessons 7-2 to 7-5]*

**27.** $\frac{1}{3} \div 4\frac{1}{2}$ _____

**28.** $3 \div 1\frac{3}{4}$ _____

**29.** $2 \div 10\frac{1}{2}$ _____

**30.** $4\frac{1}{2} \div 15$ _____

**31.** $2 \div 3\frac{3}{4}$ _____

**32.** $2\frac{2}{5} \times 6$ _____

**33.** $4\frac{3}{4} \div 1\frac{1}{5}$ _____

**34.** $6\frac{1}{2} \times 7\frac{1}{2}$ _____

Solve. *[Lesson 7-6]*

**35.** $\frac{1}{9}q = \frac{1}{6}$

**36.** $k \div \frac{1}{6} = \frac{7}{9}$

**37.** $g \div 1\frac{3}{4} = 4$

**38.** $p \div 2\frac{1}{2} = 2\frac{1}{4}$

*q* = _____

*k* = _____

*g* = _____

*p* = _____

**39.** $p \div \frac{1}{4} = \frac{7}{9}$

**40.** $\frac{1}{4}n = 2\frac{2}{3}$

**41.** $v \div \frac{1}{5} = 3$

**42.** $f \div \frac{5}{9} = 2\frac{1}{2}$

*p* = _____

*n* = _____

*v* = _____

*f* = _____

Name _____

# Classifying Lines

Draw an example of each.

**1.** $\overline{GH}$            **2.** $\overrightarrow{GH}$            **3.** $\overleftrightarrow{GH}$

**4.** $\overrightarrow{PQ}$            **5.** $\overleftrightarrow{PQ}$            **6.** $\overline{PQ}$

Describe the relationship between the lines, rays, or segments.

**7.** _____    **8.** _____

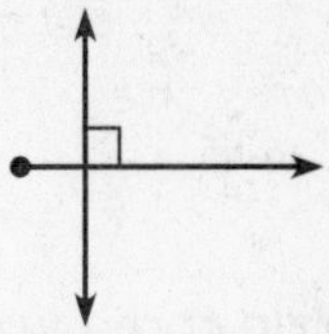

**9.** 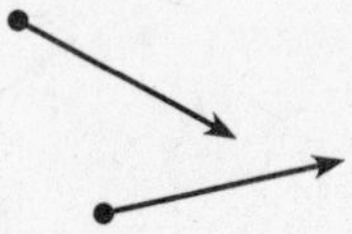 _____    **10.** _____

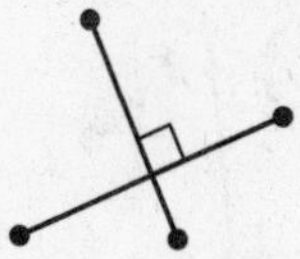

Tell whether each statement is always, sometimes, or never true.

**11.** Perpendicular lines intersect.            _____

**12.** Rays that are not parallel intersect.        _____

**13.** The blue lines on a sheet of standard notebook
paper are perpendicular.                            _____

**14.** The diagram shows a simplified drawing of a truck.

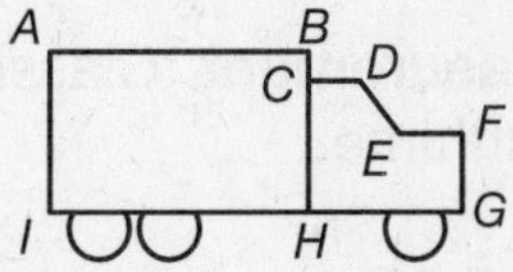

   **a.** Name two pairs of parallel line segments.

   _____

   **b.** Name two pairs of perpendicular line segments.

   _____

   **c.** Name two line segments that intersect but are not perpendicular.

   _____

Name ______________________________

**Practice 8-2**

# Classifying Angles

Classify each angle as acute, right, obtuse, or straight.

**1.** __________ **2.** __________ **3.** __________ **4.** __________

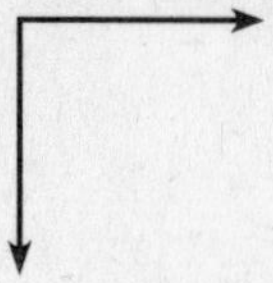
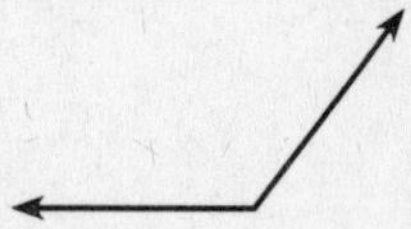
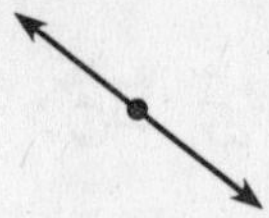
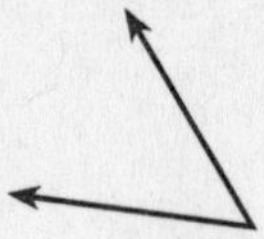

**5.** __________ **6.** __________ **7.** __________ **8.** __________

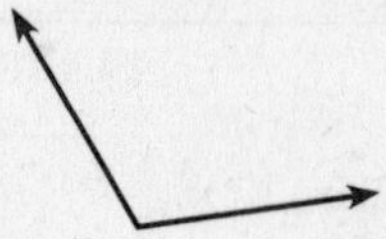
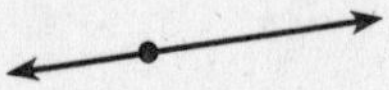
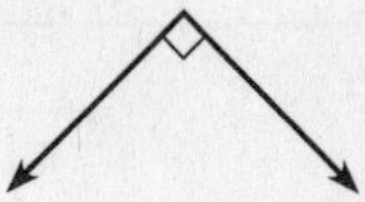
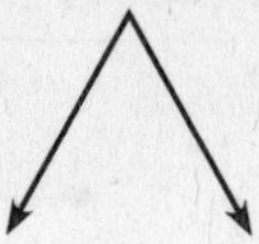

Name each angle three ways.

**9.** ______________ **10.** ______________ **11.** ______________

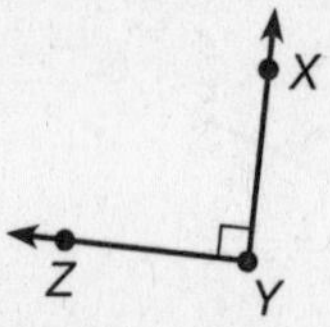

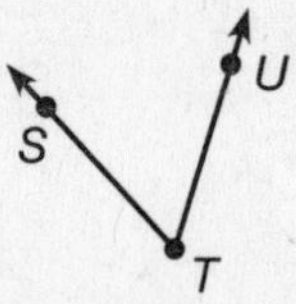

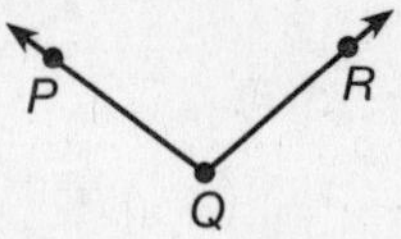


Tell whether each statement is always, sometimes, or never true.

**12.** The sides of a straight angle lie on the same line. __________

**13.** The sides of an acute angle are parallel. __________

**14.** The sides of a right angle are perpendicular. __________

**Measurement** Classify the angle made by the hands of a clock at each time.

**15.** 2:00 __________ **16.** 5:00 __________ **17.** 7:45 __________

**18.** 9:00 __________ **19.** 10:15 __________ **20.** 4:40 __________

**21.** Use the figure at the right. Name two angles of each type.

Acute: __________ Right: __________

Obtuse: __________ Straight: __________

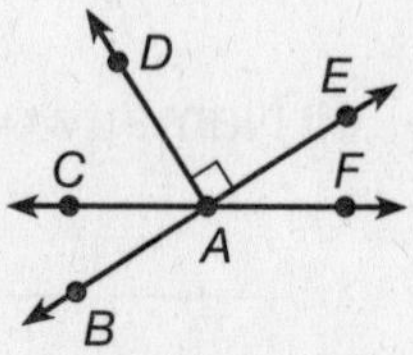

# Measuring Angles

Estimate the measure of each angle. Then measure each with a protractor.

1. _____  2. _____  3. _____  4. _____

Draw an angle of each measure. Then classify each as acute, obtuse, or right.

**5.** 60° _____  **6.** 105° _____  **7.** 90° _____  **8.** 15° _____

State the angle measure that is complementary to the given angle.

**9.** 18° _____  **10.** 88° _____  **11.** 32° _____  **12.** 60° _____

**13.** 41° _____  **14.** 26° _____  **15.** 7° _____  **16.** 78° _____

State the angle measure that is supplementary to the given angle.

**17.** 85° _____  **18.** 100° _____  **19.** 23° _____  **20.** 163° _____

**21.** 135° _____  **22.** 36° _____  **23.** 120° _____  **24.** 71° _____

Read each statement and tell if it is always, sometimes, or never true.

**25.** An obtuse angle and an acute angle are complementary. _____

**26.** A pair of supplementary angles includes an obtuse angle and an acute angle. _____

**27.** Name a pair of complementary angles and a pair of supplementary angles in the figure.

Complementary: _____

Supplementary: _____

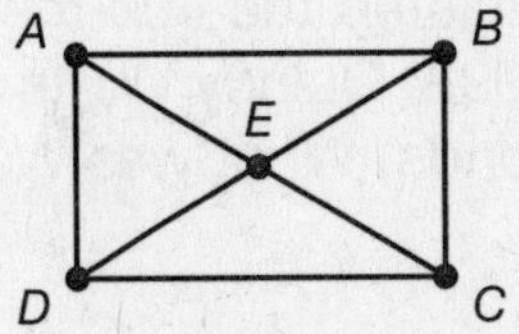

# Section 8A Review

Describe the relationship between the lines, rays, or segments.

1. _____    2. _____

3. _____    4. _____

Classify each angle as acute, right, obtuse, or straight.

5. _____    6. _____    7. _____    8. _____

Measure each angle and find its complement and supplement.

9. measure: _____    10. measure: _____    11. measure: _____

complement: _____    complement: _____    complement: _____

supplement: _____    supplement: _____    supplement: _____

12. **Science** The gar is an armored fish that has survived since the age of dinosaurs. It is 150 centimeters long. How many meters is this? *[Lesson 4-2]*

_____

13. During the 1896 Olympic Games, Thomas Burke completed the 400-meter dash in $54\frac{1}{5}$ seconds. In 1992, Quincy Watts beat this time by $10\frac{7}{10}$ seconds. What was Watts' time? *[Lesson 6-6]*

_____

# Exploring Angles in a Triangle

For Exercises 1–8, classify each triangle as acute, right, or obtuse.

1. _____    2. _____    3. _____    4. _____

5. $m\angle T = 47°$, $m\angle U = 87°$, $m\angle V = 46°$    6. $m\angle D = 73°$, $m\angle E = 90°$, $m\angle F = 17°$

_____      _____

7. $m\angle G = 51°$, $m\angle P = 68°$, $m\angle Z = 61°$    8. $m\angle A = 67°$, $m\angle R = 13°$, $m\angle F = 100°$

_____      _____

Use a protractor to determine the measures of all angles in each triangle.

9. _____    10. _____    11. _____    12. _____

Find the measure of the missing angle in each triangle.

13. $m\angle G = 94°$, $m\angle H = 47°$,      14. $m\angle K = 81°$, $m\angle L = 53°$,

   $m\angle I =$ _____               $m\angle M =$ _____

15. $m\angle P = 38°$, $m\angle Q = 45°$,      16. $m\angle B = 30°$, $m\angle S = 60°$,

   $m\angle R =$ _____               $m\angle U =$ _____

For Exercises 17–20, decide whether the angle measurements can form a triangle. If a triangle can be formed, draw and classify it.

17. $35°, 65°, 90°$                       18. $70°, 55°, 55°$

_____      _____

19. $30°, 40°, 110°$                     20. $45°, 55°, 65°$

_____      _____

Name _____

# Exploring Sides of a Triangle

For Exercises 1–8, classify each triangle as scalene, equilateral, or isosceles.

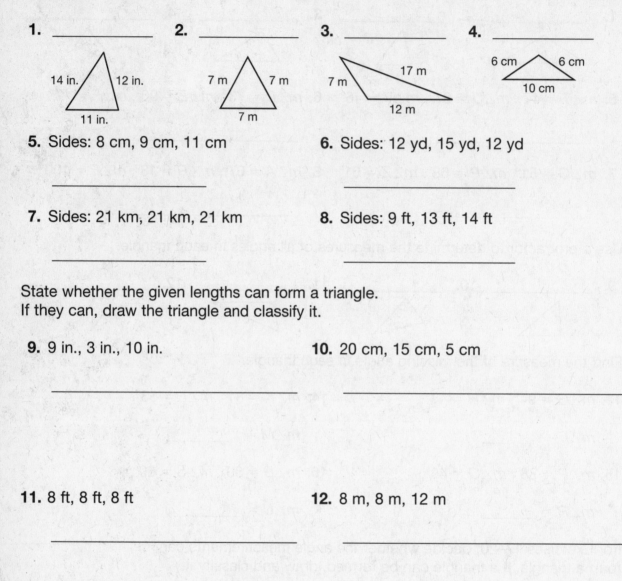

1. _____

2. _____

3. _____

4. _____

14 in.   12 in.
11 in.

7 m   7 m
7 m

7 m   17 m
12 m

6 cm   6 cm
10 cm

5. Sides: 8 cm, 9 cm, 11 cm

6. Sides: 12 yd, 15 yd, 12 yd

7. Sides: 21 km, 21 km, 21 km

8. Sides: 9 ft, 13 ft, 14 ft

State whether the given lengths can form a triangle.
If they can, draw the triangle and classify it.

9. 9 in., 3 in., 10 in.

10. 20 cm, 15 cm, 5 cm

11. 8 ft, 8 ft, 8 ft

12. 8 m, 8 m, 12 m

13. Carolyn made a triangular painting and measured its sides.
The numbers she wrote down were 35 cm, 55 cm, and 95 cm.
She said, "That can't be right. I must have made a mistake."
How did she know?

_____

Name _____

# Polygons

Name each polygon and tell if it is regular or irregular.

1. _____

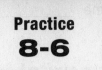

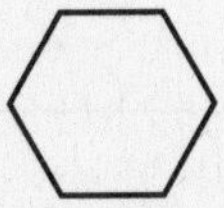

2. _____

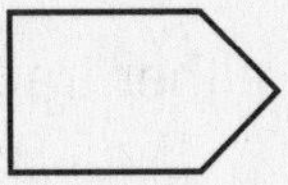

3. _____

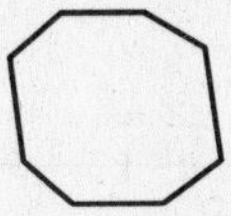

4. _____

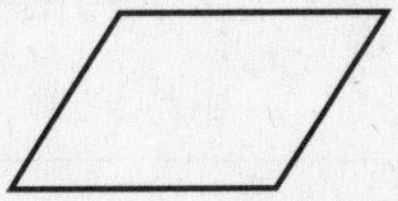

Draw an example of each figure and classify each of the angles in your drawing.

**5.** Irregular hexagon

**6.** Regular quadilateral

_____

_____

**7.** Irregular triangle

**8.** Regular octagon

_____

_____

What kind of polygon is each mask?

9. _____ 10.  _____ 11.  _____ 12. _____

**13. Social Science** The offices of the U.S. Department of Defense
are located in an Arlington, Virginia, building called the Pentagon.
How many sides do you think the shape of this building has? _____

# Quadrilaterals

Answer true or false.

**1.** Some rectangles are also rhombuses.          _____

**2.** All quadrilaterals are either trapezoids or parallelograms.          _____

**3.** A square is a kind of trapezoid.          _____

Classify each figure in as many ways as possible.

**4.** _____          **5.** _____

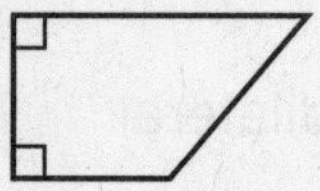

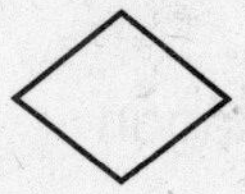

_____          _____

Draw an example of each figure. Classify each of the angles in your drawing.

**6.** A rhombus that          **7.** A rectangle that          **8.** A parallelogram that is not
is not a square          is not a square          a rectangle or a rhombus

_____          _____          _____

_____          _____          _____

**Measurement** Given the information, can you determine the lengths
of each figure's sides? If so, give the lengths.

**9.** A rhombus with a perimeter of 44 inches.          _____

**10.** A trapezoid with three 5-meter sides          _____

**11.** Classify each shape in the jack-o-lantern in as many ways as possible.

Eyes _____

Nose _____

Mouth _____

Name ______________________

**Practice**

# Section 8B Review

Use the letters to name each angle in three ways.

1. ______________

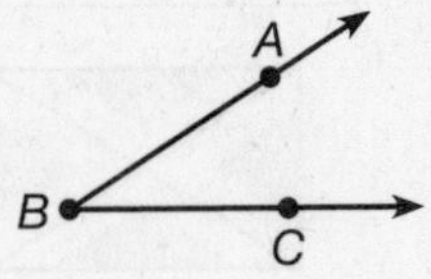
A
B
C

2. ______________

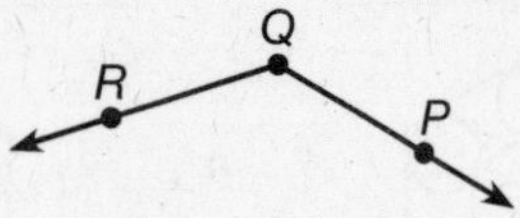
Q
R
P

3. ______________

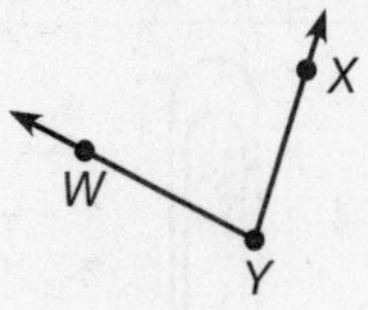
X
W
Y

Classify each triangle by its sides. Find the measure of each missing angle.

4. ______________

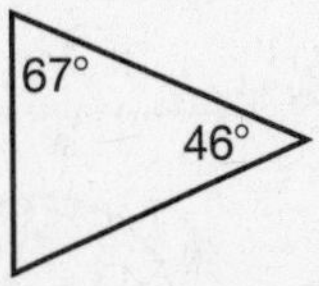
67°
46°

5. ______________

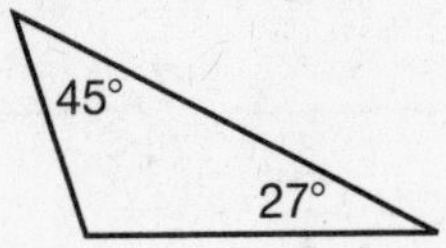
45°
27°

6. ______________

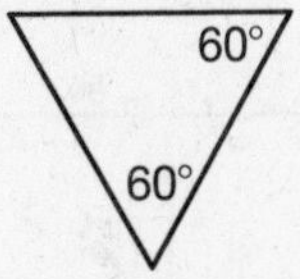
60°
60°

Draw an example of each figure.

7. Irregular octagon

8. Regular triangle

9. Irregular pentagon

Classify each figure in as many ways as possible.

10. 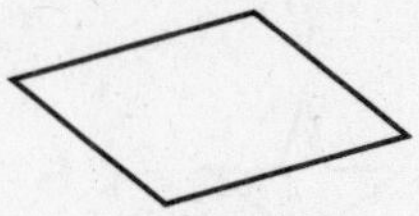

______________________________

______________________________

11. 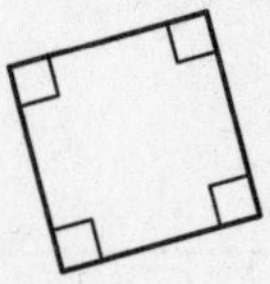

______________________________

______________________________

12. **Geography** The figure at the right shows the approximate shape of Manitoba, Canada. Find the approximate area of Manitoba. *[Lesson 4-9]*

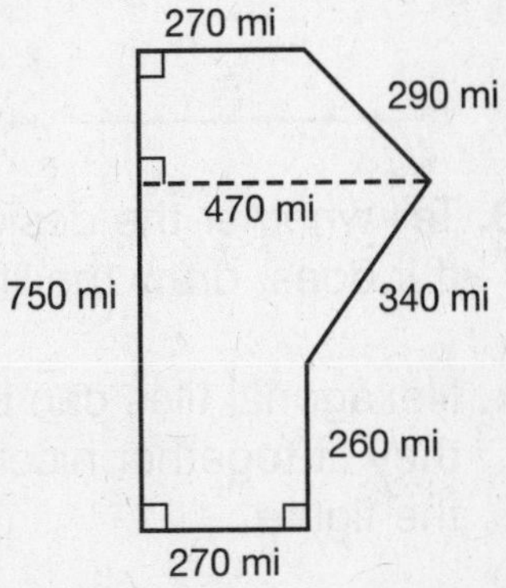
270 mi
290 mi
470 mi
750 mi
340 mi
260 mi
270 mi

______________________

13. **Science** A typical female swallowtail butterfly weighs about $\frac{11}{20}$ gram. Find the weight of 12 female swallowtails. *[Lesson 7-2]*

______________________

# Flips and Line Symmetry

Tell if the picture has line symmetry. If it does, tell how many lines of symmetry it has.

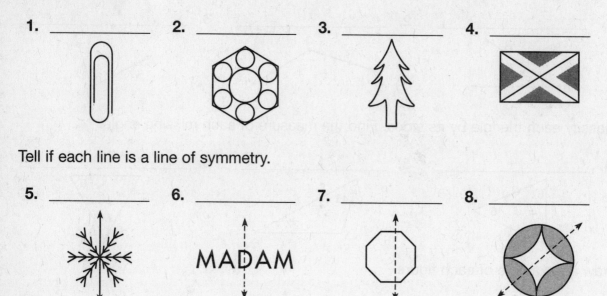

1. _____    2. _____    3. _____    4. _____

Tell if each line is a line of symmetry.

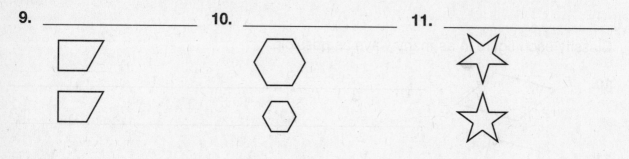

5. _____    6. _____    7. _____    8. _____

Tell if each pair of figures are congruent. If *not,* draw a figure congruent to each.

9. _____    10. _____    11. _____

Use the design for Exercises 12 and 13.

**12.** Name the congruent figures in the design.

_____

**13.** Tell whether the design has line symmetry.
If it does, draw the line(s) of symmetry.

**14.** Hexagonal tiles can be used to cover floors because
they fit together nicely. Draw all lines of symmetry in
the figure.

Name _____

# Turns and Rotational Symmetry

What is the least rotation that will land the figure on top of itself?

1. _____   2. _____   3. _____   4. _____

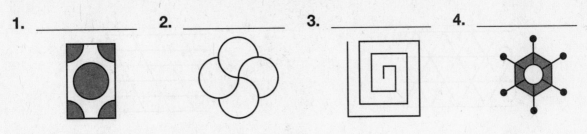

Draw a 45° clockwise rotation of the figure.

5.

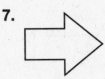

6.

7.

8.

Estimate the number of degrees and state the direction in which each figure has been rotated.

9. _____   10. _____

11. _____   12. _____

13. **Fine Arts** A mirror illustrated in Jan van Eyck's *The Betrothal of the Arnolfini* has the shape shown at the right. If the mirror is rotated 360°, how many times will it land on itself?

_____

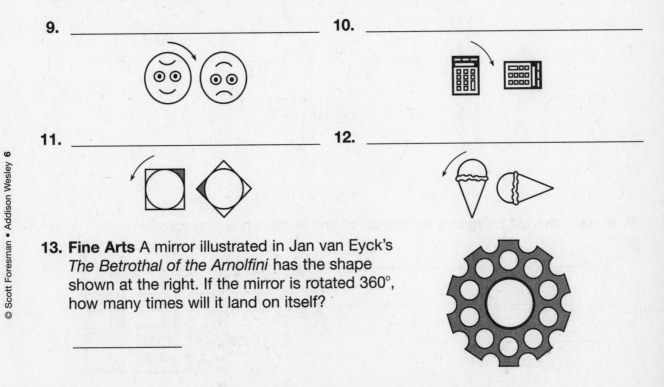

Name _____

# Tessellations

Name the polygon that is tessellated in each design.

1. _____    2. _____

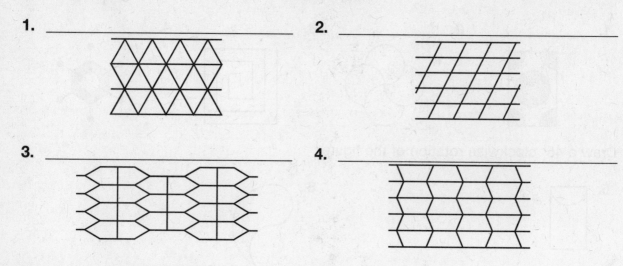

State if each figure tessellates. Make a drawing to show your answer.

5. _____    6. _____

7. _____    8. _____

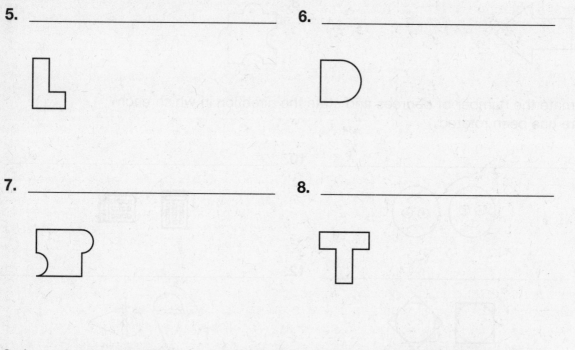

**9.** Is each shaded polygon a translation of one of the white polygons?

_____

_____

_____

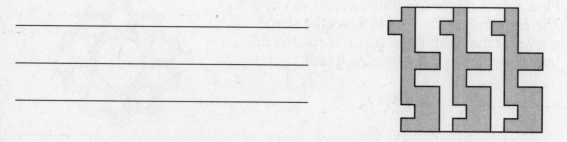

# Section 8C Review

Name each polygon and tell if it has line symmetry. If it does, tell how many lines of symmetry it has.

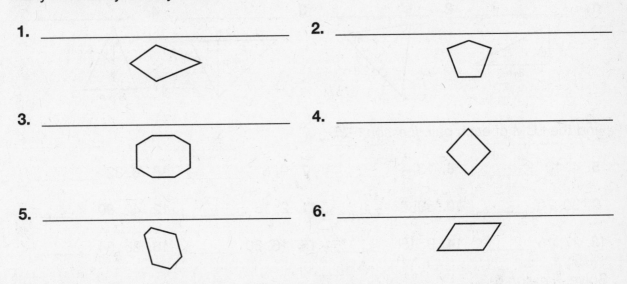

1. _____

2. _____

3. _____

4. _____

5. _____

6. _____

State if each figure will tessellate. Make a drawing to show your answer.

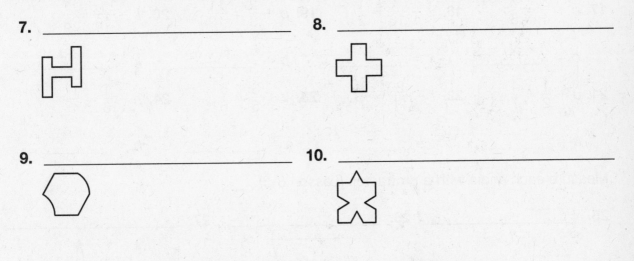

7. _____

8. _____

9. _____

10. _____

11. **Science** A running cheetah completed one stride (23 feet) in 0.28 seconds. Using the formula distance = rate × time, write and solve an equation to find this cheetah's speed in feet per second. *[Lesson 3-12]*

_____

12. A $7\frac{3}{4}$-pound tomato was grown in Oklahoma in 1986. Write and solve an equation to find the number of $\frac{3}{8}$-pound servings that could be made from this tomato. *[Lesson 7-6]*

_____

# Cumulative Review Chapters 1–8

Find the area. *[Lesson 4-6]*

**1.** _____    **2.** _____    **3.** _____    **4.** _____

4 in.
8 in.

2.3 cm
2.8 cm

12 ft
7 ft

6.2 m
5.5 m

Find the LCM of each pair. *[Lesson 5-3]*

**5.** 4, 10 _____    **6.** 13, 4 _____    **7.** 9, 6 _____    **8.** 8, 32 _____

**9.** 30, 70 _____    **10.** 50, 6 _____    **11.** 2, 15 _____    **12.** 42, 60 _____

**13.** 27, 16 _____    **14.** 9, 15 _____    **15.** 16, 30 _____    **16.** 36, 54 _____

Solve. *[Lesson 6-3]*

**17.** $c + \dfrac{3}{4} = \dfrac{7}{8}$    **18.** $x - \dfrac{3}{16} = \dfrac{1}{2}$    **19.** $p + \dfrac{2}{3} = \dfrac{11}{12}$    **20.** $k - \dfrac{1}{16} = \dfrac{1}{3}$

$c =$ _____    $x =$ _____    $p =$ _____    $k =$ _____

**21.** $u + \dfrac{1}{2} = \dfrac{4}{7}$    **22.** $t - \dfrac{2}{11} = \dfrac{2}{3}$    **23.** $v + \dfrac{3}{5} = \dfrac{5}{6}$    **24.** $h - \dfrac{1}{6} = \dfrac{1}{4}$

$u =$ _____    $t =$ _____    $v =$ _____    $h =$ _____

Measure each angle with a protractor. *[Lesson 8-3]*

**25.** _____    **26.** _____    **27.** _____

Classify each triangle as scalene, equilateral, or isosceles. *[Lesson 8-5]*

**28.** _____    **29.** _____    **30.** _____

7 in.
5 in.
7 in.

4.8 cm    3.8 cm
4.2 cm

2.8 m    2.8 m
2.8 m

Name _____

# Understanding Integers

Locate each integer on the number line.

**1.** 1    ←——+——+——+——+——+——+——+——+——+——→ $x$
                −4 −3 −2 −1   0   1   2   3   4

**2.** −3    ←——+——+——+——+——+——+——+——+——+——→ $x$
                   −4 −3 −2 −1   0   1   2   3   4

**3.** −1    ←——+——+——+——+——+——+——+——+——+——→ $x$
                   −4 −3 −2 −1   0   1   2   3   4

**4.** 4    ←——+——+——+——+——+——+——+——+——+——→ $x$
                −4 −3 −2 −1   0   1   2   3   4

Compare using $>$ or $<$.

**5.** 7 ◯ −7     **6.** −5 ◯ −6     **7.** 0 ◯ −3     **8.** 16 ◯ −17

**9.** −12 ◯ 9     **10.** 4 ◯ 0     **11.** −11 ◯ −7     **12.** 14 ◯ −12

**13.** −6 ◯ 8     **14.** 12 ◯ −11     **15.** −8 ◯ 0     **16.** 5 ◯ −1

Order from greatest to least.

**17.** 17, −15, −20, 19

**18.** −74, −83, −62, −77

_____

**19.** 5, 0, −8, 3, −6

**20.** −66, 78, 42, −58

_____

Write each number as an integer.

**21.** Jason has $318 in his bank account.

**22.** The temperature is 9°F below zero.

_____

**23.** Rover weighs 36 pounds.

**24.** Sylvia owes $520.

_____

**25.** The Aslam family made $253 at their garage sale, but they
had to pay $18 for advertising and signs. Write the money
amounts as integers. _____

**26. Science** High and low tide levels are reported using positive
and negative numbers. The tides for June 6, 1997, in Broad
Creek, South Carolina, were −12, 232, −17, and 272 centimeters.
Write these numbers in order from the lowest tide to the highest.

_____

# Adding Integers

State each number's opposite.

**1.** −2 _____   **2.** 7 _____   **3.** 14 _____   **4.** −52 _____

**5.** −16 _____   **6.** 11 _____   **7.** −23 _____   **8.** 36 _____

State if the sum is positive, negative, or zero.

**9.** −5 + 5      **10.** 9 + (−12)      **11.** −38 + 5      **12.** −3 + 17

_____      _____      _____      _____

**13.** 21 + (−9)      **14.** −2 + 1      **15.** 6 + (−6)      **16.** −64 + 38

_____      _____      _____      _____

**17.** 7 + (−3)      **18.** 17 + (−3)      **19.** −47 + 47      **20.** 43 + (−35)

_____      _____      _____      _____

Add.

**21.** −7 + 12 _____   **22.** 35 + (−1) _____   **23.** −10 + (−12) _____

**24.** −6 + (−5) _____   **25.** 0 + (−6) _____   **26.** 50 + (−2) _____

**27.** 1 + (−7) _____   **28.** −15 + 15 _____   **29.** 2 + (−9) _____

**30.** −31 + 3 _____   **31.** 4 + (−12) _____   **32.** −23 + 8 _____

**33.** 10 + (−15) _____   **34.** 42 + 16 _____   **35.** −1 + (−4) _____

**36.** −9 + (−14) _____   **37.** 12 + (−12) _____   **38.** 25 + 6 _____

**39.** 5 + (−65) _____   **40.** −20 + 0 _____   **41.** 3 + (−8) _____

**42.** −4 + 27 _____   **43.** −8 + 4 _____   **44.** 8 + 2 _____

**45.** Which height is higher, −83 feet or the opposite of −88 feet?

_____

**46.** U.S. business inventories decreased 10 billion dollars in 1991,
then increased 7 billion dollars the next year. What was the
overall change in business inventories for the two years? _____

Name _____

# Subtracting Integers

Write a subtraction equation that shows the distance between *P* and *Q*
on each number line.

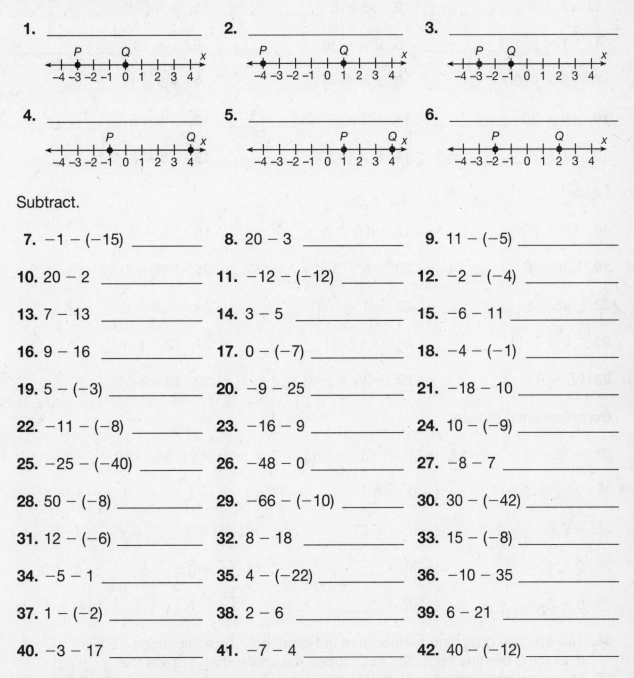

1. _____

2. _____

3. _____

4. _____

5. _____

6. _____

Subtract.

**7.** $-1 - (-15)$ _____

**8.** $20 - 3$ _____

**9.** $11 - (-5)$ _____

**10.** $20 - 2$ _____

**11.** $-12 - (-12)$ _____

**12.** $-2 - (-4)$ _____

**13.** $7 - 13$ _____

**14.** $3 - 5$ _____

**15.** $-6 - 11$ _____

**16.** $9 - 16$ _____

**17.** $0 - (-7)$ _____

**18.** $-4 - (-1)$ _____

**19.** $5 - (-3)$ _____

**20.** $-9 - 25$ _____

**21.** $-18 - 10$ _____

**22.** $-11 - (-8)$ _____

**23.** $-16 - 9$ _____

**24.** $10 - (-9)$ _____

**25.** $-25 - (-40)$ _____

**26.** $-48 - 0$ _____

**27.** $-8 - 7$ _____

**28.** $50 - (-8)$ _____

**29.** $-66 - (-10)$ _____

**30.** $30 - (-42)$ _____

**31.** $12 - (-6)$ _____

**32.** $8 - 18$ _____

**33.** $15 - (-8)$ _____

**34.** $-5 - 1$ _____

**35.** $4 - (-22)$ _____

**36.** $-10 - 35$ _____

**37.** $1 - (-2)$ _____

**38.** $2 - 6$ _____

**39.** $6 - 21$ _____

**40.** $-3 - 17$ _____

**41.** $-7 - 4$ _____

**42.** $40 - (-12)$ _____

**43. Geography** The elevation of New Orleans, Louisiana, is 8 feet below
sea level. The elevation of Lake Champlain, Vermont, is 95 feet above
sea level. How much higher is Lake Champlain than New Orleans? _____

**44.** In Fairbanks, Alaska, a typical January temperature is $-13°F$ and a
typical April temperature is $30°F$. What is the difference between
these temperatures? _____

Name _____

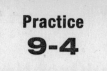

# Multiplying and Dividing Integers

Multiply.

**1.** $-2 \times 4$ _____

**2.** $-5 \times 6$ _____

**3.** $4 \times (-5)$ _____

**4.** $-1 \times (-13)$ _____

**5.** $2 \times (-8)$ _____

**6.** $5 \times 19$ _____

**7.** $-3 \times (-6)$ _____

**8.** $7 \times (-4)$ _____

**9.** $-8 \times 11$ _____

**10.** $-6 \times 20$ _____

**11.** $-3 \times (-12)$ _____

**12.** $-4 \times 5$ _____

**13.** $-7 \times 7$ _____

**14.** $6 \times (-10)$ _____

**15.** $-8 \times (-15)$ _____

Divide.

**16.** $-8 \div (-4)$ _____

**17.** $-20 \div 4$ _____

**18.** $-6 \div 2$ _____

**19.** $-12 \div 3$ _____

**20.** $-5 \div 5$ _____

**21.** $-18 \div (-3)$ _____

**22.** $-45 \div (-5)$ _____

**23.** $-4 \div (-1)$ _____

**24.** $-48 \div 6$ _____

**25.** $-6 \div (-2)$ _____

**26.** $0 \div (-5)$ _____

**27.** $12 \div (-6)$ _____

**28.** $56 \div 8$ _____

**29.** $-35 \div (-7)$ _____

**30.** $48 \div (-8)$ _____

Complete each pattern.

**31.** $-15 \div 5 = -3$

  ____ $\div 5 = -2$

  $-5 \div$ ___ $= -1$

  $0 \div 5 =$ ____

  $5 \div 5 =$ ____

**32.** $(-3)^1 = -3$

  $(-3)^2 = 9$

  $(-3)^3 = -27$

  $(-3)^4 =$ _____

  $(-3)^5 =$ _____

**33.** $-7 \times (-3) = 21$

  $-7 \times (-2) =$ ___

  ___ $\times (-1) = 7$

  $-7 \times$ ___ $= 0$

  ___ $\times 1 = -7$

**34.** $-12 \div (-4) = 3$

  $-8 \div (-4) =$ ___

  ___ $\div (-4) = 1$

  ___ $\div (-4) = 0$

  ___ $\div (-4) =$ ___

**35.** The average daily high temperature in Rome, Italy, typically drops 15°F over the 3 months from July to October. Assuming that it drops the same amount every month, how many degrees does it drop in one month? _____

**36.** Ricky is playing a game in which blue chips are worth 8 points each and red chips are worth −5 points each. Ricky has 7 blue chips and 11 red chips. Find the value of the blue chips and the red chips.

  Blue _____     Red _____

Name _____

# Section 9A Review

Simplify.

**1.** −3 + 15 _____   **2.** 3 × (−7) _____   **3.** 4 − (−9) _____

**4.** 28 ÷ (−7) _____   **5.** 10 + (−4) _____   **6.** −10 × 4 _____

**7.** 15 − (−6) _____   **8.** −100 ÷ (−10) _____   **9.** −6 + (−12) _____

**10.** −6 × (−4) _____   **11.** 8 − 21 _____   **12.** −63 ÷ 9 _____

**13.** 7 + (−11) _____   **14.** 12 × (−3) _____   **15.** −7 − 5 _____

**16.** The CD Recyclery sells used CDs for $10 each and buys them for $6 each. Bob paid $20 when he bought and sold the same number of CDs. How many CDs did he buy?   _____

For Exercises 17–20, solve each problem and state the operation you used.

**17.** Raymond lost $800 on the stock market each month for 5 months in a row. What was the overall change in the value of his stock account?   _____

**18.** Shelly tossed a ball from the top of a cliff. The ball rose 16 feet, and then fell 40 feet to the bottom of the cliff. How tall was the cliff?   _____

**19.** Taylor wrote a check for $18 on the same day his bank paid interest to his account. If his account balance changed $13 that day, how much interest did he earn?   _____

**20.** A feather fell 10 feet in 5 seconds. How far did it fall in 1 second?   _____

**21.** A recipe for bread includes $\frac{1}{4}$ cup of oil, $\frac{1}{2}$ cup of sugar, and $\frac{2}{3}$ cup of milk. Write each measurement as a decimal. *[Lesson 5-7]*

Oil _____   Sugar _____   Milk _____

**22.** The flag of Finland is shown. Does this flag have line symmetry? If so, draw the line or lines of symmetry. *[Lesson 8-8]*

_____

# The Coordinate Plane

Give the coordinates of each point.

**1.** H _____      **2.** Q _____

**3.** A _____      **4.** L _____

**5.** T _____      **6.** C _____

**7.** M _____      **8.** X _____

**9.** F _____      **10.** N _____

State which quadrant each point is in.

**11.** (3, −21) _____   **12.** (−15, −42) _____   **13.** (18, 10) _____

**14.** (−24, 29) _____   **15.** (35, 11) _____   **16.** (−6, 17) _____

Plot and label each point.

**17.** J(3, −2)      **18.** E(3, 2)

**19.** W(−1, −4)      **20.** R(1, 0)

**21.** B(−2, 2)      **22.** Z(2, 3)

**23.** P(−4, 1)      **24.** G(−3, −1)

**25.** Y(0, −3)      **26.** S(2, −4)

Describe how to locate each point.

**27.** (21, −36) _____

**28.** (−14, −25) _____

**29. Geometry** Plot these points: (−1, 1), (2, 5), (5, 1), (2, −3).

    **a.** Connect the points to form a quadrilateral.

    **b.** Classify the quadrilateral in as many ways as possible.

_____

Name _____

# Graphing Slides and Flips

For Exercises 1–2, use the point P(2, −1) to plot and label P′.

**1.** Slide P 2 units left and 3 units up.

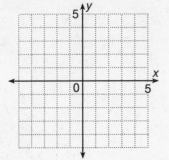

**2.** Reflect P across the x-axis.

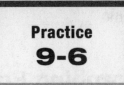

For Exercises 3–4, plot the image of quadrilateral GHIJ.

**3.** Translate GHIJ 2 units right and 2 units down.

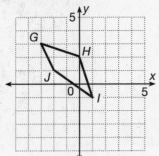

**4.** Slide GHIJ 4 units right and 2 units up.

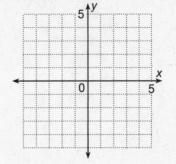

**5.** △ABC has vertices at A(−3, 4), B(1, 3), and C(−2, 0).

**a.** Draw the graph of △ABC.

**b.** Create △A′B′C′ by translating △ABC 3 units right and 4 units down.

**c.** Give the coordinates of the vertices of △A′B′C′.

A′ _____   B′ _____   C′ _____

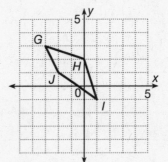

**6.** △LMN has vertices at L(−2, 4), M(1, 2), and N(−4, −1).

**a.** Draw the graph of △LMN.

**b.** Create △L′M′N′ by reflecting △LMN across the y-axis.

**c.** Give the coordinates of the vertices of △L′M′N′.

L′ _____   M′ _____   N′ _____

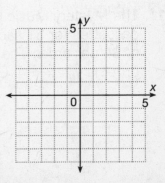

# Graphing Equations

For Exercises 1–4, make a T-table with five $(x, y)$ pairs for each.

**1.** $y = x + 12$     **2.** $y = -8x$     **3.** $y = x - 20$     **4.** $y = 15x$

Graph each equation.

**5.** $y = x - 1$     **6.** $y = x + 5$     **7.** $y = -2$

**8.** $y = -3x$     **9.** $y = x - 2$     **10.** $y = 2 - x$

**11.** The Mystery Music Company sells "grab bag" cassettes for $1 each. There is a shipping charge of $4 per order. The equation for the cost of an order is $y = x + 4$. Graph this equation.

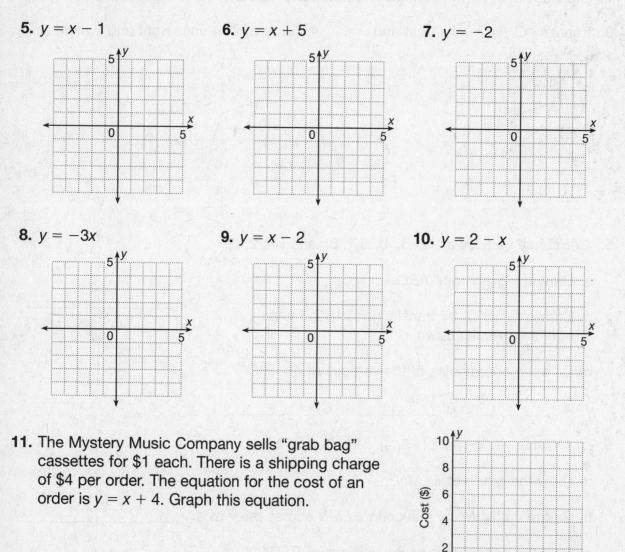

Name _____

# Section 9B Review

For Exercises 1–3, use the coordinate grid.

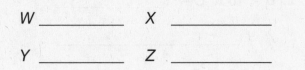

1. What are the coordinates of each point?

   W _____     X _____

   Y _____     Z _____

2. If point Y were translated left 3 units and down
   2 units, what would be the coordinates of Y'?     _____

3. If point X were reflected across the x-axis, what
   would be the coordinates of X'?     _____

Graph each equation.

4. $y = 4x$     5. $y = x + 3$     6. $y = 4$

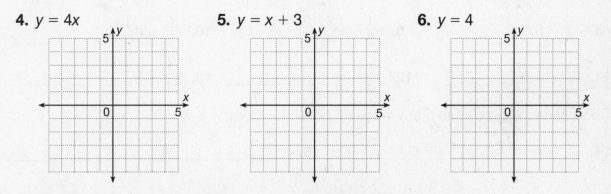

7. **Geometry** The coordinates of two opposite vertices of a square
   are $(-1, -1)$ and $(-4, 2)$. If the square is reflected across the
   y-axis, what are the coordinates of the four vertices of its image?

   _____

8. Graph the lines $y = -3$ and $y = 4 - x$.
   Do the lines have a point in common? Explain.

   _____

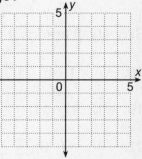

9. **Career** Drafters use a tool shaped like a triangle to make
   accurate drawings. If the base of this tool has length 4.25 in.
   and the height is 8.23 in., what is the area? *[Lesson 4-6]*     _____

10. Classify the shape of the sign in as many ways as possible.
    *[Lesson 8-7]*

    _____

    _____

Name _____

# Cumulative Review Chapters 1–9

Find the circumference C and the area A of each circle where
r = radius and d = diameter. Use 3.14 for π. *[Lessons 4-7, 4-8]*

**1.** r = 7 cm, C ≈ _____,

A ≈ _____

**2.** d = 10 ft, C ≈ _____,

A ≈ _____

**3.** r = 11 in., C ≈ _____,

A ≈ _____

**4.** r = 7.3 m, C ≈ _____,

A ≈ _____

Subtract. Write the answer as a whole or mixed number in lowest terms. *[Lesson 6-6]*

**5.** $9\frac{1}{4} - 6\frac{1}{8}$ _____

**6.** $3\frac{1}{2} - 1\frac{1}{3}$ _____

**7.** $4\frac{1}{5} - 3\frac{1}{4}$ _____

**8.** $7\frac{5}{8} - 5\frac{1}{2}$ _____

**9.** $6\frac{1}{3} - 2\frac{3}{4}$ _____

**10.** $7\frac{2}{3} - 4\frac{1}{6}$ _____

**11.** $4\frac{3}{5} - 4\frac{1}{10}$ _____

**12.** $3\frac{1}{3} - \frac{1}{5}$ _____

**13.** $8\frac{1}{4} - 5\frac{4}{5}$ _____

Classify each figure in as many ways as possible. *[Lesson 8-7]*

**14.** _____

**15.** _____

_____

_____

Simplify. *[Lessons 9-2, 9-3, 9-4]*

**16.** $-7 \times (-4)$ _____

**17.** $10 - 17$ _____

**18.** $21 \div (-7)$ _____

**19.** $-12 + (-11)$ _____

**20.** $3 \times (-8)$ _____

**21.** $8 - (-9)$ _____

**22.** $-48 \div (-6)$ _____

**23.** $-4 + 22$ _____

**24.** $-5 \times 8$ _____

Plot and label each point. *[Lesson 9-5]*

**25.** W(−3, −2)

**26.** H(1, −3)

**27.** L(2, −5)

**28.** M(3, 2)

**29.** B(−2, 4)

**30.** D(−4, 0)

**31.** G(4, 3)

**32.** Q(−1, 1)

**33.** Z(4, −3)

# What is a Ratio?

For Exercises 1–4, use the shapes pictured.

1. What is the ratio of triangles to circles?  _____

2. What is the ratio of triangles to stars?  _____

3. Give the ratio of circles to squares.  _____

4. What is the ratio of triangles to the whole group?  _____

A box contains 6 green chips, 10 blue chips, and 7 white chips.
Give each ratio in three ways.

5. Green chips to blue chips

6. Blue chips to white chips

_____

_____

7. White chips to green chips

8. Green chips to white chips

_____

_____

For Exercises 9–11, refer to the animals pictured.

9. The ratio of which animal to the whole group is 4 : 15?

_____

10. The ratio of which animal to the whole group is 1 : 5?

_____

11. Which two animals are compared in a ratio of $\frac{4}{3}$?

_____

12. **Social Science** In 1995, the U.S. Senate consisted
    of 46 Democrats and 54 Republicans.

    a. Give the ratio of Democrats to Republicans
       in lowest terms.  _____

    b. Give the ratio of Republicans to all Senators
       in lowest terms.  _____

13. At Jackson High School, 14 out of 35 students
    in the marching band are sophomores.
    Write this as a ratio in lowest terms.  _____

Name _____

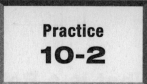

# Equal Ratios

Give two ratios equal to the given ratio.

**1.** 8 to 12 _____

**2.** $\dfrac{3}{5}$ _____

**3.** 9 to 3 _____

**4.** 15 : 35 _____

**5.** $\dfrac{8}{10}$ _____

**6.** $\dfrac{7}{8}$ _____

State if the ratios are equal.

**7.** 4 : 8; 1 : 2 _____

**8.** $\dfrac{3}{6}, \dfrac{5}{8}$ _____

**9.** 12 to 15, 4 to 5 _____

**10.** $\dfrac{10}{12}, \dfrac{15}{18}$ _____

**11.** 15 : 20, 20 : 25 _____

**12.** 10 to 8, 20 to 15 _____

**13.** $\dfrac{5}{9}$, 8 to 13 _____

**14.** 8 : 14, $\dfrac{4}{7}$ _____

**15.** 12 to 28, 18 : 42 _____

For exercises 16–19, give three equal ratios.

**16.** A third grade class has 4 boys for every 3 girls.           _____

**17.** A pet store has 5 cat collars for every 8 dog collars.           _____

**18.** A corporation has 2 secretaries for every executive.           _____

**19.** A carnival game has 2 winners for every 7 losers.           _____

Complete each table of equal ratios.

**20.** 8 snakes for every 3 turtles

| Snakes |   |   |   |    |
|--------|---|---|---|----|
| Turtles | 3 | 6 | 9 | 12 |

**21.** 7 dogs out of 12 pets

| Dogs | 7 |    | 21 |    |
|------|---|----|----|----|
| Pets |   | 24 |    | 48 |

**22.** 12 pizzas to 9 lasagnas

| Pizzas | 4 | 8 |   |    |
|--------|---|---|---|----|
| Lasagnas |  |   | 9 | 12 |

**23.** 16 cars to 20 trucks

| Cars |   |    | 12 | 16 |
|------|---|----|----|----|
| Trucks | 5 | 10 |    |    |

**24. Social Science** The ratio of Delaware residents to Maine
residents was about 55 : 100 in 1970 and about 66 : 120
in 1990. Are these ratios equal?           _____

# What is a Rate?

State if the ratio is a unit rate.

1. $\dfrac{3 \text{ cats}}{5 \text{ dogs}}$ _____

2. $\dfrac{1 \text{ ounce}}{\$0.15}$ _____

3. $\dfrac{12 \text{ inches}}{1 \text{ foot}}$ _____

4. $\dfrac{20 \text{ miles}}{1 \text{ hour}}$ _____

5. $\dfrac{6 \text{ pounds}}{1 \text{ dollar}}$ _____

6. $\dfrac{125 \text{ miles}}{5 \text{ hours}}$ _____

7. $\dfrac{1 \text{ table}}{6 \text{ chairs}}$ _____

8. $\dfrac{1 \text{ dollar}}{3 \text{ oranges}}$ _____

9. $\dfrac{2 \text{ cups}}{1 \text{ pint}}$ _____

10. $\dfrac{3 \text{ quarts}}{2 \text{ pounds}}$ _____

11. $\dfrac{4 \text{ books}}{1 \text{ dollar}}$ _____

12. $\dfrac{13 \text{ feet}}{1 \text{ foot}}$ _____

For each situation, give two equal rates.

13. Robert drove 20 miles in 30 minutes.

14. Helen earned $18 for working 3 hours.

_____

15. A radio station played 15 songs in 1 hour.

16. A breakfast cereal contains 75 raisins in every pound.

_____

17. Becky ran 2 miles in 14 minutes.

18. June bought 3 pounds of asparagus for $2.

_____

For Exercises 19–21, use the bar graph.

19. Give a rate that uses the number 28.

Year: _____     Rate: _____

20. Give three different rates that describe the average fuel efficiency in 1985.

**Fuel Efficiency of Average
U.S. Passenger Car**

_____

21. Use the average fuel efficiency in 1990 to give a rate that compares a distance to $\frac{1}{3}$ gallon of gasoline.

_____

22. Rhoda has 4 hours to type a 12-page report. How much time can she spend typing each page?

_____

23. Helga did 3 math problems in 5 minutes. If there are 45 similar problems in her homework assignment, how long will it take her to complete the assignment?

_____

Name _____

# Section 10A Review

1. About 160,000 of Rhode Island's 1,000,000 residents live in Providence. Write this ratio in lowest terms. _____

2. Last week a local humane society rescued 14 dogs and 10 cats. Give each ratio in lowest terms.

   **a.** Dogs to cats _____    **b.** Cats to dogs _____

   **c.** Dogs to all animals _____    **d.** Cats to all animals _____

3. Lucy has 5 quarters, 3 dimes, and 2 nickels. Give 5 ratios in lowest terms to describe the situation.

   _____

   _____

4. Complete each table of equal ratios.

| Men | 7 | 21 | 49 | 70 |
|-----|---|----|----|----|
| Women | 9 | | | |

| Telephones | 5 | 10 | | |
|------------|---|----|----|----|
| Fax Machines | | | 12 | 18 | 24 |

5. Give three ratios equal to 45 : 65. _____

6. There are 8 magazines and 15 books. Write the ratio of magazines to books in three ways. _____

For Exercises 7–8, use the figures pictured.

7. Give the ratio of circles to hexagons. _____

8. What is the ratio of hexagons and squares to circles? _____

9. Martin watched 10 movies in 25 hours. Write this as a rate in lowest terms. _____

10. The Peachy King Beverage Company advertises that its product contains "$\frac{2}{5}$ real fruit juice!" How much fruit juice is in a 16 ounce container of this drink? *[Lesson 7-2]* _____

11. **Science** An emperor penguin has been observed diving to a depth of 1584 feet below sea level. Write an integer to describe the penguin's height during its dive. *[Lesson 9-1]* _____

Name _____

# What is a Proportion?

State whether or not each pair of ratios forms a proportion.

1. $\frac{6}{12} \stackrel{?}{=} \frac{12}{14}$ _____

2. $\frac{3}{20} \stackrel{?}{=} \frac{2}{10}$ _____

3. $\frac{20}{12} \stackrel{?}{=} \frac{25}{15}$ _____

4. $\frac{27}{6} \stackrel{?}{=} \frac{36}{8}$ _____

5. $\frac{13}{11} \stackrel{?}{=} \frac{24}{20}$ _____

6. $\frac{3}{4} \stackrel{?}{=} \frac{15}{20}$ _____

7. $\frac{10}{4} \stackrel{?}{=} \frac{45}{20}$ _____

8. $\frac{15}{10} \stackrel{?}{=} \frac{3}{2}$ _____

9. $\frac{12}{21} \stackrel{?}{=} \frac{16}{28}$ _____

10. $\frac{3}{24} \stackrel{?}{=} \frac{4}{32}$ _____

11. $\frac{12}{20} \stackrel{?}{=} \frac{4}{7}$ _____

12. $\frac{2}{9} \stackrel{?}{=} \frac{5}{22}$ _____

13. $\frac{6}{15} \stackrel{?}{=} \frac{4}{12}$ _____

14. $\frac{15}{18} \stackrel{?}{=} \frac{20}{24}$ _____

15. $\frac{17}{12} \stackrel{?}{=} \frac{10}{7}$ _____

16. $\frac{25}{35} \stackrel{?}{=} \frac{15}{21}$ _____

17. $\frac{10}{9} \stackrel{?}{=} \frac{16}{14}$ _____

18. $\frac{32}{36} \stackrel{?}{=} \frac{40}{45}$ _____

19. $\frac{2 \text{ tsp}}{7 \text{ gal}} \stackrel{?}{=} \frac{6 \text{ tsp}}{21 \text{ gal}}$ _____

20. $\frac{12 \text{ cm}}{20 \text{ g}} \stackrel{?}{=} \frac{15 \text{ g}}{25 \text{ cm}}$ _____

21. $\frac{\$14}{3 \text{ hr}} \stackrel{?}{=} \frac{\$84}{18 \text{ hr}}$ _____

22. $\frac{27 \text{ lb}}{\$21} \stackrel{?}{=} \frac{14 \text{ lb}}{\$18}$ _____

23. $\frac{15 \text{ sec}}{21 \text{ sec}} \stackrel{?}{=} \frac{10 \text{ in.}}{15 \text{ in.}}$ _____

24. $\frac{6 \text{ ft}}{13 \text{ gal}} \stackrel{?}{=} \frac{7 \text{ ft}}{14 \text{ gal}}$ _____

For Exercises 25–30, choose the proportion that is written correctly.

25. a. $\frac{20 \text{ men}}{25 \text{ women}} = \frac{5 \text{ men}}{4 \text{ women}}$
b. $\frac{20 \text{ men}}{25 \text{ women}} = \frac{4 \text{ men}}{5 \text{ women}}$
c. $\frac{4 \text{ men}}{5 \text{ women}} = \frac{25 \text{ women}}{20 \text{ men}}$

26. a. $\frac{27 \text{ acres}}{\$15} = \frac{\$25}{45 \text{ acres}}$
b. $\frac{\$27}{15 \text{ acres}} = \frac{\$25}{45 \text{ acres}}$
c. $\frac{45 \text{ acres}}{\$25} = \frac{27 \text{ acres}}{\$15}$

27. a. $\frac{12 \text{ pies}}{4 \text{ cakes}} = \frac{6 \text{ cakes}}{18 \text{ pies}}$
b. $\frac{4 \text{ cakes}}{12 \text{ pies}} = \frac{6 \text{ cakes}}{18 \text{ pies}}$
c. $\frac{12 \text{ pies}}{4 \text{ cakes}} = \frac{6 \text{ pies}}{18 \text{ cakes}}$

28. a. $\frac{6 \text{ gal}}{15 \text{ gal}} = \frac{2 \text{ min}}{5 \text{ min}}$
b. $\frac{5 \text{ min}}{15 \text{ gal}} = \frac{6 \text{ gal}}{2 \text{ min}}$
c. $\frac{6 \text{ gal}}{2 \text{ min}} = \frac{5 \text{ gal}}{15 \text{ min}}$

29. a. $\frac{25 \text{ chairs}}{5 \text{ tables}} = \frac{10 \text{ tables}}{2 \text{ chairs}}$
b. $\frac{25 \text{ chairs}}{5 \text{ tables}} = \frac{2 \text{ tables}}{10 \text{ chairs}}$
c. $\frac{25 \text{ chairs}}{5 \text{ tables}} = \frac{10 \text{ chairs}}{2 \text{ tables}}$

30. a. $\frac{36 \text{ lb}}{28 \text{ ft}} = \frac{18 \text{ lb}}{14 \text{ ft}}$
b. $\frac{18 \text{ lb}}{14 \text{ ft}} = \frac{28 \text{ lb}}{36 \text{ ft}}$
c. $\frac{36 \text{ ft}}{28 \text{ lb}} = \frac{18 \text{ lb}}{14 \text{ ft}}$

31. During the butterfly stroke competitions at the 1972 Summer Olympic Games, Mayumi Aoki swam 100 meters in 64 seconds, and Karen Moe swam 200 meters in 136 seconds. Do these rates form a proportion? _____

32. At Deliah's Hardware, you can buy 5 feet of PVC pipe for $1.10, or 8 feet for $1.76. Are these prices proportional? _____

# Solving Proportions
# Using Cross Products

Solve each proportion.

**1.** $\dfrac{12}{a} = \dfrac{16}{20}$

$a =$ _____

**2.** $\dfrac{2}{8} = \dfrac{t}{20}$

$t =$ _____

**3.** $\dfrac{30}{a} = \dfrac{20}{18}$

$a =$ _____

**4.** $\dfrac{45}{x} = \dfrac{18}{8}$

$x =$ _____

**5.** $\dfrac{u}{5} = \dfrac{6}{3}$

$u =$ _____

**6.** $\dfrac{15}{5} = \dfrac{6}{a}$

$a =$ _____

**7.** $\dfrac{m}{8} = \dfrac{12}{16}$

$m =$ _____

**8.** $\dfrac{40}{y} = \dfrac{16}{2}$

$y =$ _____

**9.** $\dfrac{16}{36} = \dfrac{g}{45}$

$g =$ _____

**10.** $\dfrac{s}{28} = \dfrac{30}{21}$

$s =$ _____

**11.** $\dfrac{4}{5} = \dfrac{8}{d}$

$d =$ _____

**12.** $\dfrac{15}{5} = \dfrac{12}{c}$

$c =$ _____

**13.** $\dfrac{16}{28} = \dfrac{h}{7}$

$h =$ _____

**14.** $\dfrac{2}{k} = \dfrac{3}{6}$

$k =$ _____

**15.** $\dfrac{30}{3} = \dfrac{j}{2}$

$j =$ _____

**16.** $\dfrac{3}{r} = \dfrac{2}{8}$

$r =$ _____

**17.** $\dfrac{20}{8} = \dfrac{f}{2}$

$f =$ _____

**18.** $\dfrac{2}{20} = \dfrac{z}{10}$

$z =$ _____

**19.** $\dfrac{20}{d} = \dfrac{4}{5}$

$d =$ _____

**20.** $\dfrac{4}{q} = \dfrac{2}{7}$

$q =$ _____

**21.** $\dfrac{z}{15} = \dfrac{2}{6}$

$z =$ _____

**22.** $\dfrac{2}{3} = \dfrac{b}{6}$

$b =$ _____

**23.** $\dfrac{y}{2} = \dfrac{6}{4}$

$y =$ _____

**24.** $\dfrac{2}{5} = \dfrac{4}{n}$

$n =$ _____

**25.** $\dfrac{10}{m} = \dfrac{8}{4}$

$m =$ _____

**26.** $\dfrac{27}{6} = \dfrac{j}{8}$

$j =$ _____

**27.** $\dfrac{g}{3.5} = \dfrac{1.6}{1.4}$

$g =$ _____

**28.** $\dfrac{8}{36} = \dfrac{p}{9}$

$p =$ _____

**29.** $\dfrac{14}{16} = \dfrac{28}{p}$

$p =$ _____

**30.** $\dfrac{t}{24} = \dfrac{10}{16}$

$t =$ _____

**31.** $\dfrac{45}{u} = \dfrac{27}{12}$

$u =$ _____

**32.** $\dfrac{10}{45} = \dfrac{2}{x}$

$x =$ _____

**33.** $\dfrac{25}{q} = \dfrac{15}{12}$

$q =$ _____

**34.** $\dfrac{15}{20} = \dfrac{v}{4}$

$v =$ _____

**35.** $\dfrac{p}{6} = \dfrac{3}{2}$

$p =$ _____

**36.** $\dfrac{3}{7} = \dfrac{12}{a}$

$a =$ _____

**37. Measurement** If 5 pints of water weigh 80 oz,
find the weight of 12 pints of water.

_____

**38.** In 1967, a minimum wage worker would receive $84
for 60 hours of work. How much would the worker
receive for 75 hours of work?

_____

# Solving Proportions Using Unit Rates

Find the unit rate for each.

1. $\dfrac{12 \text{ books}}{3 \text{ shelves}}$ _____

2. $\dfrac{14 \text{ tsp}}{7 \text{ gal}}$ _____

3. $\dfrac{108 \text{ pages}}{9 \text{ hours}}$ _____

4. $\dfrac{6 \text{ gal}}{2 \text{ min}}$ _____

5. $\dfrac{30.48 \text{ cm}}{12 \text{ in.}}$ _____

6. $\dfrac{40 \text{ mice}}{8 \text{ rats}}$ _____

7. $\dfrac{28 \text{ cats}}{4 \text{ dogs}}$ _____

8. $\dfrac{\$315}{35 \text{ hr}}$ _____

9. $\dfrac{10 \text{ CDs}}{5 \text{ tapes}}$ _____

10. $\dfrac{90 \text{ cars}}{15 \text{ trucks}}$ _____

11. $\dfrac{14 \text{ cups}}{42 \text{ sec}}$ _____

12. $\dfrac{18 \text{ boys}}{18 \text{ girls}}$ _____

13. $\dfrac{576 \text{ pt}}{72 \text{ gal}}$ _____

14. $\dfrac{120 \text{ mi}}{3 \text{ hr}}$ _____

15. $\dfrac{35 \text{ carrots}}{10 \text{ potatoes}}$ _____

16. $\dfrac{36 \text{ cups}}{18 \text{ bowls}}$ _____

17. $\dfrac{68 \text{ men}}{17 \text{ women}}$ _____

18. $\dfrac{375 \text{ ft}^2}{25 \text{ people}}$ _____

Solve each proportion using unit rates.

19. $\dfrac{}{20 \text{ moose}} = \dfrac{14 \text{ cows}}{10 \text{ moose}}$

20. $\dfrac{25 \text{ pt}}{10 \text{ ft}^2} = \dfrac{}{8 \text{ ft}^2}$

21. $\dfrac{7 \text{ hits}}{2 \text{ innings}} = \dfrac{}{6 \text{ innings}}$

22. $\dfrac{4 \text{ ft}}{12 \text{ sec}} = \dfrac{}{6 \text{ sec}}$

23. $\dfrac{\$15}{9 \text{ lb}} = \dfrac{}{3 \text{ lb}}$

24. $\dfrac{15 \text{ meals}}{3 \text{ days}} = \dfrac{}{5 \text{ days}}$

25. $\dfrac{5 \text{ drops}}{50 \text{ gal}} = \dfrac{}{30 \text{ gal}}$

26. $\dfrac{}{2 \text{ hr}} = \dfrac{15°}{3 \text{ hr}}$

27. $\dfrac{}{4 \text{ hr}} = \dfrac{16 \text{ gal}}{2 \text{ hr}}$

28. $\dfrac{45 \text{ in.}}{5 \text{ lb}} = \dfrac{}{2 \text{ lb}}$

29. $\dfrac{12 \text{ lb}}{4 \text{ sec}} = \dfrac{}{1 \text{ sec}}$

30. $\dfrac{\$6}{2 \text{ hr}} = \dfrac{}{3 \text{ hr}}$

31. $\dfrac{35 \text{ mi}}{10 \text{ L}} = \dfrac{}{8 \text{ L}}$

32. $\dfrac{}{4 \text{ in}^3} = \dfrac{21 \text{ oz}}{6 \text{ in}^3}$

33. $\dfrac{27 \text{ min}}{24 \text{ ft}} = \dfrac{}{8 \text{ ft}}$

34. In 1909, French workmen removed a white stork's nest weighing 660 kilograms from the top of a cathedral. The nest also weighed 1452 pounds. Using these measurements, find the number of pounds in a kilogram. _____

35. **History** The Northrop XB–35 aircraft used in World War II had a wingspan of 172 feet. Melba's model of this aircraft has a wingspan of $21\frac{1}{2}$ inches. How many feet does one inch of the model represent? _____

Name _____

# Similar Figures

Find the missing side lengths.

**1.** A = _____ B = _____ C = _____

**2.** A = _____ B = _____

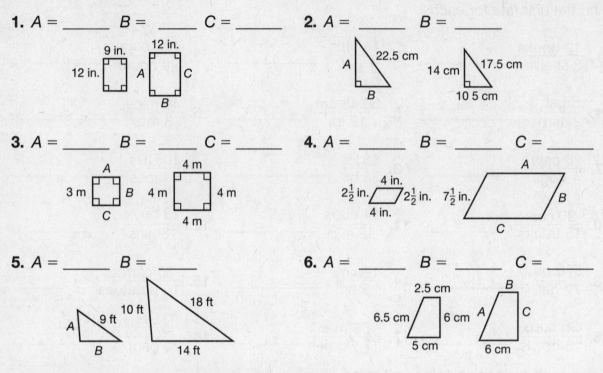

**3.** A = _____ B = _____ C = _____

**4.** A = _____ B = _____ C = _____

**5.** A = _____ B = _____

**6.** A = _____ B = _____ C = _____

**7.** On the map, 1 inch equals 850 actual miles.

  **a.** What are the actual distances between the cities?

    New York to New Orleans

    _____

    New Orleans to Miami

    _____

    Miami to New York

    _____

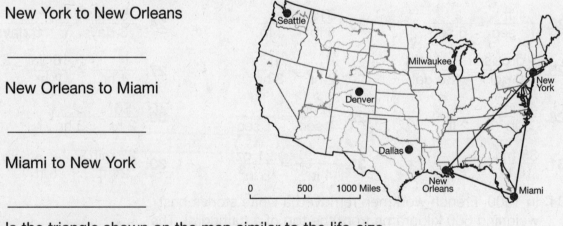

  **b.** Is the triangle shown on the map similar to the life-size triangle? Explain.

_____

**8.** The lengths of the sides of a triangle are 45 cm, 55 cm, and 70 cm. The shortest side of a similar triangle has length 27 cm. What are the lengths of the other two sides of the similar triangle?

_____

# Section 10B Review

Find the unit rate for each ratio.

1. $\dfrac{45\text{ kg}}{15\text{ m}}$ _____

2. $\dfrac{48\text{ lemons}}{\$8}$ _____

3. $\dfrac{105\text{ mi}}{3\text{ hr}}$ _____

4. $\dfrac{108\text{ cows}}{6\text{ acres}}$ _____

5. $\dfrac{20\text{ windows}}{4\text{ doors}}$ _____

6. $\dfrac{100\text{ cars}}{25\text{ min}}$ _____

Solve each proportion.

7. $\dfrac{15}{\phantom{00}} = \dfrac{3}{10}$

8. $\dfrac{3}{18} = \dfrac{2}{\phantom{00}}$

9. $\dfrac{\phantom{00}}{12} = \dfrac{21}{18}$

10. $\dfrac{4\text{ dogs}}{9\text{ cats}} = \dfrac{\phantom{000}}{18\text{ cats}}$

11. $\dfrac{18\text{ rings}}{\$20} = \dfrac{\phantom{000}}{\$30}$

12. $\dfrac{25\text{ gal}}{5\text{ min}} = \dfrac{\phantom{000}}{4\text{ min}}$

13. In 1996, a chocolate chip cookie with an area of 5240 square feet was made by Cookie Time of New Zealand. It contained about 5600 pounds of chocolate. This equals how many pounds of chocolate per square foot of cookie?

_____

14. If Chester can type 75 words in 100 seconds, how many words could he type in 5 minutes?

_____

In each pair of similar figures, find the missing side lengths.

15. $A =$ _____ $B =$ _____ $C =$ _____

16. $A =$ _____ $B =$ _____

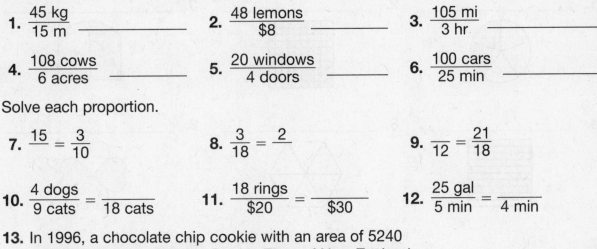

17. An instant pasta dinner package contains a packet of plain pasta plus a flavor packet weighing $\frac{1}{8}$ pound. If the entire package weighs $\frac{7}{16}$ pound, what is the weight of the plain pasta? *[Lesson 6-3]*

_____

18. Mildred always has $200 of her monthly salary transferred automatically to a savings account. The equation $y = x - 200$ gives the amount of her paycheck, where $x$ is her after-tax income. Graph this equation. *[Lesson 9-7]*

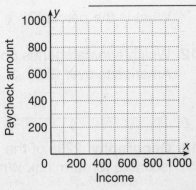

# The Meaning of Percent

Give the percent of each figure that is shaded.

1. _____   2. _____   3. _____

4. _____   5. _____   6. _____

7. _____   8. _____   9. _____

The circle graph shows the educational attainment of Americans over 25 years old in 1994. Use the graph for Exercises 10–12.

**Educational Attainment of Americans**

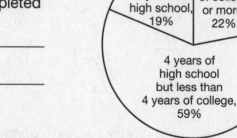

10. What percent of the population has completed

    less than 4 years of high school?   _____

    4 years of high school or more?   _____

11. Which category includes the highest
    percent of Americans over 25?

    _____

    What is the percent?   _____

12. Which two categories combined amount for 41% of
    Americans over 25?

    _____

13. **Geography** 22% of the land in Vietnam is arable
    (suitable for farming). What percent is not arable?   _____

# Estimating Percents

Estimate what percent of each figure is shaded.

1. _____

2. _____

3. _____

4. _____

5. _____

6. _____

7. _____

8. _____

9. _____

Estimate the percent.

**10.** 13 out of 66 _____    **11.** 31 out of 118 _____    **12.** 18 out of 21 _____

**13.** 73 out of 80 _____    **14.** 47 out of 77 _____    **15.** 93 out of 190 _____

**16.** $\frac{312}{420}$ _____    **17.** $\frac{59}{84}$ _____    **18.** $\frac{25}{240}$ _____    **19.** $\frac{45}{148}$ _____

**20.** $\frac{59}{74}$ _____    **21.** $\frac{88}{116}$ _____    **22.** $\frac{41}{47}$ _____    **23.** $\frac{61}{99}$ _____

**24.** In 1989, the EarthGrains Bakery in Fort Payne, Alabama, set a world record by baking a cake weighing 128,000 lb. The cake included 16,000 lb of icing. About what percent of the cake was icing?

_____

**25.** Patents are issued to inventors to prevent others from stealing their ideas. In 1965, 37,000 out of 63,000 patents were issued to U.S. corporations. About what percent is this?

_____

Name _____

# Converting Percents to Fractions and Decimals

Convert to a fraction in lowest terms.

**1.** 80% _____  **2.** 25% _____  **3.** 78% _____  **4.** 98% _____

**5.** 32% _____  **6.** 30% _____  **7.** 45% _____  **8.** 118% _____

**9.** 65% _____  **10.** 185% _____  **11.** 63% _____  **12.** 28% _____

**13.** 275% _____  **14.** 84% _____  **15.** 104% _____  **16.** 18% _____

Convert to a percent.

**17.** $\frac{7}{10}$ _____  **18.** $\frac{37}{50}$ _____  **19.** $\frac{1}{2}$ _____  **20.** $\frac{18}{25}$ _____

**21.** 0.41 _____  **22.** 0.03 _____  **23.** 0.74 _____  **24.** 0.92 _____

**25.** $\frac{123}{300}$ _____  **26.** $\frac{15}{20}$ _____  **27.** $\frac{31}{20}$ _____  **28.** $\frac{1}{10}$ _____

**29.** 0.67 _____  **30.** 4.10 _____  **31.** 0.8 _____  **32.** 0.137 _____

Give the shaded part of each figure as a percent, fraction, and decimal.

**33.**  percent: _____  **34.**  percent: _____

 fraction: _____  fraction: _____

 decimal: _____  decimal: _____

**35.**  percent: _____  **36.**  percent: _____

 fraction: _____  fraction: _____

 decimal: _____  decimal: _____

**37.** In 1993, about $\frac{1}{50}$ of American children lived with relatives other than their parents. Convert this value to a percent.

_____

**38.** In 1950, $\frac{2}{25}$ of the American population was at least 65 years old. What percent is this?

_____

# Finding a Percent of a
# Whole Number

Simplify. Round your answer to the nearest hundredth.

**1.** 28% of 11 _____    **2.** 44% of 46 _____    **3.** 66% of 21 _____

**4.** 95% of 49 _____    **5.** 12% of 8 _____    **6.** 14% of 37 _____

**7.** 29% of $16.50 _____    **8.** 1% of 32 _____    **9.** 15% of 60 _____

**10.** 42% of 4 _____    **11.** 17% of 2.89 _____    **12.** 39% of 83.75 _____

**13.** 11% of 18 _____    **14.** 3% of 15 _____    **15.** 24% of 100 _____

**16.** 20% of 7.63 _____    **17.** 19% of $21.95 _____    **18.** 6% of 53 _____

**19.** 36% of 21 _____    **20.** 30% of 69 _____    **21.** 35% of 35 _____

**22.** 61% of 41 _____    **23.** 7% of 12.8 _____    **24.** 68% of 84 _____

**25.** 9% of 64.88 _____    **26.** 56% of 98 _____    **27.** 73% of 79 _____

Find the total amount.

**28.** 24% of _____ is 38.4   **29.** 30% of _____ is 14.4   **30.** 16% of _____ is 52

**31.** 79% of _____ is 402.9   **32.** 41% of _____ is 24.6   **33.** 38% of _____ is 114

**34.** 5% of _____ is 14.25   **35.** 84% of ____ is $74.76   **36.** 62% of _____ is 775

**37.** 55% of _____ is 40.7   **38.** 25% of _____ is 21   **39.** 12% of _____ is 10.32

**40.** 36% of _____ is 63   **41.** 8% of _____ is 9.6   **42.** 68% of _____ is $17

**43.** 65% of _____ is 140.4   **44.** 32% of _____ is 12   **45.** 88% of _____ is 132

**46. Consumer** Molly bought a video game that was priced
at $24.95. She had to pay 6.5% sales tax. Find the sales
tax amount and the total price.

     tax: _____      total: _____

**47.** The population of Chula Vista, California increased
from 83,927 in 1980 to 135,163 in 1990. Find the
percent increase.

                    _____

# Section 10C Review

Estimate the percent of each figure that is shaded.

1. _____  2. _____  3. _____

Convert each percent to a decimal and a fraction.

4. 37% _____  5. 40% _____  6. 84% _____

7. 35% _____  8. 170% _____  9. 12% _____

10. 68% _____  11. 8% _____  12. 38% _____

Convert to a percent.

13. 0.47 _____  14. 0.1 _____  15. 0.95 _____  16. 0.74 _____

17. $\frac{7}{10}$ _____  18. $\frac{19}{25}$ _____  19. $\frac{14}{40}$ _____  20. $\frac{27}{50}$ _____

21. 0.02 _____  22. 2.73 _____  23. 0.462 _____  24. 0.87 _____

25. $\frac{11}{2}$ _____  26. $\frac{8}{5}$ _____  27. $\frac{9}{10}$ _____  28. $\frac{8}{25}$ _____

Simplify.

29. 28% of 64 _____  30. 70% of 51 _____  31. 68% of 94 _____

32. 43% of 83 _____  33. 4% of 23 _____  34. 86% of 28.5 _____

35. 225% of 74 _____  36. 94% of 46 _____  37. 63% of 37 _____

38. **Measurement** One grain is to equal $\frac{1}{20}$ of a scruple.
Write and solve an equation to find the number of
scruples in 70 grains. *[Lesson 7-6]*

_____

39. **Science** Temperatures on Mercury are as high as 510°C
and as low as −210°C. Find the difference between these
temperatures. *[Lesson 9-3]*

_____

# Cumulative Review Chapters 1–10

Write in lowest terms. *[Lesson 5-5]*

**1.** $\frac{9}{15}$ _____    **2.** $\frac{20}{25}$ _____    **3.** $\frac{24}{36}$ _____    **4.** $\frac{10}{22}$ _____

**5.** $\frac{14}{49}$ _____    **6.** $\frac{8}{64}$ _____    **7.** $\frac{6}{21}$ _____    **8.** $\frac{12}{90}$ _____

**9.** $\frac{35}{75}$ _____    **10.** $\frac{24}{42}$ _____    **11.** $\frac{8}{18}$ _____    **12.** $\frac{33}{57}$ _____

Simplify. *[Lessons 7-3, 7-5]*

**13.** $3\frac{2}{7} \times 2\frac{2}{3}$ _____    **14.** $\frac{1}{9} \div 6\frac{2}{3}$ _____    **15.** $4\frac{4}{5} \times 1\frac{1}{5}$ _____    **16.** $\frac{2}{3} \div \frac{1}{3}$ _____

**17.** $5\frac{1}{2} \times \frac{1}{4}$ _____    **18.** $1\frac{5}{6} \div \frac{3}{10}$ _____    **19.** $1\frac{2}{3} \times 1\frac{1}{4}$ _____    **20.** $7\frac{1}{2} \div 4$ _____

**21.** $\frac{5}{7} \times \frac{14}{15}$ _____    **22.** $\frac{5}{7} \div 2\frac{2}{3}$ _____    **23.** $1\frac{1}{5} \times 4\frac{1}{3}$ _____    **24.** $4\frac{1}{2} \div 12\frac{1}{2}$ _____

Classify each triangle as acute, right, or obtuse. *[Lesson 8-4]*

**25.** _____    **26.** _____    **27.** _____    **28.** _____

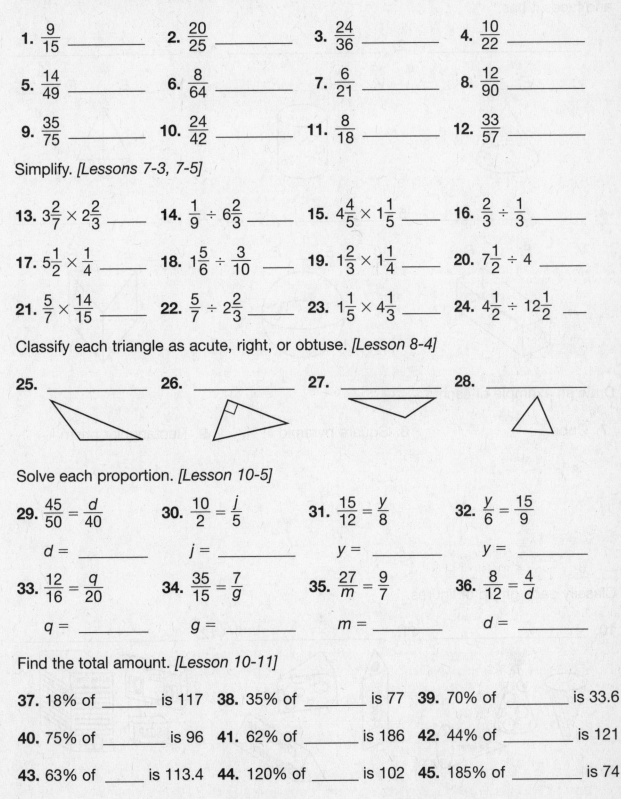

Solve each proportion. *[Lesson 10-5]*

**29.** $\frac{45}{50} = \frac{d}{40}$    **30.** $\frac{10}{2} = \frac{j}{5}$    **31.** $\frac{15}{12} = \frac{y}{8}$    **32.** $\frac{y}{6} = \frac{15}{9}$

    $d =$ _____       $j =$ _____       $y =$ _____       $y =$ _____

**33.** $\frac{12}{16} = \frac{q}{20}$    **34.** $\frac{35}{15} = \frac{7}{g}$    **35.** $\frac{27}{m} = \frac{9}{7}$    **36.** $\frac{8}{12} = \frac{4}{d}$

    $q =$ _____       $g =$ _____       $m =$ _____       $d =$ _____

Find the total amount. *[Lesson 10-11]*

**37.** 18% of _____ is 117    **38.** 35% of _____ is 77    **39.** 70% of _____ is 33.6

**40.** 75% of _____ is 96    **41.** 62% of _____ is 186    **42.** 44% of _____ is 121

**43.** 63% of _____ is 113.4    **44.** 120% of _____ is 102    **45.** 185% of _____ is 74

Name _____

# Classifying Solids

Classify each solid. If it is a polyhedron, tell how many vertices, edges, and faces it has.

1. _____

V: ___ E: ___ F: ___

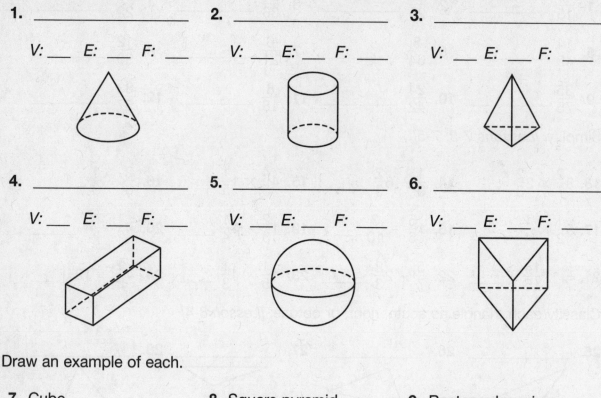

2. _____

V: ___ E: ___ F: ___

3. _____

V: ___ E: ___ F: ___

4. _____

V: ___ E: ___ F: ___

5. _____

V: ___ E: ___ F: ___

6. _____

V: ___ E: ___ F: ___

Draw an example of each.

**7.** Cube

**8.** Square pyramid

**9.** Rectangular prism

Classify each group of figures.

10. _____

11. _____

12. _____

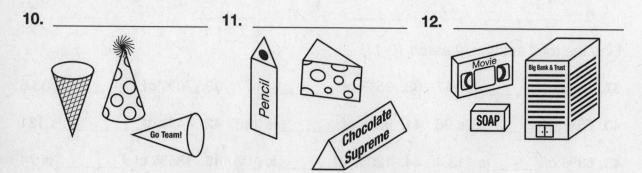

# Exploring Surface Area

Find the area of each net. Classify the solid.

**1.** SA: _____

**2.** SA: _____

**3.** SA: _____

_____

_____

_____

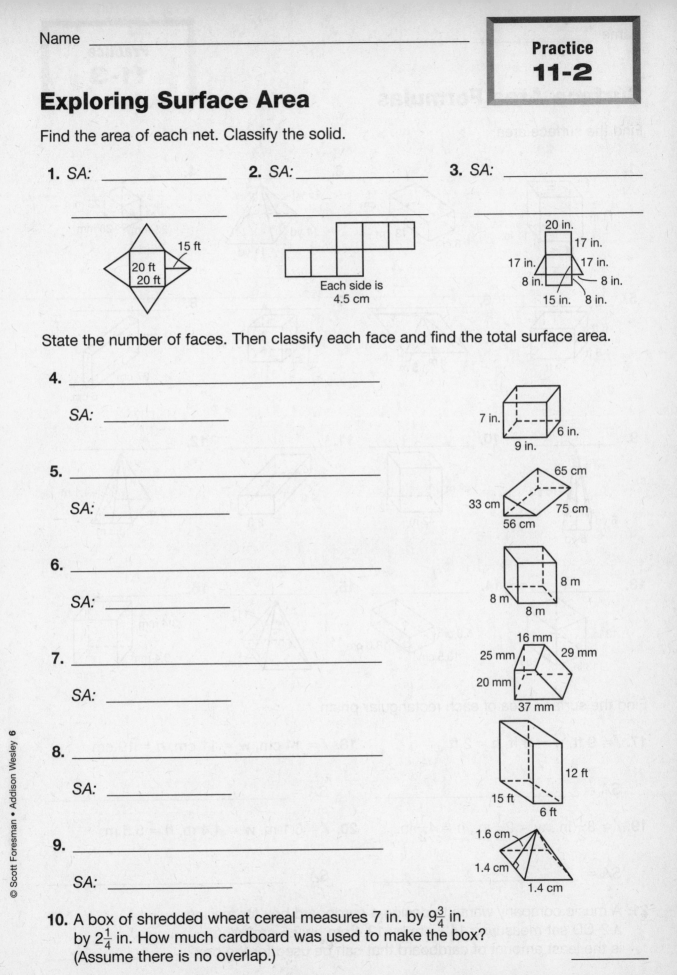

15 ft

20 ft
20 ft

Each side is
4.5 cm

20 in.
17 in.
17 in. 17 in.
8 in. 8 in.
15 in. 8 in.

State the number of faces. Then classify each face and find the total surface area.

**4.** _____

SA: _____

7 in.
6 in.
9 in.

**5.** _____

SA: _____

65 cm
33 cm
75 cm
56 cm

**6.** _____

SA: _____

8 m
8 m
8 m

**7.** _____

SA: _____

16 mm
25 mm 29 mm
20 mm
37 mm

**8.** _____

SA: _____

12 ft
15 ft
6 ft

**9.** _____

SA: _____

1.6 cm
1.4 cm
1.4 cm

**10.** A box of shredded wheat cereal measures 7 in. by $9\frac{3}{4}$ in.
by $2\frac{1}{4}$ in. How much cardboard was used to make the box?
(Assume there is no overlap.)

_____

# Surface Area Formulas

Find the surface area.

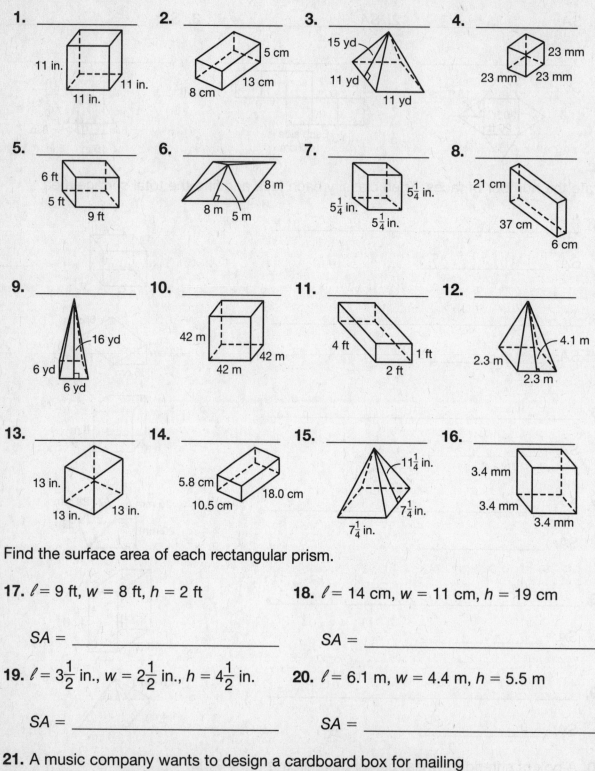

1. _____
11 in.
11 in.
11 in.

2. _____
5 cm
13 cm
8 cm

3. _____
15 yd
11 yd
11 yd

4. _____
23 mm
23 mm   23 mm

5. _____
6 ft
5 ft
9 ft

6. _____
8 m
8 m   5 m

7. _____
$5\frac{1}{4}$ in.
$5\frac{1}{4}$ in.
$5\frac{1}{4}$ in.

8. _____
21 cm
37 cm
6 cm

9. _____
16 yd
6 yd
6 yd

10. _____
42 m
42 m
42 m

11. _____
4 ft
2 ft   1 ft

12. _____
4.1 m
2.3 m
2.3 m

13. _____
13 in.
13 in.   13 in.

14. _____
5.8 cm
10.5 cm   18.0 cm

15. _____
$11\frac{1}{4}$ in.
$7\frac{1}{4}$ in.
$7\frac{1}{4}$ in.

16. _____
3.4 mm
3.4 mm
3.4 mm

Find the surface area of each rectangular prism.

**17.** $l$ = 9 ft, $w$ = 8 ft, $h$ = 2 ft

SA = _____

**18.** $l$ = 14 cm, $w$ = 11 cm, $h$ = 19 cm

SA = _____

**19.** $l$ = $3\frac{1}{2}$ in., $w$ = $2\frac{1}{2}$ in., $h$ = $4\frac{1}{2}$ in.

SA = _____

**20.** $l$ = 6.1 m, $w$ = 4.4 m, $h$ = 5.5 m

SA = _____

**21.** A music company wants to design a cardboard box for mailing
a 2-CD set measuring 14.2 cm by 12.4 cm by 2.5 cm. What
is the least amount of cardboard that can be used for the box? _____

# Surface Area of a Cylinder

Find the surface area of each cylinder. Use 3.14 for π.

**1.** _____
6 ft — 32 ft

**2.** _____
6 in. 12 in.

**3.** _____
4 m 9 m

**4.** _____
7 cm 17 cm

**5.** _____
18 mm 7 mm

**6.** _____
3 yd 4 yd

**7.** _____
16 cm 21 cm

**8.** _____
$2\frac{1}{4}$ in. $6\frac{1}{2}$ in.

**9.** _____
2.9 cm 2.2 cm

**10.** _____
10 ft 2 ft

**11.** _____
13 mm 42 mm

**12.** _____
15 in. 18 in.

**13.** _____
1.6 m 1.8 m

**14.** _____
7 yd 6 yd

**15.** _____
$3\frac{3}{4}$ in. 8 in.

**16.** _____
41 cm 98 cm

Given the radius and height of each cylinder, find the surface area.
Use 3.14 for π.

**17.** $r = 3.8$, $h = 15$

SA ≈ _____

**18.** $r = 21$, $h = 4$

SA ≈ _____

**19.** $r = 12$, $h = 13$

SA ≈ _____

**20.** $r = 2.1$, $h = 4.9$

SA ≈ _____

**21.** $r = 7.1$, $h = 40$

SA ≈ _____

**22.** $r = 18$, $h = 11.5$

SA ≈ _____

**23.** An oatmeal box has the shape of a cylinder with diameter
$3\frac{7}{8}$ in. and height 7 in. What is the surface area of the box? _____

# Section 11A Review

Classify each solid. If it is a polyhedron, tell how many vertices, edges, and faces it has.

1. _____    2. _____    3. _____

V: ___  E: ___  F: ___    V: ___  E: ___  F: ___    V: ___  E: ___  F: ___

4. _____    5. _____    6. _____

V: ___  E: ___  F: ___    V: ___  E: ___  F: ___    V: ___  E: ___  F: ___

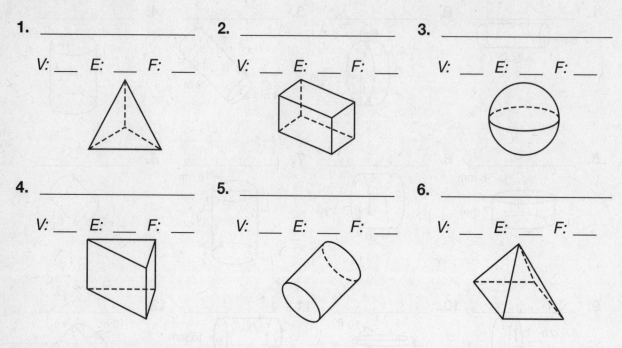

Find the surface area of each figure.

7. _____    8. _____    9. _____    10. _____

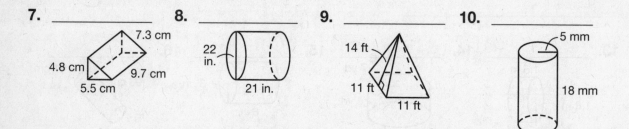

11. Find the surface area of a rectangular prism that measures 15 in. by 21 in. by 24 in.

_____

12. The symbol at the right is used to represent "clubs" in a deck of playing cards. Tell whether the symbol has line symmetry. If it does, draw all the lines of symmetry. *[Lesson 8-8]*

_____

13. The distance from Berlin, Germany, to Rome, Italy, is about 734 miles. It is also 1181 kilometers. Using these measurements, find the number of kilometers in a mile. *[Lesson 10-6]*

_____

# Three-Dimensional Figures

Draw the front, side, and top views of each solid. There are no hidden cubes.

**1.**

**2.**

**3.**

**4.**

Describe each pattern. How many cubes are in the eighth solid of each pattern?

**5.** _____

_____

_____

**6.** _____

_____

_____

**7.** Each cube in the solid shown is 5 in. by 5 in. by 5 in.

   **a.** How many cubes are in the solid?    _____

   **b.** How tall is the solid at its highest points?    _____

   **c.** How wide is the solid at its widest point?

# Exploring Volume

Find the volume of each solid.

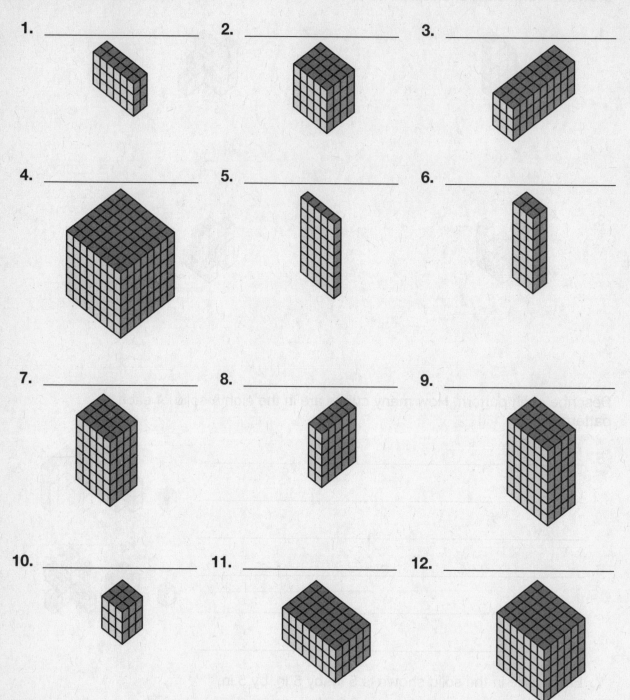

1. _____

2. _____

3. _____

4. _____

5. _____

6. _____

7. _____

8. _____

9. _____

10. _____

11. _____

12. _____

**13.** A farmer is loading bales of hay onto a wagon. The bales can fit 4 across, and there are 9 rows of bales from the front to the back of the truck. If each stack is to be 5 bales high, how many bales will fit in the wagon?

_____

# Calculating Volume

Find the volume of each solid.

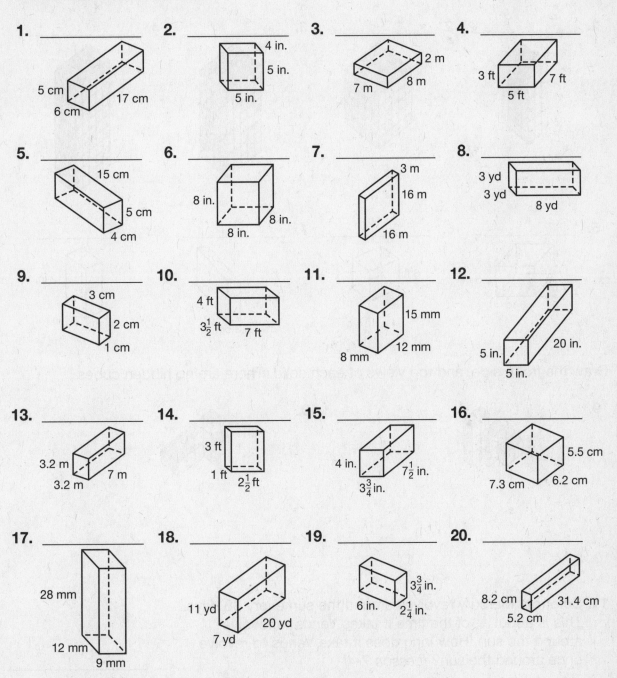

**1.** _____
5 cm  6 cm  17 cm

**2.** _____
4 in.  5 in.  5 in.

**3.** _____
2 m  7 m  8 m

**4.** _____
3 ft  7 ft  5 ft

**5.** _____
15 cm  5 cm  4 cm

**6.** _____
8 in.  8 in.  8 in.

**7.** _____
3 m  16 m  16 m

**8.** _____
3 yd  3 yd  8 yd

**9.** _____
3 cm  2 cm  1 cm

**10.** _____
4 ft  $3\frac{1}{2}$ ft  7 ft

**11.** _____
15 mm  8 mm  12 mm

**12.** _____
20 in.  5 in.  5 in.

**13.** _____
3.2 m  3.2 m  7 m

**14.** _____
3 ft  1 ft  $2\frac{1}{2}$ ft

**15.** _____
4 in.  $7\frac{1}{2}$ in.  $3\frac{3}{4}$ in.

**16.** _____
5.5 cm  7.3 cm  6.2 cm

**17.** _____
28 mm  12 mm  9 mm

**18.** _____
11 yd  7 yd  20 yd

**19.** _____
$3\frac{3}{4}$ in.  6 in.  $2\frac{1}{4}$ in.

**20.** _____
8.2 cm  5.2 cm  31.4 cm

**21.** The Panama Canal has a length of 89,200 yd, a width of 37 yd, and a depth of 14 yd. Estimate the volume of water in the canal by assuming it has the shape of a rectangular prism.

_____

# Section 11B Review

Find the volume of each solid.

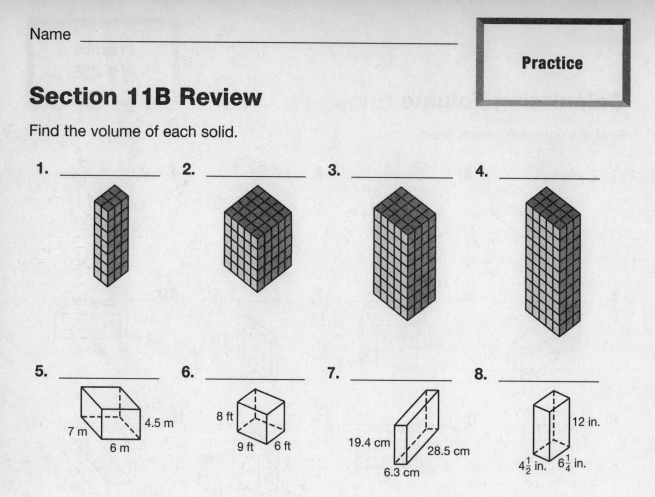

1. _____
2. _____
3. _____
4. _____

5. _____
6. _____
7. _____
8. _____

5. 7 m, 6 m, 4.5 m

6. 8 ft, 9 ft, 6 ft

7. 19.4 cm, 28.5 cm, 6.3 cm

8. 12 in., $4\frac{1}{2}$ in., $6\frac{1}{4}$ in.

Draw the front, side, and top views of each solid. There are no hidden cubes.

9.

10.

11. **Science** Mercury revolves around the sun every 88 days. This is about $\frac{11}{28}$ of the time it takes Venus to revolve around the sun. How long does it take Venus to revolve once around the sun? *[Lesson 7-4]*

_____

12. A rectangle has sides of 10 cm and 15 cm. A similar rectangle has a base that is 24 cm long. There are two possible values for the height of the larger rectangle. What are they? *[Lesson 10-7]*

_____

© Scott Foresman • Addison Wesley 6

Name _____

# Cumulative Review Chapters 1–11

Solve. *[Lesson 6-3]*

**1.** $x + \dfrac{3}{7} = \dfrac{3}{4}$　　**2.** $k - \dfrac{2}{3} = \dfrac{1}{6}$　　**3.** $m + \dfrac{11}{8} = \dfrac{9}{5}$　　**4.** $z - \dfrac{7}{10} = \dfrac{2}{15}$

$x =$ _____　　$k =$ _____　　$m =$ _____　　$z =$ _____

Estimate what percent of each figure is shaded. *[Lesson 10-9]*

**5.** _____　　**6.** _____　　**7.** _____　　**8.** _____

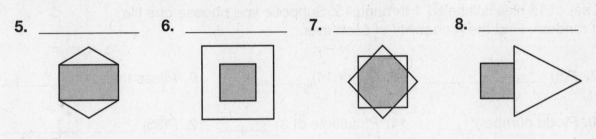

Convert to a percent. *[Lesson 10-10]*

**9.** 0.16 _____　　**10.** 0.03 _____　　**11.** 0.816 _____　　**12.** 0.56 _____

**13.** $\dfrac{7}{10}$ _____　　**14.** $\dfrac{3}{25}$ _____　　**15.** $\dfrac{63}{100}$ _____　　**16.** $\dfrac{3}{8}$ _____

**17.** $\dfrac{17}{20}$ _____　　**18.** $\dfrac{3}{40}$ _____　　**19.** $\dfrac{2}{5}$ _____　　**20.** $\dfrac{3}{4}$ _____

Classify each solid. If it is a polyhedron, tell how many vertices, edges, and faces it has. *[Lesson 11-1]*

**21.** _____　　**22.** _____　　**23.** _____

V: ___  E: ___  F: ___　　V: ___  E: ___  F: ___　　V: ___  E: ___  F: ___

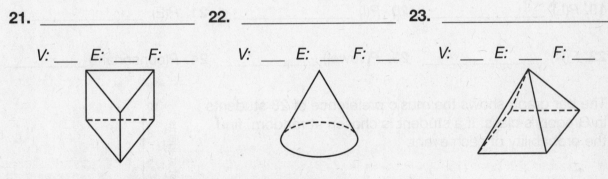

Find the volume of each solid. *[Lesson 11-7]*

**24.** _____　　**25.** _____　　**26.** _____　　**27.** _____

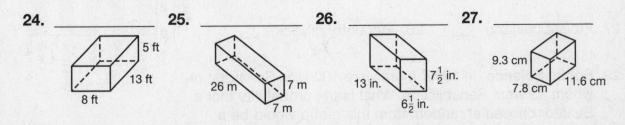

# Probability

A set of 12 cards is labeled 1 through 12. Suppose you choose one
card at random. Find the probability of each event.

**1.** $P(5)$ _____
**2.** $P$(even number) _____
**3.** $P$(multiple of 5) _____

**4.** $P(12)$ _____
**5.** $P$(less than 9) _____
**6.** $P$(multiple of 3) _____

A set of 15 tiles is labeled 1 through 15. Suppose you choose one tile
at random. Find the probability of each event.

**7.** $P(8)$ _____
**8.** $P$(7 or 11) _____
**9.** $P$(less than 20) _____

**10.** $P$(odd number) _____
**11.** $P$(multiple of 3) _____
**12.** $P(35)$ _____

Suppose you roll a number cube. Find the probability of each event.

**13.** $P(4)$ _____
**14.** $P(8)$ _____
**15.** $P$(2 or 5) _____

**16.** $P$(less than 4) _____
**17.** $P$(greater than 5) _____
**18.** $P$(multiple of 5) _____

There are 13 cards that spell out L I E C H T E N S T E I N. Suppose
you choose one card. Find the probability of each event.

**19.** $P(L)$ _____
**20.** $P(I)$ _____
**21.** $P(E)$ _____

**22.** $P(N)$ _____
**23.** $P$(vowel) _____
**24.** $P$(consonant) _____

The bar graph shows the music preference of 28 students
in Gregory's class. If a student is chosen at random, find
the probability of each event.

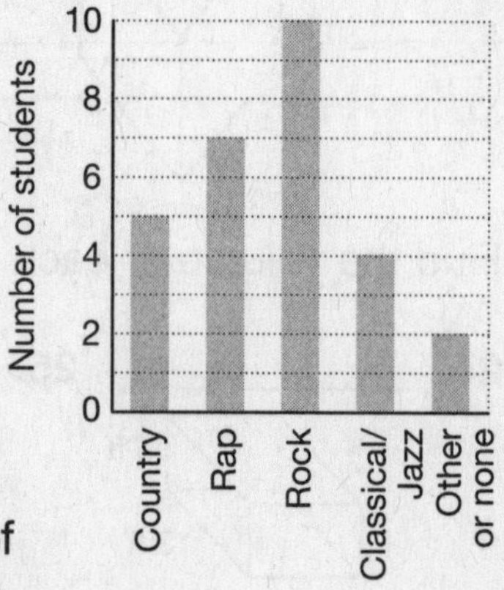

**25.** $P$(country) _____
**26.** $P$(rock or rap) _____

**27.** $P$(classical/jazz) _____
**28.** $P$(country or rock) ___

**29. Social Science** In 1992, there were 100 U.S. Senators, of
whom 43 were Republicans. What is the probability that a
Senator chosen at random from this group would be a
Republican? Express your answer as a decimal and a percent. _____

Name _____

# Making Predictions

Use the data recorded in the chart for Exercises 1–3.

| Trial | 1 | 2 | 3 | 4 | 5 | 6 | 7 | 8 |
|---|---|---|---|---|---|---|---|---|
| Outcome | square | circle | square | triangle | circle | square | square | circle |

**1.** How many different outcomes were there? _____

**2.** How many times was the outcome a circle? _____

**3.** What is the probability of the outcome being a square? _____

Use the data recorded in the chart for Exercises 4–6.

| Trial | 1 | 2 | 3 | 4 | 5 | 6 | 7 | 8 |
|---|---|---|---|---|---|---|---|---|
| Outcome | blue | yellow | red | blue | green | red | yellow | blue |

| Trial | 9 | 10 | 11 | 12 | 13 | 14 | 15 |
|---|---|---|---|---|---|---|---|
| Outcome | blue | green | red | blue | blue | green | red |

**4.** How many different outcomes were there? _____

**5.** How many times was the outcome red? _____

**6.** What is the probability of the outcome being yellow or green? _____

One day, 40 members who came to an athletic club were asked to complete a survey.

| Question | Result |
|---|---|
| Are you male or female? | 28 male, 12 female |
| Are you under 26 years old? | 24 yes, 16 no |
| Do you use weight machines? | 32 yes, 8 no |
| Do you participate in aerobics classes? | 14 yes, 26 no |

If the athletic club has 870 members, use the survey results to estimate the number of members who:

**7.** are male _____     **8.** are 26 or older _____

**9.** use weight machines _____     **10.** take aerobics classes _____

# Geometric Models of Probability

Suppose you drop a token on each shape in Exercises 1–16. Find the probability of the token landing on the shaded area.

1. _____

2. _____

3. _____

4. _____

5. _____

6. _____

7. _____

8. _____

9. _____

10. _____

11. _____

12. _____

13. _____

14. _____

15. _____

16. _____

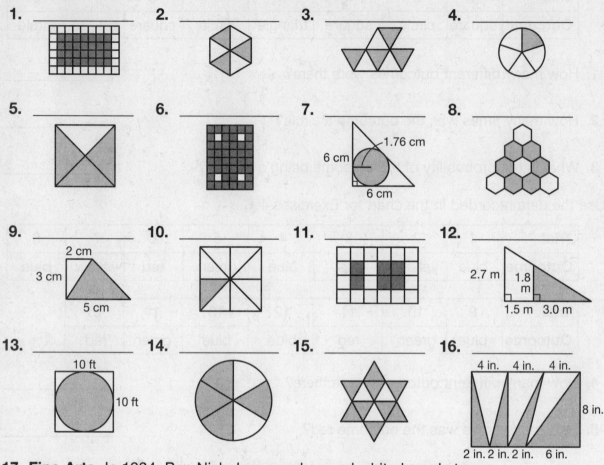

17. **Fine Arts** In 1934, Ben Nicholson used carved white boards to create a work of art resembling the drawing at the right. Suppose a speck of dust lands randomly on this work of art.

a. What is the probability that it lands in one of the smaller labeled rectangles?

_____

b. The circle has a diameter of about 26 cm. What is the probability that the dust speck lands in the circle?

_____

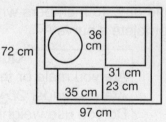

18. If you throw 500 darts at the hexagonal dart board shown, how many should you expect to land in the shaded area?

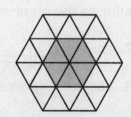

_____

# Section 12A Review

A set of 8 tiles is numbered 1 through 8. Suppose you choose one tile at random. Find the probability of each event.

**1.** $P(5)$ _____

**2.** $P$(odd number) _____

**3.** $P$(multiple of 3) _____

**4.** $P(10)$ _____

**5.** $P$(3 or 5) _____

**6.** $P$(prime number) _____

Use the spinner to find each probability.

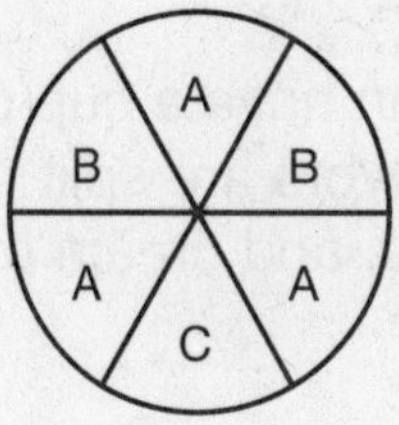

**7.** $P(A)$ _____

**8.** $P(B)$ _____

**9.** $P(C)$ _____

**10.** $P$(consonant) _____

**11.** $P$(not C) _____

**12.** $P$(A or C) _____

**13.** The probability that a Sloth Airlines flight will be on time is $\frac{2}{15}$. What is the probability that a flight will be late? _____

**14.** If 160 tokens were dropped on the figure shown, how many would you expect to hit the shaded region?

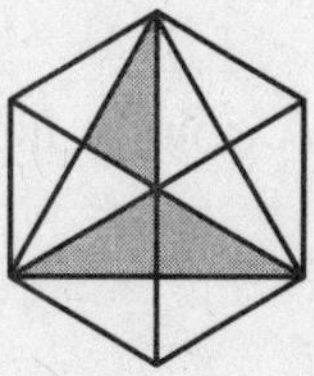

_____

**15.** Which probability is greater, 13 out of 35 or 21 out of 57? Explain. _____

_____

**16.** In Detroit, Michigan, the average probability that it will rain on any given day is about $\frac{9}{25}$. About how many rainy days will there be in a 365-day year? _____

**17.** If $P(X) = \frac{3}{20}$, $P(Y) = 18\%$, and $P(Z) = 0.2$, which event has the greatest probability of occurring? _____

**18. Geography** The shaded portion of the figure represents the percent of land used for crops in Ukraine. What percent of Ukraine's land is used for crops? *[Lesson 10-8]*

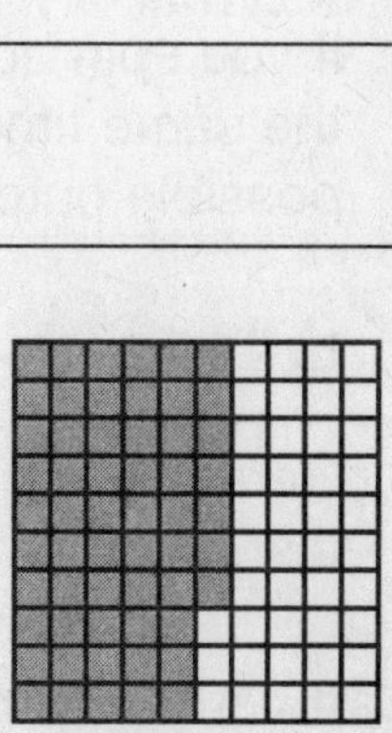

_____

**19. Measurement** A carton measuring $5\frac{1}{2}$ in. by 6 in. by 7 in. holds exactly one gallon of liquid. How many cubic inches are in a gallon? *[Lesson 11-6]*

_____

# Tree Diagrams

For Exercises 1–4, draw a tree diagram for each situation.

**1.** A club is choosing a girl (Kathy, Linda, or Meg) and a boy (Warren or Xavier) to represent the club at a student council meeting.

**2.** You can have a cup or a bowl of soup. The flavors are split pea, minestrone, tomato, and cream of broccoli.

**3.** A coin is flipped three times in a row.

**4.** You are going horseback riding. You can choose one of 8 horses, and you may go to any one of 5 destinations. How many different ways can you make your selection? _____

**5.** If you spin both spinners at the same time, how many possible outcomes are there?

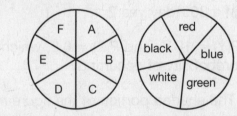

_____

**6.** Gerald is taking a multiple-choice test in his Spanish class. The test has four questions, and each question has 5 possible answers.

**a.** How many different ways can Gerald complete his answer sheet? _____

**b.** Gerald forgot to study. If he guesses randomly, what is the probability that he will get the first problem right? _____

# Compound Events

Five cards numbered 1, 2, 3, 4, and 5 are in a paper bag. Each time a card is drawn it is replaced. Find the probability of each event.

**1.** *P*(even, then even) ___   **2.** *P*(even, then odd) ____   **3.** *P*(odd, then even) _____

**4.** *P*(odd, then odd) ____   **5.** *P*(odd, odd, odd) _____   **6.** *P*(even, even, odd) ____

For Exercises 7–10, the spinner is spun twice.

**7.** Find the probability of spinning N both times.   _____

**8.** Find the probability of spinning E then R.   _____

**9.** Find the probability of spinning a vowel then a consonant.   _____

**10.** Find the probability of not spinning B either time.   _____

**11.** Suppose you flip a coin and spin the spinner from Exercise 7.
What is the probability that the coin lands heads and you spin M?   _____

**12.** Suppose you roll 5 number cubes while playing Yahtzee®. What
is the probability of getting a number less than 5 on all of the
number cubes?   _____

**13.** A Thai restaurant offers the curry special shown
at the right. If a customer makes all choices
randomly, what is the probability that she orders
a yellow or green tofu curry with tea?

| Curry Special $5.99 |
| --- |
| Curried vegetables with your choice of beef, chicken, tofu, or shrimp. |
| Choose yellow curry, green curry, or red curry. |
| Drink included: tea or soda. |

_____

**14.** A standard deck of 52 playing cards includes 26 black cards
(13 clubs and 13 spades) and 26 red cards (13 hearts and
13 diamonds). Suppose you draw a card, put it back, and then
draw again. Find each probability.

**a.** *P*(black, then red) ___   **b.** *P*(red, then spade) ___   **c.** *P*(heart, then heart) ____

**15.** The game of Scrabble® includes 100 lettered tiles. 42 of the tiles
represent vowels. If you select a tile, put it back, and select again,
what is the probability of getting a vowel both times?   _____

# Fairness and Unfairness

For Exercises 1–9, determine if the game is fair. If it is *not*, tell which player has the higher probability of winning.

1. A number cube is tossed. Evan wins if the number is even. Otherwise, Arnold wins.

   _____

2. Tina and Jody use a computer to select two random numbers from 1 to 10. Tina wins if both numbers are prime or neither is prime. If one number is prime and the other is not, Jody wins.

   _____

3. Kim and Lance played a coin toss game 25 times. Kim won 60% of the games and Lance won 40%.

   _____

4. Two number cubes are tossed. If both numbers are even, Amy wins. If both numbers are odd, Brad wins. Otherwise, Cheryl wins.

   _____

5. A random number from 1 to 9 is selected. If the number is 5 or greater, Kelly wins. If it is less than 5, Hoang wins.

   _____

6. Three coins are tossed. If there are more heads than tails, Beth wins. Otherwise, Dara wins.

   _____

7. **Fine Arts** The color pairs on opposite sides of the spinner shown (such as blue and orange) are called *complementary colors*. The spinner is spun twice. If the two colors are the same or complementary, Steve wins. Otherwise, Anson wins.

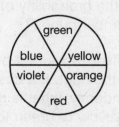

   _____

8. The spinner in Exercise 7 is spun twice. If the two colors are the same or next to each other on the spinner, Kyle wins. Otherwise, Francis wins.

   _____

9. Carol, James, Nancy, and Tara played a card game 28 times. Tara made a bar graph to show how many times each player won. Can you be certain that the game was fair?

   _____

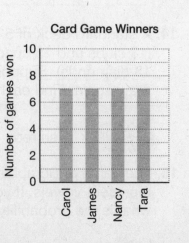

Card Game Winners

# Section 12B Review

1. Suppose you roll three different-colored number cubes.

   **a.** How many outcomes are there? _____

   **b.** What is the probability for each outcome? _____

2. A fast-food restaurant gives you one of 5 different drinking glasses with each meal. If you order 2 meals, what is the possibility that your drinking glasses will match? _____

3. Eileen is making cupcakes. Each cupcake is made with either chocolate or vanilla cake and chocolate, vanilla, or mint frosting. Each cupcake also has either chopped nuts or colored sprinkles. How many different kinds of cupcakes can Eileen make? _____

4. Your uncle tells you that his license plate has 5 digits, and each digit is either 2, 4, or 6.

   **a.** How many different license plates can match this description? _____

   **b.** If you try to guess the license plate, what is the probability that you guess correctly? _____

5. A random 2-digit number (10 to 99) is chosen. Anthony wins if the tens digit is greater than the units digit. Otherwise, Carlos, wins. Is the game fair? Explain.

   _____

   _____

6. Two nickels and a dime are tossed. Candy wins if the value of the coins that come up heads is greater than the value of the coins that come up tails. Otherwise, Frederick wins. Is the game fair? Explain.

   _____

   _____

7. The average daily minimum temperature for January is −14°F in Gulkana, Alaska, and 3°F in Minneapolis, Minnesota. How much warmer is the temperature in Minneapolis than in Gulkana? *[Lesson 9-3]* _____

8. A can of fancy mixed nuts has diameter 10.0 cm and height 9.3 cm. Find the surface area of the can. *[Lesson 11-4]* _____

Name _____

# Cumulative Review Chapters 1–12

What is the least rotation that will land the figure on top of itself? *[Lesson 8-9]*

1. _____  2. _____  3. _____  4. _____

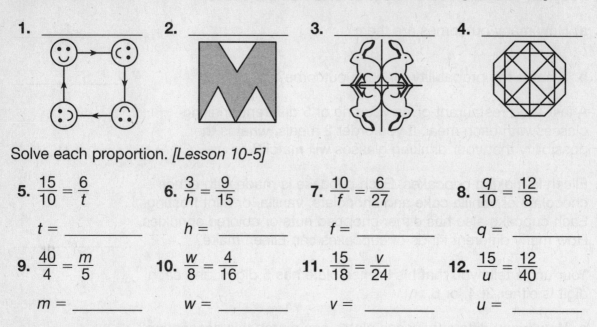

Solve each proportion. *[Lesson 10-5]*

5. $\frac{15}{10} = \frac{6}{t}$   6. $\frac{3}{h} = \frac{9}{15}$   7. $\frac{10}{f} = \frac{6}{27}$   8. $\frac{q}{10} = \frac{12}{8}$

$t =$ _____  $h =$ _____  $f =$ _____  $q =$ _____

9. $\frac{40}{4} = \frac{m}{5}$   10. $\frac{w}{8} = \frac{4}{16}$   11. $\frac{15}{18} = \frac{v}{24}$   12. $\frac{15}{u} = \frac{12}{40}$

$m =$ _____  $w =$ _____  $v =$ _____  $u =$ _____

Find the surface area. *[Lesson 11-3]*

13. _____  14. _____  15. _____  16. _____

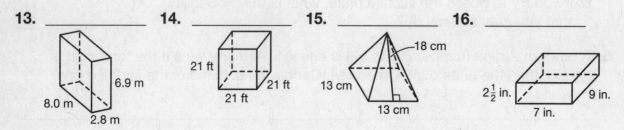

There are 12 cards that spell out C O N S T I T U T I O N. Suppose you choose one card. Find the probability of each event. *[Lesson 12-1]*

17. $P$(C) _____  18. $P$(O) _____  19. $P$(T) _____

20. $P$(vowel) _____  21. $P$(N or O) _____  22. $P$(consonant) _____

23. $P$(Z) _____  24. $P$(T or I) _____  25. $P$(not a T) _____

Suppose you drop a token on each shape. Find the probability of the token landing on the shaded area. *[Lesson 12-3]*

26. _____  27. _____  28. _____  29. _____

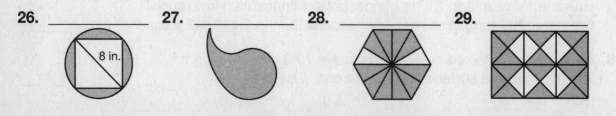